Caribbean Transnational Experience

Harry Goulbourne

Pluto Press

LONDON • STERLING, VIRGINIA

ARAWAK

publications

Kingston   Jamaica

First published 2002 by Pluto Press
345 Archway Road, London N6 5AA
and 22883 Quicksilver Drive, Sterling, VA 20166–2012, USA

www.plutobooks.com

and
A R A W A K publications
17 Kensington Crescent
Kingston 5, Jamaica

British Library Cataloguing in Publication Data
A catalogue record for this book is available from the British Library

ISBN 0 7453 1763 4 hardback PLUTO
ISBN 0 7453 1762 6 paperback PLUTO
ISBN 976 8189 15 0 paperback A R A W A K

Library of Congress Cataloging in Publication Data
Goulbourne, Harry.
    Caribbean transnational experience / Harry Goulbourne.
      p. cm.
    ISBN 0–7453–1763–4 — ISBN 0–7453–1762–6 (pbk.)
    1. West Indians—Great Britain. 2. Caribbean Area—Relations—Great
Britain. 3. Great Britain—Relations—Caribbean Area. 4. Caribbean
Area—Emigration and immigration. 5. West Indians—Foreign countries.
I. Title.
    DA125.W4 G72 2002
    303.48'2729041—dc21

                                                                    2001006413

National Library of Jamaica Cataloguing in Publication Data
Goulbourne, Harry
    Caribbean transnational experience / Harry Goulbourne
      p. ; cm. – (Caribbean contemporary series)
    Includes bibliographical references and index
    ISBN 976–8189–15–0
    1. Great Britain – Race relations 2. West Indians – Great Britain
3. West Indian – Immigrants I. Title II. Series
305.896072042   dc.20

Reprints: 10   9   8   7   6   5   4   3   2   1   0

Designed and produced for Pluto Press by
Chase Publishing Services, Fortescue, Sidmouth EX10 9QG
Typeset from disk by Stanford DTP Services, Towcester
Printed in the European Union by Antony Rowe, Chippenham, England

Contents

List of Figures and Tables

FIGURES

TABLES

Preface and Acknowledgements

This book is an attempt to encourage the development of theoretically relevant and empirically informed knowledge about the living connections between Caribbeans in Britain and their links with the wider world across the Atlantic. The book brings together a number of central themes about the transnational characteristics of Caribbean life in Britain and in the Caribbean as they have emerged and developed in my work over several years. Unlike the general focus on broad and discursive topics found in literary and cultural studies, I am concerned about particular aspects of the lived experiences of individual and collective actors or agents. Through their thought and action there has been a radical transformation of the well-known and widely recognised historical trans-Atlantic triangular world, which was formed through mercantilism, the slave trade and the settler colonialism of the first British empire. In other words, whilst in the first part of the development of an Atlantic world, Europe called all the shots ('discovery', settlement/colonisation, development, etc.), in the contemporary period a transformation is occurring whereby relatively new groups become active participants in cross-Atlantic life.

Each chapter of this book was written within a specific context, and it is worth mentioning these briefly here to convey the overall relevance of the themes to current debates about Britain in the new century. The contents of Chapter 2 were first presented on three occasions on which there were demands for more knowledge and understanding of Caribbeans in Britain and their continuing links with the Caribbean: part of the chapter is from a very long paper initially written for a small group of European and American scholars concerned about transnational communities in Europe and America and loosely discussed at meetings held at the European University Institute in Florence and later in Berlin in 1997 and 1998, respectively; another part is drawn from a public lecture given at Gresham College, London to mark the fiftieth anniversary of sizeable migration to the UK, after the docking of the *Empire Windrush* at Tilbury in June 1948; the third part of the chapter draws on, and develops, a public lecture delivered at Bristol City Museum in

January 1999 to launch that city's assessment of its part in the slave trade and an exhibition in March 1999 on the subject. Accordingly, I am grateful to the following persons and their respective institutions for providing me with the opportunity to clarify my thinking about the issues condensed in this chapter: Josh deWind of the Social Science Research Council, New York and Aristide Zolberg of the New School, New York; Peter Fraser, then of Goldsmith's College, London and the staff of Gresham College, London; members of the Magpie Society, Bristol, the Director of Bristol Gallery and Museum, and Madge Dresser.

Some of the subsequent chapters also draw upon public lectures I have given over the years and on earlier published pieces. An earlier version of Chapter 3 appeared in Goulbourne and M. Chamberlain (eds) *Caribbean Families in Britain and the Trans-Atlantic World* (Macmillan, 2001). A section of Chapter 4 was delivered as the second David Nicholls Memorial Lecture in October 2000 as part of Black History Month, at Littlemore, Oxford, where David had been vicar as well as being an Oxford political theorist and theologian. I am grateful to the David Nicholls Memorial Trust, including his widow Gillian Nicholls, Robin Cohen, Bernard Crick, James Ferguson, Kenneth Leech, John Muddiman, Christopher Rowland, Jane Shaw and Paul Sutton, for the invitation to pay my respect to a distinguished Caribbeanist.

The materials for Chapter 4 and Chapter 6 were collected when, as a member of the Economic and Social Research Council's Centre for Research in Ethnic Relations at the University of Warwick, I conducted research into the political action of new minority ethnic communities. The materials I use from this period of research have never been published, but with the passing of time the story they inform has become more relevant to an understanding of the making of post-imperial Britain. I am grateful to numerous individuals who helped me with both gathering and understanding the data, particularly about the Black Unity and Freedom Party, Bogle L'Ouverture Publications, New Beacon Books, and the Joshua Francis Defence Committee. Only a few of the many who helped me are specifically mentioned here, namely, the late Emil Chang, Sonia Joseph, Ken 'Bubbles' Williams, Eric Huntley, Jessica Huntley and John LaRose.

Chapter 5 was initially written as an expert witness statement in the case involving the boxers Frank Bruno and Lennox Lewis and the *Observer* and *Guardian* newspapers in 1994/95; it is included here because it is a clear illustration of the close connections between US and British Caribbean communities. My thanks to Veena Vasista for her valuable research for this chapter. Chapters 7 and 8 draw on material collected in a major ESRC research project that I led with Mary Chamberlain of Oxford Brookes University entitled *Living Arrangements, Family Structure and Social Change of Caribbeans in Britain* (ESRC Award No. L315253009) in their *Population and Household Change in Britain Programme* (1995–98). An earlier version of Chapter 7 appeared in Susan McRae (ed.) *Changing Britain: Families and Households in the 1990s* (Oxford University Press, 1999); an earlier version of Chapter 8 appeared in *Policy Studies*, vol. 20, no. 3, 1999. I am grateful to the many individuals and families in Britain, Barbados, Jamaica and Trinidad who helped us better to understand continuities and change across the Atlantic-Caribbean communities. I am also grateful to the many government officials and spokespersons for returning resident associations in each of these countries who provided us with relevant data. In particular, I am grateful to Steve Batchelor, Lloyd Bradshaw, Don Brice, Charles Corbin, Melvin Drayton, Arthur Harper, Beverley Miller, Peter Phillips, Jennifer Sampson and John Small.

My sincere thanks to Roger van Zwanenberg, his colleagues at Pluto Press and their anonymous readers for some very pertinent and critical questions about my perspectives on the issues raised, and, of course, for their efforts to bring this project to fruition.

Finally, as always, my thanks to Selina for critical remarks which had to be addressed.

In general, the overall analyses in this book are informed by my experience of teaching and researching in Africa, Britain and the Caribbean from 1972 to the present, and by a concern to maintain a continuity in my understanding of social science theory as derived or induced from empirical social research. Obviously, therefore, the responsibility for this work remains mine alone.

Harry Goulbourne
Baginton
October 2001

1 Questions of Theory, Definition, Purpose

INTRODUCTION

The spread of Caribbean people across the North Atlantic world is a central and significant aspect of both the Caribbean and the wider African diaspora. However, the notion of a Caribbean diaspora is more problematic than it might first appear, touching as it does not only on the African but also other well-recognised diasporas, such as the Jewish and Chinese, as well as those which are now being recognised, such as the Indian and Irish diasporas. The question may therefore be asked as to whether groups from the Caribbean, who have spread across the Atlantic world over the last half of the twentieth century, constitute a diaspora or are simply the further growth of other diasporas, principally the African diaspora, but also the Chinese, Indian and Irish.

In short, the notion of a Caribbean diaspora raises a number of intriguing questions about the meaning of the concept, individual and collective or group identities, and questions about the mechanisms whereby social action, structures and beliefs and perceptions are articulated, identified and analysed by scholars interested in this ancient but also postmodern phenomenon. The chapters in this book mark a deliberate attempt to focus on a number of particular aspects of Caribbean diasporic or transnational experiences. By way of introduction, however, I want in this chapter to direct attention to what I understand by the notion of diaspora, Caribbean diaspora, and related notions such as transnationality and globalisation. Particular attention is drawn to aspects of cultural studies because of the sometimes crippling grip that the culturalist persuasion exerts over matters pertaining to Caribbean diasporic experiences as well as the concept itself.

DIASPORAS, TRANSNATIONALISM, GLOBALISATION

The concept of diaspora, as Marienstras (1989, p. 125) suggests, is 'adventurous, for it applies to a human adventure subject to the fortunes of history and fate'. Unfortunately, however, this spirit of adventure has been taken almost to the point of recklessness by some theorists so that the concept now runs the risk of becoming valueless in attempts to understand the kinds of human experiences it was meant to demarcate and clarify.

Of course, this is not surprising. From time to time there emerges a word, phrase or concept which forcefully or succinctly expresses something about the phenomena we seek to understand. It is in the nature of things that these words, phrases or concepts embark on careers of secure employment in and out of seasons. For example, the better part of the 1960s and 1970s saw development studies providing full employment for the phrase 'centre and periphery' so that there were times when some people could speak of the 'centre' and the 'periphery' of almost any kind of human experience. The decade from the mid-1970s to the mid-1980s was dominated by the notion of political economy (often bolstered by relatively vague minor themes such as 'crisis'); it hardly mattered what was being written about or discussed in a wide range of disciplines in the humanities and social sciences – writers tended to emphasise 'the political economy of ...'. This was true in radical economics and politics as in law, history and other humanities. Earlier, drawing from Hegel and the young Marx, there had been 'negation' (and sometimes negation of the negation), 'alienation' and 'anomie' from Marx and Durkheim. More recently, over the last decade or so, concepts such as 'discourse', 'identity' and 'negotiation' have come to form a readily recognised litany for those who have been initiated into one or other of a number of academic circles which are as tightly held together as any minor religious sect. The difference between this form of initiation and religious sects lies in the degree of their fidelity; like religious belief, these academic sects are not easily shaken by verifiable facts; unlike religious convictions, it is fashion which leads to the periodic boom and bust of these circles.

Academically popular key words and concepts have a way of exhausting their usefulness, as they eventually become shibboleths embodying or encoding such earth-shattering insights into human affairs to the point that usually the writers who employ them find it difficult to explain themselves and usually declare their statements to be entirely original. Their descriptive, evaluative or explanatory powers are liable to be spent once the scope of their original meanings are expanded beyond recognition. In other words, they become over-stretched. And, rather like a page of script being repeatedly photocopied, the copy becomes less and less true to the original, with the last copy exaggerating the faults of the one before it: blurred letters, meaningless spaces between unrecognisable words, indistinct forms. So too with over-employed concepts, suggesting that a little under-employment of genuinely useful social and/or analytical concepts may not be amiss.

The concept of diaspora, not unlike many concepts in the social sciences over the last thirty years or so, may now be at the juncture where it collapses so many different experiences into a seemingly common whole that the concept is losing its meaning or usefulness in social analysis. This may be occurring because of its over-employment by those who are intellectually cosy or those who seek salvation and comfort through intellectually vicarious living. For example, the concept is now in regular employment by cultural theorists, many of whom use a vocabulary borrowed from archaeology and architecture or any other discipline which is 'chic' and is in a boom phase, or more appropriately, is 'sexy' at the point of putting pen to paper, face on the screen, or simply vocalising the 'biting' phrase which grabs the circus's attention.

At the moment it is almost impossible to separate the concept of diaspora from the experiences of migration, the experiences of asylum seekers and refugees or even from the experiences of the transient, the traveller or the tourist. Increasingly, therefore, writers seek to abandon the traditional understanding of what the concept of diaspora may have evoked, validated or sustained in the experiences of groups of people. It may mean as little as the movement from one place to another, irrespective of geographical or cultural distances between these points. As one authoritative text in the field of cultural studies expresses the point, a diaspora is 'the movement, whether forced or voluntary, of a nation or group of people from one homeland to another' (Mirzoeff, 2000, p. i) and, drawing on the considerable authority of a founding father, Stuart Hall, diasporic identities are said to be where people are perceived to be 'constantly producing and reproducing themselves' (p. 4). If it appears a little far-fetched to restrict the concept to the first part of this formulation, it must also be obvious that it is equally absurd to extend it to the almost meaningless notion of people involved in the exercise of forever changing: even the amoeba eventually takes on a form sufficiently long to be recognised, described and analysed. And while the postmodern condition may be said to be characterised by uncertainty and rapid changes, these do not occur at a rate that makes it impossible for social science to analyse patterns of continuity as well as change.

The Meaning of Diaspora

It must be clear that I want to rescue the hitherto useful concept of diaspora from its vogue status, its over-employment and its impending exhaustion or even atrophy. After all, atrophy is usually what follows from this kind of over-use: who today speaks about 'political economy', 'crisis', 'alienation', anomie' and so forth, apart perhaps from those theorists who were never taken in in the first place by chic or vogue scholarship? The game is to be at something called the 'cutting edge' of academic work or to be 'hip' with the latest notions of a selection of gurus or priests who alone can 'speak in tongues' and interpret the mysteries. It is also part of the game, however, for one new high priest to deprecate the last, standing on the shoulder of one who had been hitherto overlooked. Thus, for some of these theorists the trick for a would-be new priest is to discover such an overlooked worthy and promote their work to a new level, endowing them with sainthood and elevate their work to iconic status. Here, egos and reputations, salvation and acceptance, are involved and at seminars it is always painful to see young scholars straining to please established gurus and being careful to identify who will next be elevated to this status. Consequently, the dominance that cultural studies enjoys in the academy today and its close association with sociology gives the impression that discussions in the social sciences are little more than an exercise of a merry-go-round in a playing field misnamed academia.

The meaning of diaspora that I employ in the following chapters may be distinguished from the often Delphic statements enunciated by the high priests of cultural studies. My understanding and use of the concept diaspora and/or diasporic experiences are therefore closer to its traditional meaning. This understanding involves a combination of some of the following: forced or voluntary dispersal or scattering; the development of a broadly social and political consciousness of interconnectedness between more or less distinct groups sharing certain identifiable factors (language, religion, distinct past historical or mythical events, colour, etc.); the feeling of being in exile and a desire to return somewhere at some indefinite point in time; the sense of community/belongingness that transcends the nation-state community; a sense of *angst* because of absence from 'home' or absence of a notional communal wholeness. It is not enough for just one of these experiences to exist for high priests to enunciate the existence of a diaspora; the notion of combination is an important defining factor. It is possible for each of these characteristics to be individually experienced, and for the status of diaspora to be absent. After all, there have been several voluntary and forced dispersals of people in prehistory as well as in history, without the emergence of a diaspora occurring. If all scatterings were diasporas, then the vast majority of humanity (if the biologists, physical anthropologists and archaeologists are correct about the origins of humankind) would be properly described as an African diaspora irrespective of where societies have emerged on the globe. Second, a wide variety of groups develop social and political consciousness on the basis, for example, of occupation, class, gender, generation, geography, and the accident of experience and contact between groups.

Third, exile is a common experience for intellectuals, artists, politicians, social outcasts and criminals. Consider for a moment the experience of the prisoner: the individual is expelled for a fixed time from the larger social whole and in some earlier social orders he (more or less always males and sometimes their dependants) was punished by being sent into 'exile', with rehabilitation involving the permission to 'return home'. As the works of Marx, Durkheim, Soren Kierkegaard, Albert Camus and Jean-Paul Sartre in economics, sociology, religion/theology, literature and philosophy show, the individual's experience of alienation, anomie or angst are encountered by the individual or group in a variety of life's pathways.

Of course, the concept of diaspora as a figure of speech could embrace aspects of these instances of individual and collective experience, but to go beyond this is to rush to over-use and weakening of the concept, and thereby to deny the plurality, diversity and sense of the human condition. Usually, a social phenomenon involves the combination of a number of factors and not just one element. Exile, as the experience of absence from home or the experience of not 'being at home', is not of itself the making of a diaspora.

Transnationalism

Transnationalism and globalisation should not be confused with diaspora. To be sure, all three are closely intertwined, but they are different experiences. The processes of globalisation involve the breaking down of factors that separate groups of people and political units such as states in the international community; globalisation brings production units and markets closer so that they cohere more easily; in short, globalisation makes for greater ease of communication in almost every department of life on a world scale. In some circles, such as among the anti-capitalist/anti-globalisation demonstrators at international meetings, there is an implied view that globalisation should entail the eradication of inequality, unfairness, dishonesty and amorality in the world community. It is important, however, to recognise that none of the processes and experiences being discussed here – globalisation, transnationalism, diaspora – necessarily entails equality; they are as divisive along class, gender, generation and other lines as any other generalised process or community such as the migration process or the nation-state community. Similarly, these processes may generate salutary practices (such as bringing people closer together or maintaining existing bonds) as well as undesirable practices (for example, atrocities, such as the bombing of the World Trade Centre and the Pentagon on 11 September 2001).

It follows, therefore, that the process of transnationalism is varied. For example, transnationalism may involve groups of people who are connected in some significant ways to maintain the close links across the boundaries of nation-states; it may involve the enjoyment of more than one citizenship or belonging to more than one society; it may also involve the easy movement of people across states and societies. This situation may come about as a result of large-scale migration, wars and natural disasters, which in turn create streams of refugees and asylum seekers who maintain close and living links with their 'homelands'. For some, these continuing links may be a threat to national loyalty and even security, because the often desired goal of the newcomers' integration into the host society is thwarted. The embrace of the philosophy of multiculturalism (the recognition, toleration and celebration of a diversity of cultures within the boundaries of a nation-state) as ideology and as policy in societies such as Britain may be said to reinforce transnationalism.

But transnationalism can stand on its own, and has several features. In the first place, it may be described as popular where it involves ordinary people. Whereas in the past it was mainly elites who may have enjoyed transnational experiences, today very many people experience migration, engage in cross-national family rela-tionships such as marriage, and so forth. In the economic sphere, transnationalism involves the easy flow and ownership of capital and exploitation of natural resources without barriers being erected by nation-states. Economic transnationalism also undermines the sovereignty of the nation-state, because vital and far-reaching decisions about economic activities are taken independently of the concerns of particular nation-states. In the political sphere, transnationalism – such as regional integration – compromises the sovereignty of nation-states. For example, the regionalism represented by the European Union makes the whole stronger, ensures greater security to smaller and weaker members and allows for greater freedom of movement across national boundaries, but it thereby lessens the force of individual member-states.

Obviously, the processes of both transnationalism and globalisation are closely intertwined with the formation and maintenance of diasporas. A diaspora can come into existence without there being any significant increase or development of either transnationalism or globalisation. Historically, however, the processes have been closely connected, and in the chapters that follow I will be referring sometimes interchangeably to these processes.

Historical Diasporas and the Experiences of Caribbeans

Of course, the historical experiences which have defined the concept of diaspora are relatively few, principally the Jewish and African dispersals, and later the Chinese and Indian; some ancient groups, such as the Armenians or the Kurds, have also been considered to have experienced diasporas. In these instances, diaspora formation has been closely allied to both processes of globalisation and transnationalism, where these are understood to mean territorial and cultural expansion and transgression of the political and cultural boundaries erected to demarcate groups of people. The breakup of the Israelite confederacy by the Babylonians, the transfer into captivity in Babylon, and the return to Jerusalem to rebuild Yahweh's Temple formed the experience of the first dispersal as well as the formation of a distinctively Jewish collective identity. The second great dispersal, following Titus's destruction of Jerusalem in AD 70 formed the traumatic experience which went into the making of the Jewish diaspora over the last two millennia. African-Atlantic slavery, plantation or estate exploitation and the beginnings of modern capitalism formed the original elements of the African diaspora. Both groups have been subjected to further dispersals, which may have helped to cement their collective experience of belonging to a diaspora. The Jews were dispersed from unifying Spain in the sixteenth century, from Tsarist Russia, Poland and other parts of East and Central Europe at various times in the nineteenth and twentieth centuries, and in recent decades have chosen to leave North Africa and Ethiopia.

Caribbean Africans have arguably been the most mobile members of the African diaspora within the Atlantic world, and migrations within the Caribbean, the Americas, and North-west Europe (Britain, France and The Netherlands) have characterised its expansion and continuing construction. It is not, however, the case that other groups of Africans in the diaspora have not been mobile; rather, it has been a case of moving within a politically unified territory, such as the great northward migration of African Americans from the former Confederacy States in the wake of the Depression in the 1930s and post-Second World War search for greater economic opportunities. In contrast, Africans in the islands of the seas had to move across deep and expansive waters in search of similar opportunities in the more open post-imperial centres of Europe, namely, England, France and The Netherlands. Slavery, dispossession and resultant poverty, but particularly the tremendous desire or urge to improve and secure social justice, transformed groups of people who were not before known as seafarers to become world travellers.

There are, of course, significant similarities and differences within and between the defining African and the Jewish diasporic historical experiences. In both cases force, compulsion and destruction punctuated the dispersal; as Robin Cohen (1997) has pointed out, both groups became highly creative: exile is a condition of loneliness, misery but also opportunity. In the process, members of the diaspora develop world-views which transcend their beginnings and their locations, and it is not surprising that some of the main thinkers, artists, performers and so forth in all areas of human endeavours have emerged from the cultures thrown up within the uncertainties of diaspora. In other words, Babylon has been oppressive and uncomfortable, but Babylon has also been the site of liberation from past entrenched encumbrances, the site at which new identities are forged, as Malinowski (1961) pointed out early in the last century (when he spoke about culture-contact resulting in culture-change) and culturalists were to 'discover' later. This is a point that is generally overlooked in treatises about the Caribbean diaspora or Babylonian practical experiences; 'Inside Babylon' – the title of the well-received James and Harris collection (1993) – is not generally seen as a moment of opportunity and creativity, but a moment almost exclusively of oppression and exclusion as the Rasta-

present for a diaspora to emerge, but there needs at the very least to be a collective consciousness of belonging to such a collectivity. The articulation of such consciousness is largely the work of intellectuals (poets, novelists, artists), religious leaders and politicians. It is not surprising therefore that attention nearly always turns to such figures when attempts are made to trace the contours of the emergence and development of a diaspora. As the chapters in this book suggest, however, the transnational lives of Caribbean people involve far more than intellectual formulations, and far more than the careers of outstanding individuals such as a C.L.R. James, a Claudia Jones, a Marcus Garvey or a George Padmore in the last century, and in the century before, a Martin Delany or an Edward Blyden. After all, the very careers and lives of such individuals are to a significant degree predicated on the presence of ordinary folks who go about their ordinary lives independently of the thoughts of these great figures. While it is important to restate repeatedly the significance of these personalities, it is at the very least as significant to explore the impact of ordinary people on the creation of the Caribbean diaspora, and the chapters which follow are a plea in that direction.

Diasporic consciousness nearly always involves the aspiration of establishing or re-establishing an original homeland and a degree of commitment to an eventual return, whether permanently or simply as a referent of spiritual or emotional renewal. Like nationalism, diasporic consciousness is a powerful stimulus of myths, historical reconstruction and the redefinition of collective identity. In the Jewish diaspora, like the African diaspora, the vast majority of people have not necessarily wished to return to Palestine or to Africa – 'home' is not necessarily Zion or Africa/Ethiopia; in practical, lived terms 'home' is where the hearth is, and for Jews this may be more in New York than in Israel, as for the Irish the hearth may be as much in London and Liverpool as in Dublin or Belfast. But the important point is that in both experiences, there has occurred from time to time such an urge and partial fulfilment. It is not only Zionists who wished to return to Zion (thereby territorialising swathes of Palestine in an image of the ancient Mosaic, Joshuaic or Davidic confederacy). Although only a handful of Africans returned to Africa (Sierra Leone, Liberia, and ports and rivers along the West African coast), there is the ever-present interest in Africa by diasporic Africans, most of whom do not plan ever to visit the continent, which for many is still the forbidding 'dark continent' that it was for nineteenth-century European imperialists, the 'area of darkness' conjured by Conrad and reinforced by Hollywood and the brutish behaviour of most post-colonial presidents who saw the former colonial governor as their model in the exercise of power.

There are at least two important ways in which the treatment of diaspora in this discussion differs from its current use by hegemonic cultural theorists. First, the concept is taken here to relate to collectively lived experiences that can be examined and documented. The concept is not used as mere metaphor and representation of imagery. It is of course true that when we attempt to describe what Durkheim called a 'social fact' it is not as simple and as straightforward as some of his disciples sometimes appeared to have thought, largely because any 'social fact' or 'thing' may be variously described, depending on our individual moral and ethical standpoint, as is well established in the wider sociological tradition from Weber (1995) to Myrdal (1944, 1969) to C. Wright Mills (1959) and beyond. However, there are degrees to which we can accept the description of particular social phenomena, without recourse to first principles because, as C. Wright Mills already in the late 1950s reminded sociologists, the purpose of sociological investigation, or the 'sociological imagination' as he chose to describe it, is to help people in the modern age to understand their situations and relate these to those of others and thereby seek common answers to their common troubles. While there is comparatively little that can be described as a shared Kuhnian paradigm between some of the sub-fields of contemporary sociology, there is none the less a modicum of shared understanding (at least in the sociological tradition associated with such founding figures of the discipline as Marx, Weber and Durkheim and a good many of their disciples) about some characteristics of social life. In the discussions which follow this chapter, I make this assumption and proceed to analyse aspects of what I consider to be Caribbean diasporic or transnational experiences in an increasingly globalised world.

These experiences tend to be broadly social and not individual-orientated as much of the discussion in cultural studies emphasises. In other words, the emphasis on individual consciousness, feelings and expressions tends to be the focus of such theorists, and this has been widely and enthusiastically embraced. But this is not the focus of the discussion in this book. Whatever its strengths or weaknesses, the discussion about diasporas from the perspective of the individual psyche ultimately relates to a highly subjective and relativistic articulation of life. This is often exciting and brings to centre stage the subjective and the speculative and its warm reception may be due to its juxtaposing one weakness with another. In other words, the culturalist's glorification of relativism points up the drawbacks of the extreme empiricism and sometimes over-optimistic positivism of much traditional sociology; the one weakness is pitched against the other and in such a contest the situation may be six of one and half-a-dozen of the other. Unfortunately, however, it also underplays the empirical and the verifiable which are vital if we are to arrive at general statements about society.

My interest is more in the direction of collective social experience which transcends the individual's or the individualistic perspective of social life. It is, after all, well established in philosophy – and even Emile Durkheim would admit in his less positivistic moods that the social sciences are grounded in philosophy – that the aggregate social total is more than the simple addition of the individual parts. Individual subjective feelings and perceptions pursued by cultural theorists – who ultimately derive their intellectual bearings from considerations of the wholly subjective as developed in creative prose and poetry, films, music and other self-expressions of the perceptible, the felt, the tactile – are, of course, valid sources about the human condition in themselves. We do not have to be of the Comtean positivist persuasion, however, to recognise that a sociology entirely rooted in the personal and the subjective is very limited and limiting.

Solipsism and Culturalist Epistemology

It would be harsh to say that the starting-point of much cultural theory is the philosophy of solipsism (the view that the only thing of which we can be certain or attain certain knowledge about, is the self), but it is difficult to separate the profound scepticism inherent in solipsism from some of what is presented as method in cultural theory. After all, statements about the social are often ultimately justified by reference to particular experience, usually the experience of the writer, without reference to the experiences of social others. It is not surprising therefore that the validity of statements rests not so much on empirical evidence (limited as these may be) but on the cultist or iconic status of the writer. The underplay of collective experience, of empirical evidence, and the overwhelming dependence on individual sense experience reinforces the charismatic authority of each high priest or priestess, which after all, is not subject to external (even if independent) scrutiny or validation.

I do not wish to leave an impression that I view the subjectivity of social analysis that cultural theorists remind us of as irrelevant to our understanding of society. After all, over the last decade or more the culturalists have brought a refreshing breath of life into what had become a sometimes stultifying social science of the 1980s where dogmas, often from the previous century, held sway. The singular strength of the culturalist persuasion has been its power to communicate a message; the culturalist persuasion is able to make understanding of complex issues accessible, to bring a kind of freedom from the rigours of any particular discipline, and the persuasion endows an ability to address anything that pertained to the human condition. For a generation of students this appeared not only refreshing but also liberating.

In a sense, the culturalist persuasion has been a useful reminder of a kind of Weberian caution or nuance to the more assertive certainty of Durkheimian sociology. But this has become a new orthodoxy; the caution has become the central matter of analysis, and it insists that each new text or writer must, as a kind of *rite de passage*, comment on the last person who commented on one of the gurus of the persuasion, and then genuflect to one or two of the founding figures such as Stuart Hall and one or other of the French *grandes maîtres* such as Jacques Derrida. In general, readers of these texts must be prepared to invest much time and effort going through the labyrinth of those considered worthy of respect in the sect, before coming to anything beyond untestable assertions, which, because of their vagueness, are then declared to be 'theoretical'. There is therefore a tendency to offer commentary upon commentary, and little space exists for considering aspects of actual moments of social action, structures and continuity in human affairs beyond individual sense experience. As one would-be researcher of this persuasion put it to me some years ago, he could not conduct 'research' into a particular problem because no one had written about the problem we were discussing: his view of research was restricted to commentary on other sect members' commentaries. My discussion of Caribbean diasporic experiences is not about commenting on what others have commented upon. Nor is it about commenting on what others have not done, as supposed explanation of the exclusivism of educational institutions – something that some academics are still fond of doing in order to excuse the absence of a willingness to conduct verifiable work (see, for example, Hesse, 2000).

I want then to distinguish my discussion of Caribbean diasporic experiences from the view that because human beings are always caught up in an endless activity of change and flux – a central plank in the culturalist's platform – there can be few if any empirically verifiable statements. Always is a strong word here. To be sure, social structures, beliefs and so on do not remain constant. Indeed, the fact that change occurs is one of the central concerns of sociology, and it was the attempt by Marx, Durkheim, Weber and others to explain this fact of social life that gave rise to the discipline we loosely call sociology. Social changes do not, however, occur at such a rate that we cannot see the contrary patterns of continuity, making it possible to isolate aspects of social life in order better to describe, explain and understand them. Changes occur but not at the frantic, constant, everyday intensity or flux suggested by cultural theory. Even if some *individuals* constantly reconstruct themselves on a daily basis, this is not necessarily change at a *social* level; indeed, such rearrangements on the part of the individual must be more like Ervine Goffman's (1956) character who changes the presentation of self depending on the audience. It may be a mistake to assume that this change of face on or off stage amounts to social change; one face or mask may be set aside now for another to be worn, but that too will be put aside later for the replacement of an earlier one. This is more of a circular set of events than of a changing nature. The cultural theorist's insistence on the playing out of an endless negotiation over roles and self, may be a little more than Goffman's dramaturgical representation of the individual subject: observations of the monotony of everyday life and of conformity, not social change.

The work of cultural theorists who focus on individual experience and consciousness, must therefore be set aside from the kind of discussion that I want to invite here about the presence of Caribbean diasporic or transnational experiences across the Atlantic. It is important to make this point because the Caribbean experience is often cited as representation of what many cultural theorists wish to talk about, and consequently much mischief and misunderstanding are wrought or conjured when there is mention of the region and its people abroad.

THE NOTION OF A CARIBBEAN DIASPORA

This leads to a consideration of the notion of a Caribbean diaspora or diasporic experiences. In other words, to what extent is it valid to speak of a Caribbean diaspora as an independent entity, in the ways that we speak about a Jewish, African, Chinese or Indian Diaspora? In the first place, some of these other diasporas appear to be characterised by kinship or national communal bonding which coincide with the juridical-political unit, the nation-state. Of course, these are themselves loose and sometimes vague categories. For example, the notion of the Indian diaspora cannot be restricted to the modern nation-state of India, but must properly refer to different groups of people from the Indian sub-continent, or the earlier construction of Hindustan. None the less, it is the post-Raj state of India which is often celebrated as the Indian diaspora (see, for example, ESRC 2000).

More than most diasporas, the Caribbean one refers to a highly fragmented geographical region which has little or no coherence at home or abroad. At home, the Caribbean is several: Anglophone/Commonwealth, Francophone, Hispanic, Dutch, American and Danish. This is reflected outward into the wider world: in Europe there are at least three Caribbeans (French, Dutch and British); in North America the situation is much the same (Hispanic, Haitian, British). They share, in the main, a heritage of slavery, colonialism and indentureship, although these are also different in important respects. Outward from the region, there is at least one significant aspect of the making of a diaspora involved, namely, the scattering or spread of groups of people who share certain identifiable characteristics. But this one necessary condition for the construction of a diaspora is insufficient.

The second difficulty with the notion of a Caribbean diaspora is the glaring fact that the Caribbean abroad is not a singular but a very plural world or community, which looks outwards to different worlds. Consider the fact that people from the region are themselves committed to groping for their identities to places outside the Caribbean. In the main they look to Africa and to the Indian sub-continent as both the points of their departures and their historical, mythical or aspirational homes, if not necessarily their eventual destinations as actual 'home' of abode. Caribbeans crossing the Atlantic may therefore be caught up in different diasporas: Indian, Jewish, Irish, English, African.

In Britain they make a stance on this point. Thus, the whites who came to Britain during the period of decolonisation in the 1950s and 1960s have not generally become part of a Caribbean diaspora, but have completed their circle of a return 'home', and national census returns do not record their offspring as 'Caribbean'. This would also be true for whites returning during the same period from South Asia and Africa where they had a shorter historical stay than in the Caribbean. People of South Asian backgrounds who migrated from the Caribbean to Britain have either voluntarily or forcibly been removed from the Caribbean world, and may be in the process of renewing links with other communities with a claim to descent from South Asia. The significant presence of communities in Britain and The Netherlands with historic connections to South Asia provides one of the bases for the formation of an Indian diaspora, but this diaspora is also intricately intertwined with the African-Caribbean diaspora, and cannot clinically be disentangled.

Perhaps the most significant development over the last half-century in the Atlantic world is that Caribbeans of African backgrounds in Britain have come to redefine themselves and been accepted as African Caribbeans, and sometimes the 'African' quali-fication is left out of the reckoning because it has become unnecessary to state it. It is understood that Caribbean means African. First, this is so partly because the demographic majority in the Commonwealth Caribbean are predominantly of African ancestry and this fact has strongly marked migration flows from the region since the Second World War. Second, this is so because the definition of African in Britain has been determined largely by Caribbeans, not Africans directly from the continent.

The notion of a Caribbean diaspora, therefore, is problematic. It must be understood to be a community in formation. Crucially, it must be understood to be a new dimension of a wider diaspora, principally the African diaspora. This wider collectivity reaches out not only back to the Caribbean, but also to North America and to Africa, as some of the chapters in this book illustrate. However, it is worth remembering that Alexander Herzen's territorialising of Zion for European Jews could, by a quirk of history (had the discussions to usher in the new European order at the end of the First World War at Versailles in 1919 taken a different turn), have been located as far from Palestine as Uganda. So too could the notion of 'home' for diaspora Africans have been over-generously interpreted with respect to the African continent, particularly as narrated by the Rastafarian myth.

A third problematic point warrants brief consideration. Increas-ingly, the Caribbean-derived population in Britain is becoming mixed with members from other communities, principally the white, European or historically indigenous population. The 1991 census of population and subsequent Labour Force Surveys suggest that about a third of ostensibly Caribbean households are of mixed backgrounds, as discussed in a later chapter. Exogenous marriage or partnerships have a basis in Caribbean societies themselves, but in the open and liberal social context of post-imperial Britain, the freedom of choice that exists has given rise to the present situation. This has led Orlando Patterson (1999) to suggest that the presence of a Caribbean community in Britain by the middle of the present century is unlikely. But mixing of populations and the resultant racial redesignation of groups do not of themselves mean the erad-ication of collective identities. After all, all populations change their composition, and even continuity of geographical location and nomenclature do not guarantee sameness through time. For example, the Jewish dispersal resulted in the radical raciation of those communities that consider themselves to be Jewish. In other words, it has been more the consciousness of being Jewish (through religious belief and practice) that has kept disparate groups aware of their uniqueness and collective identity. Jewish raciation has resulted in the groups which claim to be Jewish displaying a range of racial types, and currently there is a discussion in parts of the Jewish diaspora and in Israel about what makes a person a member of the Jewish community.

This process of raciation is also true for Africans in the diaspora – these Africans are not always distinguished by uniformity of colour or other racial features; their intermixing over time has resulted in a range of physical appearances that have little to do with Africa. It is possible, therefore, that Caribbeans in Britain in the next five or more decades may radically change their appearance (as well as a sizeable proportion of the overall population of the British Isles) but there might still exist a strong sense of being Caribbean. In other words, just as today Jewishness displays a range of racial types, Caribbean racial types will continue to be diverse, and ethnic iden-tification may become more significant than racial identity.

Of course, by racial identity I refer to such palpable phenotypic and therefore visible factors as colour (of skin, eyes, hair, etc.) and structure (various parts of the body) of groups of people, and by ethnic identity I refer to socially acquired attributes as culture, including language, religion, aesthetics, values, and so on. The first of these is inherited through the accident of ancestry, parentage, biology; the second is acquired through accident of cultural location or belongingness of parents. Whilst the first can only exceptionally be changed by the individual, the second can be relatively easily changed and has been changed through a variety of social actions such as conquest and domination, individual choice, migration, intermarriage, and so on. Of course, these two dominant lines of individual and collective identities are usually conflated and intertwined, thereby resulting in a complex social and conceptual situation (see H. Goulbourne, 2001). Cultural and postmodernist theorists are generally fond of exploiting these complexities as if to fulfil a desire to wreck attempts at comprehension in discussions about them, and this is very prevalent in race and ethnicity as well as diasporic studies both of which frequently draw on Caribbean situations and experiences.

The general point here, however, is that it is not possible to predetermine the future of the Caribbean diaspora at this point in post-imperial Britain, and the future must be kept as an open question, as I stress in the concluding chapter to this volume. For now it is enough to appreciate the problematic nature of the notion of a Caribbean diaspora in the making, particularly as distinct from other diasporas and in its own terms. At this point in the discussion it is of considerable significance to locate the formation of the Caribbean diaspora and diasporic experiences within a wider context of social structure in the Atlantic world.

DIFFERENTIAL INCORPORATION OF CARIBBEANS

Turning to this broader question, I want to suggest that it is not so much a situation of what Gilroy calls 'double consciousness' that is of significance in structural terms within the Caribbean diaspora, but the process of differential incorporation of these communities into the wider world of the Atlantic. After all, this 'double consciousness' is not exceptional or unique to Africans in the West or the wider Atlantic world; it is not difficult to imagine that this must also be true for other groups.

Consider the situation of the Irish: dispersed across the Atlantic by the English, are they not also caught up in the *angst* of being Irish, being British, being European, as well as whatever they have become depending on what point they are located in the Atlantic world? What other group has been as subversive of English hegemony in the visual arts, literature and politics across the Atlantic world, while using the very tools or pathways initiated by the English themselves? And what is there to be said of these groups that cannot be more astonishingly stated about Jews who have integrated into the social, economic and political fabrics of social orders in varied time and space in the Atlantic world and yet also developed a sharp consciousness of themselves? The experiences of other groups in the Americas are not necessarily significantly less complex: the privileged Scots and English, the politically less successful French in the Mississippi Delta and Quebec, and very many other scattered groups from Europe and the Middle East, all of whom have created futures for themselves in the Americas and the Caribbean. The concept of double consciousness and its apparent subversiveness (of modernity) may be a general, not a particular, situation; these are not qualities that are exceptional to any group, and I for one am not convinced that they significantly advance our understanding of Africans and Caribbeans across the Atlantic world.

What distinguishes Africans in the West from other groups, however, is their structural positions within the social order. The 'West' in this respect includes the Caribbean, which can be distinguished from other parts of the Western world only by levels of development and differences in racial population distribution: the essential elements constituting the social order are not significantly different between large swathes of the United States, Europe and the Caribbean. When, however, commentators see phenotypical differences, they tend also to see all kinds of differences which do not structurally exist. In this cross-Atlantic world of the Caribbean, North America and Britain, what I have been speaking about as the emerging Caribbean diaspora exhibits a fundamental structural difference in the positions occupied by Africans of the Caribbean diaspora. This is what M. G. Smith described as 'differential incorporation'. The vigorous and lively debates in the 1960s that took place in Caribbean studies over Smith's theory of social and cultural pluralism in the Caribbean (see, for example, Smith, 1984; Rubin, 1960) later led to his *Corporations and Society* (1974) in which he sought to apply pluralism to a wider range of societies, including the US, and it is this development that I wish to draw upon here.

Smith argued that there are different ways in which groups are incorporated into societies, and outlined three kinds of incorporation: the universal/uniform, the segmental/equivalent, and the differential. The universal or uniform incorporation of groups involves society conferring the same rights on people of the same racial but different ethnic groups. Thus, in the US all white Europeans, irrespective of ethnic or national backgrounds, enjoyed the rights to vote, organise, publish, live where they wished and engage in economic activities. In such situations, M. G. Smith points out, 'differing ethnic cultures do not entail any differences of formal status in the public domain of political, legal, economic and ancillary activities between ethnic units' (Smith, 1988, p. 195). The distinction between the private and public domains is maintained and it appears that this is what multiculturalism aspires to in Britain. Multiculturalism, like universal incorporation 'simultaneously confers equal citizenship and identical legal rights and obligations on individuals' (ibid.). But Smith's point is that in what he called complex pluralities, such as North American and British societies, some groups may indeed enjoy uniform or universal incorporation into the social order, but in the same society other groups may simultaneously be incorporated in less favourable and inequitable ways.

Thus, whilst white groups which share the same racial typology as dominant groups have been discriminated against, with time they have come to enjoy universal incorporation with the dominant groups. The cases of the Irish in Britain and the US and the Jews in both these societies illustrate this point. On the other hand, groups of people with black or brown or yellow colours were differentially or inequitably incorporated into these societies. Segmental or differential incorporation meant that, for example, whilst black Americans may have sometimes had the same *de jure* rights as those conferred on white Americans, these could not be enjoyed by blacks because of the *de facto* situation which prohibited their participation in the mainstream of American life. Blacks were excluded from free, active and equal participation in American life despite the fact that this contradicted some of the fundamental tenets of American democracy, principally equality based on individual, not group, worth. Similarly, the indigenous Amerindian population and other groups of people such as the Chinese, Japanese, Mexicans, Polynesians and blacks from elsewhere were segmented from the rest of society by 'differing judicial provisions' (Smith, 1988, p. 196). Within the Atlantic world inhabited by Caribbeans, however, the process of incorporation may be more complex than Smith's legalistic formulation suggests.

Migration to Britain has not significantly changed the place of black Caribbeans in the social structures that obtain in the Anglo-Caribbean world which straddles the Atlantic. The Caribbean that the migrants left behind between 1948 and the early 1960s was a region in which the economy was dominated and owned by the small pockets of Europeans who remained after Emancipation from slavery in 1838, as the dominance of the West India interest in

British politics gave way to those of the nabobs of the East India interest in London following the Corn Laws of 1840. Although political independence was won in the 1960s by most of these countries, economic control failed to materialise and the vast majority of black Caribbeans remained outside the sphere of significant ownership as detailed by a generation of Caribbean scholarship. This is hardly the place to explain the patterns of ownership and control in the region; suffice it therefore to suggest that the incorporation of African Caribbeans into European or Island British society has not been significantly different from the form of their historical differential incorporation within the Caribbean itself.

Of course, within the Caribbean the situation has been significantly changed during the last four or so decades: black Caribbeans now have a stake in the economy of their countries and a more complex class system has changed significantly the racial differentiation that obtained under the colonial order. The commanding heights of the economy remain, however, in the hands of Caribbean-European or other minorities and transnational companies in agriculture, manufactures, mining (oil and bauxite) and tourism. The situation on the European side of the Atlantic is not significantly different in relation to the economy. With respect to visible representation, and participation in a range of public activities (such as sports, entertainment and politics) the Caribbean presence is abundantly clear. Whether this creativity will lead to a *de facto* realisation of uniform incorporation is an open question for the future.

CONCLUSION

It must be obvious, therefore, that while I am of the view that the theory of differential incorporation helps to explain an historical and continuing contemporary situation, it does not necessarily help us to provide answers about the future. However, before picking up in the last chapter of this book on such necessarily troubling matters, it is important to look at some aspects of the diasporic or transnational experiences being alluded to in this discussion. Thus, in the next chapter I turn to a general outline of what I see as the place of Caribbeans in a common transatlantic heritage, and in Chapter 3 I focus on the socio-political contexts of Caribbean transnationality. In Chapter 4 I discuss an aspect of how Africa and the Caribbean itself came to be restructured in the emerging Caribbean consciousness in Britain and what that meant for Caribbeans in Britain, while in Chapter 5 I suggest the relevance of popular US perceptions to this situation in Britain. The role of some publishers in the creation of a Caribbean diaspora in Britain is taken up in Chapter 6. In Chapters 7 and 8 I focus on family connections and the propensity to 'return home' from the 'Mother Country' in recent years – the situation of an experience that has come full circle.

It must be stressed that the specific topics discussed in these chapters do not by any means exhaust the range of issues that need to be researched about Caribbeans in Britain and their relations across the Atlantic. They are, however, intended to suggest some of the kinds of issues which require both theoretical and empirical attention if we are to understand the dynamic process of diasporic or transnational formation where Caribbeans are concerned.

2 A Common Transatlantic Heritage

Slavery and indenture, colonialism and migration constitute the backdrop for the formation of the Caribbean diaspora across the Atlantic. Described as *A Respectable Trade* in the BBC's television drama series of the same title towards the end of the 1990s, the slave trade was an essential part of the mercantilist system that formed one of the cornerstones of the British Industrial Revolution, as Eric Williams attempted to demonstrate in his seminal work, *Capitalism and Slavery* (1944). If not exactly the beginning of modern Caribbean societies, this trade in persons and the plantations that they worked, were to form the beginnings of post-Columbian societies in the Caribbean as well as American societies such as the US and Brazil. Labour shortage on the Caribbean plantations led to the establishment of what Hugh Tinker (1974) described as a 'new system of slavery', namely, Indian indenture labour, particularly in Trinidad and Guyana from Emancipation in 1840 to 1917.

European settlement, African slavery, Indian indenture, as well as labour from China and Madeira, and later immigration from troubled places such as Palestine and Nazi Germany all play a part in the overall construction of the Commonwealth Caribbean and the Caribbean abroad. In general, however, if we can speak meaningfully of a Caribbean diaspora across the Atlantic it must be recognised as having been defined and shaped predominantly by the demographic majority of the region, that is, people of African backgrounds.

This chapter discusses, first, how the diverse Commonwealth Caribbean has come to create living and therefore meaningful connections across national boundaries and over considerable distances in such a way that these links are increasingly described as a diaspora, and second, how the slavery past continues to cast a long and deep shadow over our present condition in the Atlantic world. By briefly describing aspects of the contemporary presence of Caribbeans in Britain, it will be possible to address the first of these questions and establish a basis for addressing the second.

THE DEMOGRAPHIC AND SOCIAL PRESENCE OF CARIBBEANS IN BRITAIN

Caribbean communities in Britain are distinguished by such factors as their size and distribution; their variation and plurality; the fact of their historical and cultural proximity to the indigenous and dominant English, Welsh, Irish and Scottish majority communities, and, finally, the fact that Caribbean communities in Britain are, like other communities, in the process of reshaping themselves alongside and in their relationship with each other. It is worth looking very briefly at each of these aspects in order better to establish the backdrop against which to understand some of the more specific features of Caribbean transnationality or diasporic experiences.

The 1991 census is generally considered to have provided the most reliable figures about the British population, because for the first time in the country's history there was what is called 'the ethnic question', asking individuals to identify the group they considered best describe their ethnicity (see, for example, Coleman and Salt, 1996, Ch. 1). The categories offered a choice between White, Black-Caribbean, Black-African, Black-Other (with an option to describe 'Other'), Indian, Pakistani, Bangladeshi, Chinese, Any Other ethnic group (with an option to describe this). In the end, ten categories were constructed from the returns. Whilst there was much heated debate over the pro and contra of including 'the ethnic question' in the census (see Bulmer, 1996), once the returns became available they proved invaluable in gaining more precise knowledge of the size, structure, distribution and so on of the majority ethnic population as well as the new minority groups. The utility of the 1991 returns has been reflected in the close discussions that have gone on about the phrasing of the ethnic question in the 2001 census. The total new minority ethnic population was found to be just over 3 million or 5.5 per cent of the British population of 54,999,844. With a total of 499,964 (Owen, 1996, pp. 85–8), people of Caribbean backgrounds accounted for 0.9 per cent of the British population. These included both those born in the Caribbean and those born in Britain, with the latter continuing to be in the majority. People of Caribbean backgrounds constituted the second largest new minority ethnic group after people of Indian backgrounds (840,000 or 2.7 per cent) and just ahead of those of Pakistani backgrounds (476,555). Asian communities (including Chinese, Vietnamese, Bangladeshis, East African Asians, etc.) account for the overwhelming majority of new minority ethnic population, making a considerable shift from the situation from the 1950s to the mid-1960s, when Caribbeans (particularly Jamaicans) formed a majority. Although people who identified themselves as 'Black-Caribbean' are the single largest group of the 890,727 (1.6 per cent) people identified as 'black ethnic groups', it must be remembered that this total black population includes 212,362 'Black-Africans' and 178,401 'Black-Others'.

It must be firmly borne in mind that the breakdown of minority ethnic representation offered by the 1991 census did not give a perfect reflection of the racial and ethnic kaleidoscope that is post-imperial Britain. For example, people of Sri Lankan, Filipino and Vietnamese backgrounds were not included in the larger Asian categories. Owen points out that North Africans, Arabs and Iranians 'cannot be separately distinguished' (p. 89) even although they constitute 22.5 per cent of the Other-Other category in the census. More significant for the purposes of this discussion is the fact that many Indo-Caribbeans may have been encouraged or forced to identify themselves as Indians or Black-Caribbeans whilst African Americans serving in Suffolk and Argyll may have identified themselves as Black-Others (ibid.).

The 1991 census confirmed what earlier censuses and intervening Labour Force Surveys had consistently surmised from answers given about an individual's place of birth (UK, Ireland, New Common-wealth, etc.), namely that the vast majority of people of Caribbean backgrounds lived in the urban areas of Greater London and the West Midlands. Whilst Black-Others, that is, mixed black people, are more widely distributed in the country, people who identify themselves as Black-Caribbeans have long been significantly con-centrated in the South East (just under 60 per cent), constitute 1.9 per cent of the population of the South East region of the country, 4.4 per cent of Greater London, 1.5 per cent of the West Midlands and 2.8 per cent of the population of the metropolitan area around the country's second city, Birmingham. In sharp contrast, the numbers of Caribbean people in Scotland (with a total population of about 6 million) and Tyne & Wear in Northern England are statisti-cally insignificant with scores of 0.0 per cent. In Wales, Caribbeans account for a mere 0.1 per cent in a population of around 3 million. To be sure, there are pockets of Caribbeans distributed throughout most of England, but outside the South-east and the West Midlands their presence accounts for less than 1 per cent.

The gender and age distributions of the Caribbean population reflects its relatively longer settlement, its pattern of migration and family characteristics when compared to other new minority ethnic communities. Whilst migration from the Caribbean was at first led by men, it soon became common for women to find their own way and often establish their own families (see, for example, Patterson, 1965; Peach, 1991; Thomas-Hope, 1992). This is in sharp contrast to the male-led migration pattern that characterised migration from South Asia (see, for example, Brown and Foot, 1994; Ballard, 1994; Bhachu, 1986). Since women generally live longer than men, there is expectedly a higher ratio of women to men in both minority and majority ethnic populations. For example, for every thousand women there were 954 men in the White, 927 in the Other-Asian and 946 in the Caribbean populations, which contrasted with the higher ratios of well over a thousand for all other categories of Asians and Africans.

In terms of age, there are significant variations between the indigenous white population and the new minorities, with the Caribbean population being closest to the white population at the 55–60 age group, reflecting their earlier migration history. The age pyramid is wide at the base (5–14 years) amongst South Asians, less wide for black communities but wider than for the white population; at the top of the pyramid (from around 56 to 85+ years) the majority white population is significantly wider than is the case with either South Asians or black people.

It must now be obvious that people of Caribbean backgrounds, like other new minority and indeed the indigenous majority ethnic groups in Britain, do not constitute a homogenous entity as is often thought to be the case. The diversity of the Caribbean-derived communities is often hidden or subsumed under the common banner of blackness, being Caribbean or being Jamaican. But the Caribbean community in Britain is comprised of people from a wide range of islands and territories stretching well over a thousand miles along the Atlantic, and separated by the other (Spanish-speaking and French-speaking) Caribbeans, and extends both north and south beyond the geographical Caribbean into the wider Atlantic and the South American continent. The Commonwealth Caribbean includes Antigua, Anguilla, the Bahamas and Barbados (both in the Atlantic proper), Belize, the British Virgin Islands, the Caymans, Dominica, Grenada, Guyana (on the South American continent), Jamaica, Montserrat, St Kitts & Nevis, St Lucia, St Vincent & the Grenadines, and Trinidad & Tobago. Moreover, both the land mass and population of this sub-region are comparatively small: Jamaica, the largest single island[1] (10,990 sq. km) has also the largest population with about 2.5 million people; Guyana, the largest country (214,970 sq. km) has a far smaller population than Trinidad & Tobago which has around 1.5 million people and is under 5,180 sq. km in size. Some of the islands are even smaller than Barbados with her 430 sq. km; for example, Anguilla is a mere 91 sq kms. In total, the population of the Commonwealth Caribbean is only roughly the same as Haiti's (about 6 million), and migration to Britain (and North America) therefore marked a significant shift of population for the main sending countries.

Second, while statistics are important in outlining population size and distribution, they do not tell the whole story about that population's general presence. In broad social terms, there are several factors to be noted about the Caribbean presence in Britain. For example, groups of Barbadians, Antiguans, Jamaicans and others retain much of their distinctiveness within British cities, even where they live cheek by jowl with others from the majority ethnic as well as other new minority ethnic communities. In terms of cuisine, music, language and other features, groups from Caribbean countries retain important aspects of their distinct national features. However, perhaps what is more interesting is that these groups also change as a result of their proximity to each other as Caribbean groups, and to others as a result of culture-contact. The changes they undergo in relation to each other as Caribbean groups occur because in the main they meet for the first time in Britain, not in the Caribbean where, for example, a Jamaican was not very likely to meet a Guyanese or a Barbadian outside the charmed circles of literature, cricket, the regional University of the West Indies and within the confluence of union and party political leadership.

It is not only the statistical returns which show that over a period of half a century, Caribbean communities in Britain have come to be defined in a manner that excludes people of Asian-Caribbean backgrounds; in general, the various Asian, and indeed, European groups found in the Commonwealth Caribbean do not significantly feature in the definition of Caribbean communities in Britain. It is important, however, immediately to note that some of the most visible in the Caribbean communities over this half-century have been from groups other than the demographically and culturally dominant African-Caribbean group. To a degree, well-known individuals (such as the publisher Arif Ali, the late Rudy Narayan who as a barrister was a thorn to the judicial system, and Sir Shridath Sonny Ramphal) are lost to the Caribbean communities in Britain, because they are from Asian (East Indian in the Caribbean) backgrounds. At best, they appear to be regarded as kinds of honorary Caribbean figures, much the same as white individuals in Britain with backgrounds or investments in the Caribbean.

This is understandable to a degree. East Indians from the Caribbean are no doubt pulled in the direction of defining themselves alongside and with the larger and very dynamic Asian presence in Britain. After all, South Asians are themselves from varied backgrounds in terms of religions, languages, geography and so on, and, like people of African backgrounds in Britain, South Asians are also engaged in redefining and reconfiguring their collective identities in much the same way as people of African backgrounds. The fact that the vast majority of people from the Caribbean (principally Jamaica and Barbados) came from the majority African countries and not the country with an East Indian overall majority (Guyana) or a country with the single largest group (Trinidad) being East Indians, also acted strongly to influence the patterns of development of the Caribbean diaspora in Britain. In another sense, however, this reconfiguring of Caribbean identity in Britain results in a loss of Caribbean diversity and cultural richness.

Second, it has been in Britain that people from the Caribbean islands have discovered much of their commonalities, and are creating and developing ethnic bonds which do not exist in the same way in the region itself. This fact is reflected in several peculiarly British practices which have come to define the Caribbean in Britain: the participation of Jamaicans in the (originally Trinidadian) Notting Hill Carnival, the growth and popularity of reggae (originally from Jamaica) in Britain, the display if not quite embrace of the Rastafarian lifestyle far beyond its narrow following in Jamaica, and the use of terms such as 'Afro-Caribbean' or 'African Caribbean' that have little or no meaning within the region itself. This creation of new collective ethnic identity in Britain has been consolidated by such factors as inter-island marriage or partnership and households, leading to offspring who feel that they have common links with more than one country in the Caribbean and are therefore migrating to the region in a reverse process to that followed by their parents in the 1950s and 1960s. Paradoxically, perhaps apart from the existence of the regional University of the

West Indies, migration to Britain has been a more powerful factor in the promotion of Commonwealth Caribbean social integration than any other single initiative within the region, including the Caribbean Common Market (CARICOM).

A final aspect of this sketchy background to Caribbean transnationality in Britain is the general cultural proximity between the indigenous European and Caribbean-derived cultural artefacts. It is hardly necessary to detail the obvious cultural presence of Caribbean people in Britain, but it is important to note that this presence continues to have a significant impact in various areas of British national life, including phrases in the popular use of language and music, style in everyday life and sports. Popular phrases (to have 'street cred', or to be 'cool'), youth dress style (the turned-around basketball cap, ever larger unlaced trainers and big soft-looking boots, baggy T-shirts), DJs and loud music in clubs and remodelled cars are examples of the visibility and audibility of the powerless. These features of black cultures in the African diaspora cannot be easily delineated according to national boundaries because they are in constant interplay in a nomad-like fashion across juridical and political borders, particularly across the Atlantic. Thus, in each of these areas membership of a cross-Atlantic African diaspora, importantly embracing the US and, of course, the Caribbean region, strengthens the presence and the impact of Caribbeans in Britain. What is observed of popular music, language and dress styles may also be observed with respect to the active participation in sports, entertainment and a presence in the advertisement of consumer goods.

No doubt, the proximity of Commonwealth Caribbean culture (language and literature, sports and entertainment, values and religion) to the dominant majority culture must be a factor in the visible and audible presence of Caribbeans in these areas in Britain. The differential incorporation, however, that M. G. Smith (1974, 1988) spoke about, as discussed in Chapter 1, has also powerfully restricted the choice of social and economic participation in British life by people of African-Caribbean backgrounds. This helps to explain the fact that despite high levels of participation in the creative spheres of cultural life Caribbean people have little or no participation in the control or ownership of cultural production. For example, with the notable exceptions of Ruud Gullit from The Netherlands and John Barnes the former Liverpool player, as late as 2001 there has been a conspicuous absence of managers and trainers of Caribbean backgrounds in football clubs. Similarly, with the exception of Linford Christie the former Olympic champion, there has also been a conspicuous absence of Caribbean sportspeople as trainers in athletics, which has been dominated by young people with Caribbean and African backgrounds. Moreover, few individuals from Caribbean backgrounds and certainly no household or recognisable names come to mind when contemplating the ownership of football and athletics clubs, and indeed leading music companies – areas of human endeavours in which the Caribbean presence as performers is glaringly obvious. These features of the background of the Caribbean presence in Britain suggest that whilst migration to Britain had the potential for upward social mobility, this experience has not significantly changed the place of Africans in the social structures that obtain in the Anglo-Caribbean world straddling the Atlantic.

Caribbeans in Britain have none the less passed from being immigrants to becoming members of a seemingly flourishing multicultural or multiracial society in the half-century from 1950 to 2000 whilst not managing significantly to change their structural position in the scheme of things. This process of national change and transatlantic continuity has been strongly mirrored by social research, and for convenience as well as for analytical purposes the emphases in the literature on race relations (in which discussions about Caribbean and other new minority ethnic groups have taken place) may be grouped into the following: an immigrant situation, a race relations situation, a cultural situation and a situation of differential incorporation. It is not necessary to discuss each of these here as there have been a number of discussions of each elsewhere (see, for example, Goulbourne, 1998). I want instead to confine myself to making some remarks about the *immigrant situation* during the period of entry and settlement, and the *multicultural situation* that characterised much of the thinking about communities and identities during the last 15 years.

AN IMMIGRANT SITUATION

What is generally regarded as the Windrush or immigrant generation from the West Indies first attracted the attention of social analysts who saw the West Indian presence as a situation involving immigrants and hosts. This view was informed by the ignorance of – or the unwillingness to acknowledge – the presence of Africans and Asians in Britain since the age of European discovery from the late fifteenth century. None the less, this earlier presence has been well documented by historians such as F. O. Shyllon (1974), James Walvin (1973, 1982), Peter Fryer (1984) and others. Earlier, Eldred Jones (1965, 1971) had conducted important and relevant work on the black presence in Elizabethan drama; there were also autobiographies, such as that of Oloudah Equaino, published in London in 1789, the year of the French Revolution. But by and large this long-standing black presence was not always taken into account in what was to become a new wisdom or orthodoxy of the black presence and British society from the 1950s. To be sure, there were some attempts to acknowledge the presence of blacks in seaports such as Liverpool and Cardiff, as the work of Kenneth Little (1947), Anthony Richmond (1955) and Michael Banton (1968) show. In the main, however, the first generation of analysts of Caribbeans (or West Indians, as they saw themselves and as others saw them) in a Britain retreating from empire sought to explore the apparent newness of this presence, including its social, economic and psychological implications for the immigrants and the host community. Adjustment and accommodation, individual prejudice and strangeness were key variables in their accounts of what they – partly correctly – saw as a new kind of encounter.

The essential characterisation was of the immigrant–host dichotomy, and the corollary was the problematic of integration or, more properly, absorption of the former into the latter society. In other words, it was generally assumed that British society was homogeneous (mainly through the agencies of colour, culture and a shared history and myths of nationhood). It was also assumed that this supposedly homogeneous culture had the capacity to integrate and absorb whatever differences might appear this side of the White Cliffs of Dover. It was, therefore, a rather static model which underplayed social conflict as well as the history of earlier encounters between different racial and cultural groups in the first and second British empire, and how these might impact on Island Britain.

This perspective may be illustrated by reference to the work of Sheila Patterson, whose *Dark Strangers: A Study of West Indians in London* was first published in 1963. A classics scholar turned social anthropologist, Patterson had conducted research in South Africa as well as on Polish immigration to Canada. She was also a product of what was to become by the 1960s, and particularly the 1970s, the disparaged 'race relations industry' started by Kenneth Little at Edinburgh University in the 1950s, which included such figures as

Michael Banton and Anthony Richmond (see Goulbourne, 1998, Ch. 6). Her work on Brixton reflected a general concern about the apparently sudden West Indian entry into the English body social. Although a work subjected to much justified criticisms, it is fair to say that, revisiting the text today, Patterson approached her subject with a greater degree of objectivity and commitment than is to be found in a good many works of social analysis that followed. Based on years of close field research, she concluded that the meeting of black and white people on British Islands soil was not as in South Africa where she saw 'a race relations situation' between different groups. None the less, the difference of people's colour (black, brown and white) marked off West Indians and Asians from Europeans such as Poles, Italians, Latvians and Cypriots. The problem was not one of numbers (for example, the Poles outnumbered West Indians at the time) but one of colour, culture and historical antecedents. The spirit and concerns of the times are clearly summarised in Patterson's statement that the 'newcomers' not only differed among themselves (different West Indians and South Asians), but the new encounter between these groups

> ... underlined the point made throughout the Brixton study – that Brixton is faced, not with an established colour or racial situation, but with a dynamic and uncrystalised immigrant situation, in which the newcomers' visibility serves mainly to draw attention to the problems inevitably found in the early years of immigrant absorption. The great divergences of culture, social organisation, and goals between the self-segregating, self-sufficient Asians and the individualist, assimilating West Indians has also led to the real-isation in the host society that different approaches and policies are needed to ease the processes of integration for different groups. [Patterson, 1965, pp. 9–10]

This perspective was fairly typical of other studies during the years of entry and settlement from the late 1950s to the late 1970s. Book titles in this period were clear reflections of the concern with what Patterson called 'immigrant-host relations' within the context of 'an immigrant situation'. Consider, for example, such titles as Ruth Glass's *Newcomers: The West Indians in London*, published in 1960, three years before Patterson's *Dark Strangers*, or Davison's *West Indian Migrants* (1962), published two years before Patterson's work. The point here is that Sheila Patterson's work was already part of a genre of social analysis on the apparently new presence of West Indians. The genre was to continue in the 1970s in works such as the American Nancy Foner's *Jamaica Farewell: Jamaican Migrants in London* (1979) and Philpott's *West Indian Migration: The Montserrat Case* (1973), as well as Collins' earlier personal account of being a migrant in *Jamaican Migrant* (1965).

Let us take the example of Glass's work to illustrate the broad concern at the time about cultural absorption of the newcomers. Glass conducted her research across London during these same years when Patterson was working in Brixton, and like Patterson, Glass noted the qualitative difference involved in this new pattern of immigration. She stressed that no 'other recently arrived minority group has aroused emotions and controversies of the same intensity and scale' (1960, p. 3), because of their colour. On the human plane, both Glass and Patterson recorded their impressions and visual intakes of the processes of change which were about to unfold in British cities, and it is worth quoting each statement extensively in order to convey the sense of anticipation they appear to have had about this particular juncture of contemporary British society. Glass describes the scene of the docking of a ship at Folkestone in November 1958 with 82 West Indians (including 44 women and 12 children) and about 50 Germans and Dutch travellers. There were a number of officials from the Caribbean Welfare Service in London and the British Council to meet and provide help to the West Indian migrants. Glass continues her account:

> The West Indian passengers came ashore last, many of them still in summer clothes, with some improvised extra covering to meet the harsh November day. They went quickly through passport control while the two London officials stood by, in case there were any special questions. Two coaches on the boat-train had been reserved for the West Indian party so that the two officials could go around and ask everyone whether they had a place to go to. The actual addresses, in many different parts of London, were not listed. The officials simply wanted to find out whether the migrants knew their destination or not. Everybody had an address to give. The officer from the British Council wrote down the names of students and young girls. If nobody came to meet them at Victoria, the British Council would look after them.
>
> But at Victoria the platform was crowded. There was a mass of dark people; about a hundred friends and relatives were waiting to

greet the newcomers. Soon they were all dispersed. No official body has a record of where they have gone to; and no official body knows for certain where they are now. [Glass, 1960, pp. 9–10]

Patterson describes a scene that she called 'colour shock' on visiting Brixton, even though she had been amongst black people in the West Indies and South Africa, and also knew that the South London area had become a site for West Indian settlement. She opens the first chapter of her book with the following description:

One afternoon, in May 1955, I went down to the South London district of Brixton to make a reconnaissance for the study of a recent West Indian migrant group which is the subject of this book. As I turned off the main shopping street, I was immediately overcome with a sense of strangeness, almost of shock. The street was a fairly typical South London side-street, grubby and narrow, lined with cheap cafes, shabby pubs, and flashy clothing-shops. All this was normal enough. But what struck one so forcefully was that, apart from some shopping housewives and a posse of teddy boys in tight jeans outside the billiards hall, almost everybody in sight had a coloured skin. Waiting near the employment exchange were about two dozen black men, most in the flimsy suits of exaggerated cut that, as I was later to learn, denoted their recent arrival. At least half of the exuberant infants playing outside the pre-fab day nursery were *café noir* or *café au lait* in colouring. And there were coloured men and women everywhere I looked, shopping, strolling, or gossiping on the sunny street-corners with an animation that most Londoners lost long ago. [Patterson, 1965, p. 13]

Thus, whilst some four decades ago, Glass's study took a broad view of the changes that were being brought about by the size and scale of the new black presence, Patterson concentrated on a clearly defined Brixton as demarcated from her surrounding areas, such as Battersea to the west, Wandsworth to the south-west and Camberwell slightly to the east. By the end of the century Brixton society exhibited new posses of young men and new fashions; in the area there were new cuisine, audible and visual arts, and much else in day-to-day life which continue to draw on cultural traditions from outside the British islands. What is true of Brixton is, of course, true for other parts of the city, such as Southall in the west (see Baumann,

1996), Tower Hamlets (see Eade, 1989) and other parts of the east and to a degree Notting Hill, Finsbury Park and other parts of London (see Phillips and Phillips, 1998). This process of interaction and change is, however, far from being the anticipated process of absorption envisaged by Patterson some forty years ago. While Jamaican hot Scotch bonnet chilli patties may not have replaced Cornish pasties in the same way as subcontinental Indian chicken tikka masala dishes have replaced the longer established battered fish and chips in the national cuisine (as the Foreign Secretary, Robin Cook, pointed out in a major speech a few days before St George's Day in April 2001) none the less several aspects of traditional British, especially London, life have been significantly changed or modified by the presence of Caribbeans and others over the last half-century.[2]

Outside London, the research of Rex and Moore (1967) followed much the same pattern of focusing on a specific area (Sparkbrook in Birmingham) in order to provide a more general statement about the transformation of the country that was about to commence. Their understanding of the changes being wrought in British cities was described as 'a race relations situation' and was later elaborated theoretically by Rex (1983) and empirically by Rex and his colleagues (Rex and Tomlinson, 1979). The theoretical perspectives of these writers were, of course, different. Where Patterson stressed notions of accommodation, absorption and integration, Rex and his associates stressed the conflictual nature of society and sought to develop a notion of class (around the specific issue of access to housing) from Max Weber rather than from Marx, as later writers such as Miles (1993) would seek to do. The 1980s and the 1990s witnessed a greater concentration on specific problems and issues pertaining to youths and the judicial system, schools and education, training and employment, and so on, and on the settlements of specific minority ethnic communities (such as Muslims, Sikhs and Punjabis). The extant literature abounds with examples of new communities which together portray the changing composition of British cities, particularly in the south of the island; however, with 'race riots' in the northern cities of Bradford and Manchester in the summer of 2001, it may be expected that more attention will be given to developments in this part of the country.

Underlying the assumption that newcomers would be absorbed by the host society was the view that the international social order was fairly fixed, firmed up by history and consistency of cultural norms. What was therefore required was for the newcomers, the migrants, to adjust to their new lot, the new situation into which they had voluntarily entered. But there was also a certainty about structures and social practices which came from the imperial experience. This imperial certainty suggested that there was a cultural norm to which all variants could strive to adjust. Thus, the values and norms of the class system extant in Britain was such that newcomers should seek to accommodate themselves. Of course, there were those such as the late Enoch Powell, MP for Wolverhampton, who believed that no amount of cultural adjustment would make a West Indian or an Asian an English person. It should not be too surprising, therefore, that there have been strong reactions to the notion of a multicultural Britain, as expressed periodically in popular newspapers since the 1970s.

But let us bear in mind that Patterson and her contemporaries were writing in a period charged by debates about the direction of a post-war, de-imperialising Britain: the recognition of American paramountcy, the end of empire, a ruined but reviving post-war economy, the emergence of a new European order within the framework of the European Community led by Germany and France. In Britain itself the period was marked by the passing of the Commonwealth Immigration Act (1962), Harold Wilson's Labour Government's White Paper on immigration (1965), the 'rivers of blood' speech by Enoch (as many West Indians, fond of their Old Testament prophets, narratives and imageries, liked to call this wayward son from the English tradition of tolerance) in Birmingham in 1968 depicting racial violence between black, brown and white peoples, the heating-up of racial tension in such places as South Africa and Southern Rhodesia (now Zimbabwe) with the declaration of UDI by the racist Ian Smith and his gang of thugs, the Kenyan Asian crisis, the first two Race Relations Acts, and so on. The 1960s was not just about Beatlemania, the Rolling Stones, rock and roll and Chubby Checker's 'let's twist again': it was a decade and an age characterised by much that would frighten a generation living in the shadow of a devastating world war, and with the threats of global nuclear catastrophe and race wars as prophesied by Ronald Segal in his 1967 book, *The Race War*, while the US civil rights movement began to influence struggles for justice and equality in other parts of the shrinking, globalising, world.

The entry of West Indians into Britain marked the end of a period of innocence on the part of all concerned: immigrants (who thought that they would be in Britain for three to five years before returning to the lands of their births); hosts (who thought the newcomers exotic, temporary and initially unthreatening because of their social and economic weakness). Of course, there were those who saw the newcomers as the fulfilment of their worst nightmares about the retribution for the excesses of empire and colony – nightmares in which white certainty and dominance would be replaced by a situation in which, as J. Enoch Powell saw it, the black man would have the upper hand over the white man: taking the white man's job, and worse, taking the white man's woman with that style and panache with which the black man was thought to be richly endowed and took every opportunity to display.

These matters also lay on the grid of what W.E.B. DuBois called the colour-line, which he saw as the major division between human communities in that century. Arthur Lovejoy's analysis of the 'great chain of being' at the end of the medieval world and the beginning of the modern age – a historical juncture at which the founder and benefactor of these lectures stood[3] – had, after all, been further transformed following the Darwinian Revolution in biology in the nineteenth century from a divine to a biological cosmology. This is, of course, part of the paradox of the European contribution to the globalisation of the modern age: the essential core of the inspiration of Gresham and his colleagues in the Renaissance, encompassing the Reformation and the Scientific Revolution, pointing to the overturning of the limitations imposed by traditions and beliefs with their essential particularisms. The participants in these epoch-making events would not themselves have necessarily envisaged this logical outcome whereby the sons and daughters of Africa and Asia are engaged in the construction of cultures and a social order in what Blake was later to describe as England's green and pleasant land. A land for which, despite the nature of their reception, many black immigrants have come to develop a strong dream-like love–hate relationship that Sigmund Freud – a man who like Joseph in Pharaoh's Egypt was much given to interpreting dreams – may have had a way of explaining to us.

A MULTICULTURAL SITUATION

I want to turn to what I have suggested we call 'a multicultural situation', which juxtaposes with the 'immigrant situation'. The multicultural situation has a two-fold expression which at first sight appears to be contradictory, but may be taken to reflect different aspects of a widely shared perspective on post-imperial Britain. First,

Roy Jenkins, speaking as Home Secretary on 23 May 1966 to the then National Committee for Commonwealth Immigrants declared that he would 'define integration not as a flattening process of assimilation but as equal opportunity, accompanied by cultural diversity in an atmosphere of mutual tolerance' (Jenkins, 1967, p. 267). This declaration marked the end of the attempts to achieve absorption of the immigrants into the host community; this was a shift of gigantic proportions that would inform much future thinking, research and policy options on the integration and adaptation of West Indians in British society. Jenkins' view was later restated by the Swann Committee Report of 1985. Swann advocated a preference for a society characterised by a pluralism that

> ... enables, expects and encourages members of all ethnic groups, both minority and majority, to participate fully in shaping the society as a whole within a framework of commonly accepted values, practices and procedures, whilst also allowing and, where necessary, assisting the ethnic minority communities in maintaining their identities within this common framework. [Swann, 1985, p. 5]

This was to take Jenkins' view one step further by suggesting, or at least hinting, that it would be sound policy for there to be public support for the maintenance of minority ethnic communities in terms of languages, religion, customs and so on, many of which may continue to be in conflict with established majority British values but some of which would also reinforce extant values.

By and large, for much of the 1990s several of the implications or questions involved in the notion of the multicultural society as defined by Swann were ignored or sidestepped, but by the end of the decade the publication, first, of the McPherson Report (1999) into the Stephen Lawrence case, and second, the publication of the Runnymede Trust's report – *The Future of Multi-Ethnic Britain* (2000) – there was a powerful restatement of the multicultural cause. McPherson significantly accepted the radical view that British institutions suffered from 'institutional racism', which he understood in terms of the delivery of professional services and equal treatment of all irrespective of race. This helped many employers to state that they were keen to uphold equal opportunities in a multicultural society. The Runnymede Trust's report was published in an atmosphere of optimism about the McPherson Report.

The Runnymede report covered nearly all aspects of British society, including education and employment, the criminal justice system, arts, media and sport, health and welfare, religion and belief, immigration and asylum, politics and representation. It went on to make recommendations pertaining to social cohesion, equality and difference, touching on most aspects of British society. As the chairperson of the Commission, Professor Lord Bhikhu Parekh, stressed in his opening comments the 'report was inspired by and intended to rethink the seminal report *Colour and Citizenship*' (Runnymede Trust, 2000, p. 4) by Jim Rose et al. which had been published some two decades earlier in 1969. On the whole, the report made a number of useful and insightful observations about contemporary post-imperial Britain, but perhaps of greater interest than the report itself was the public response of the 'chattering classes' during the first week or so of publication.

Many took exception to the suggestion that Britishness needed to be updated to include all the peoples who today make up the population; the icons of British identity were reasserted (and much was officially made of St George's Day on Monday, 23 April 2001, as a celebration of historic English identity). Much of the debate in the media, particularly the press, turned on the questions of the use of the word 'Britain' and 'British' in describing contemporary society. The report was taken to suggest that there is a need to transcend these labels, and many took exception to this misplaced idealism. The debates led to a wider discussion leading up to the national elections of June 2001, when nearly all leaders in each of the major parties participated in stressing that Britain is not a racist society but one entering the new millennium with a clear view of what it means to be multicultural.

Yet, as ideology and as policy, the philosophy of multiculturalism has several flaws which frequently need to be faced in practice. For example, the philosophy of multiculturalism is largely self-evident as well as self-contradictory: on the one hand, it is self-evident that large societies contain groups which are different in value systems and social institutions; at the same time, for such differences to become the norm of social cohesion appears nonsensical and a serious misreading of the notions of social integration. The problem is how can different cultures, where they are lodged within different and conflicting value systems, live within the same juridical-political framework that is also democratic and peacefully manages conflict of values? Additionally, how and why should public funds be used, as Swann recommended, to promote not similarities but differences between groups? The many insights and recommendations of the Runnymede Trust report, laudable as some may be, do not squarely answer these questions; moreover, the report failed to structure, guide or inform a debate about issues of transition and accommodation that are relevant to post-imperial Britain.

My concern, however, is that the issues of multiculturalism do not necessarily address the principal problems of social equality faced by members of the African diaspora, particularly those of Caribbean backgrounds in Britain. African Caribbeans have enjoyed the benefits of cultural participation in Britain, what they have lacked has been a share in the economic production of their own labour and creativity. This problem raises questions about equality and fairness that are side-stepped by multiculturalism.

West Indians in England have never fully immersed themselves in the dream that they would be participants in a US-style 'melting pot', nor is there much evidence of the dream of participating in a multicultural society. England, the 'Mother Country', was not conceived of in quite this way, although there was the hope that fair play and opportunity would be greater than in the colonial order from which they came. What occurred over the last half-century has been the sad vindication of M. G. Smith's differential incorporation: membership of a social order in which the practical enjoyment of rights has been unequally invested in groups. These are not new circumstances for Caribbean people. And their response has been to transform themselves from West Indians into Caribbean communities. This, of course, creates new divisions, resulting in a loss to the new community. As indicated earlier, the transformation from immigrants to Caribbean communities in Britain is constructed as an exclusively African or black world, when in fact it is as (or more) varied in its membership as are communities in the Caribbean itself. So, it is appropriate to ask what is the historical background to the conundrum of Caribbean communities this side of the Atlantic.

THE HISTORICAL BACKGROUND

It is not possible today for any of us to remain entirely dispassionate about the 'respectable trade' – the slave trade – the total social system to which slavery led and the aftermaths of this system that were to set the tone for relations and perceptions of Africans and Europeans or for black and white people in this shared Atlantic world. The passion aroused by the slavery past is shared by persons whose forebears may have passed through Bristol, or Liverpool or London from Africa as well as those who have forebears directly from the British Isles, or both. This is also true for many persons or families whose forebears never left British shores, but whose material well-being depended on the fortunes that the 'respectable trade' made in the West Indies.

There has long been a reluctance to admit these kinds of human connections forced by slavery, but occasionally in the more open world of the last years of the millennium there are individuals who have found it possible to face up to this past. After all, during slavery itself there were those who, like Matthew (Monk) Lewis, were heirs 'to a West India fortune', but who, unlike Monk,[4] never visited their plantations; instead, they enjoyed their wealth in London and other cities. Just as there is a theme about the West India interest and its prominence on the social scene in British history during the late eighteenth and early nineteenth centuries, so too is there a theme in Caribbean history which suggests that these societies did not benefit, unlike the southern states in the US or South American societies, from the presence of a leisured and educated class. True or false, this perception does point to what the sociologist and novelist Orlando Patterson described as 'an absence of ruins' – the title of one of his novels. Slavery and the plantation links Jane Austen's *Jane Eyre* and Patterson's *Absence of Ruins* (1967a), and much else in Caribbean history. However, the subsequent artistic creativity of people in the region in many areas of the arts, social encounters and so on suggests that the relative absence of a leisured European class in the region did not irrevocably deprive the Caribbean. But few regions, irrespective of size, can rival the Commonwealth Caribbean in its contribution to modern world culture during the last half-century.

But guilt, shame and ambiguities about slavery continue to be felt on both sides of the Atlantic. Narratives of the post-Emancipation Caribbean are logically and inextricably wrapped up with narratives of Island Britain, and it is to be welcomed that there is some recognition of the fact that Bristol,[5] as a foremost entrepreneurial city of the kingdom that both pre- and post-dates Atlantic slavery, is more appropriate a city than say Kingston in Jamaica or Bridgetown in Barbados or any other destination in the Caribbean to be the site for reminding the Atlantic world of this important chapter in its cross-oceanic and intercontinental history. This is a history which is perceived as influencing our present situation on all points of the Atlantic world, and is not a chapter in European exploration and domination that even Margaret Thatcher could unashamedly remember when she recalled in her famous Bruges speech in September 1988 that 'the story of how Europeans explored and colonised and – yes, without apology – civilised much of the world is an extraordinary tale of talent, skill and courage' (Thatcher, 1988, p. 2).

The burden of slavery has been placed not on the backs of those who profited from it and those societies which owe their initial development to capital accumulated from slavery. Rather, the burden of the slavery past has been squarely placed on the backs of descendants of slaves. This is, of course, absurd. And it may be that Europeans, Africans and Caribbeans of the first decades of the new millennium will have to face squarely the legacies of slavery as a common or shared heritage which links them in a long and unresolved historical tragedy. Recognition of this fact is also an invitation to return to the issues of slavery itself and the nature of the settlement agreed in the 1830s and 1840s, whereby the perpetrators of the system were compensated for the 'loss' of their commodities (persons) and the ex-slaves abandoned to their own devices and to make do as best they could without state assistance.

Even before ex-slaves in the British Caribbean in 1838 began to enjoy their freedom under the Emancipation Act of 1834, their fate and the society they would bring about were of profound concern to a range of interests astride the Atlantic. For the planter interests (planters, overseers, agents) there was the concern over what would happen to the production of sugar and rum. For those in London who financed these enterprises in the central areas of production in the West Indies, there was the key concern about the long term as well as new opportunities elsewhere, as John Bull turned his predatory attention away from the Caribbean and focused on Africa and Asia. On the North American rim of the Atlantic, many of the protagonists in the debate about slavery and free labour (waged in the context of the expansion of the Union to the Far West and the Southwest, occupied by Mexico until President Polk's successful war of 1846) kept a close watch on developments in the West Indian corner of the world's then superpower – Britain.

The relevance of the activities of freed Africans in the Caribbean to the debate in the US was to find expression in two seminal works of the period. First, in 1852 the New England abolitionist Harriet Beecher Stowe's novel *Uncle Tom's Cabin* was published. It was to become a classic, perhaps the first novel to sell over a million copies;

as will be seen in a later chapter, the novel's central character, Uncle Tom, was destined to have a long and often derogatory career despite Beecher Stowe's commendable purpose of attacking 'the peculiar institution' of the States south of the Mason–Dixon Line and to show that white people ought not to fear the free African. The second book first appeared as letters in the *New York Times*, and was later published on the eve of the American Civil War in 1860 as *The Ordeal of Free Labor in the British West Indies*. The author, William Sewell, a New York journalist firmly on the side of the abolitionists, sought to show that freedom in the British Caribbean was not endangering the welfare of white society in that region. There is more than a hint of reassurance to his readers (presumably, well-intentioned white folks) in his Preface to the second edition of the book, published in 1862 at the height of the Civil War:

> The writer's aim has been to give, as free from comment as possible, such statistical and other information concerning the West Indian populations, their habits and customs, their industry, their commerce, and their government, as he has been able to procure from reliable sources, or to gain from personal observation.

Stowe's optimism about the African's freedom and Sewell's positive portrayal of developments in the West Indies were opposite to the views of British commentators. Let us take two well-known examples. First, Eric Williams said of Thomas Carlyle that his *Occasional Discourse on the Nigger Question*, published in 1849 (see Williams, 1963), was 'his most infamous essay', because in this essay Carlyle vented all his venom against liberty and equality and for him the free African in the West Indies was the epitome of laziness and sloth – the results of freedom, in his view. This theme was to be picked up later by the novelist and postmaster, J. A. Froude, in *The English in the West Indies, or the Bow of Ulysses*, published in 1888. For both men, the African in the West Indies was not only lazy but also childlike, needing guidance. To paraphrase Walter Rodney (1981) – writing about the stereotypes of free Africans in Guyana – for these men, 'Qushee had become, after slavery, more indolent' and lost without the white master's guidance. It was not surprising, therefore, that the British government's response to a black and brown small landowners' petition at Morant Bay in 1865 (for more land) was one of condemnation of their supposed laziness. This was accompanied by the admonition for the hardworking free Africans to 'pull themselves up by their own efforts', as if they had not been doing so without the financial help that the state had offered to planters. This theme has continued down to our own time, and migrants from the Caribbean to Britain during the last half-century have had to confront much the same accusations[6] as the first generations of freed Africans in the West Indies.

It may be appropriate at this point to turn to aspects of the free Africans' search for self-improvement that Sewell and others documented, and to the continuing relevance of the slavery past in the Atlantic world.

AFRICAN IMPROVEMENT

Improvement – self-improvement and improvement 'of the race' – may be said to have become the hallmark of developments in the decades that followed Emancipation in 1838 in the British Caribbean. This took several forms, but I want briefly to comment on three broad aspects: the search for land space, the hunger for education, and seizing opportunities abroad. Each of these must be understood within the context of the slavery past from which Africans and their descendants were concerned to place themselves at a distance. As post-Emancipation Caribbean societies developed, they were not to be so much concerned about return to an African, European or otherwise past; nor were their spokespersons as concerned as earlier generations of Englishmen in the Thirteen Colonies in North America to create a social order in sharp distinction to those of old Europe. Establishing a place for themselves within an accepted British imperial predominance appears to have been the ambition. In this situation, the over-arching context of British political power was accepted and questions appear to have been about how to realise some aspects of Britishness, not to totally negate Britain's presence; for example, the very notion of England as 'Mother Country' was taken from English colonisers, much the same as Africans and Asians would take English values such as parliamentary democracy, the novel and poetry as their own. It is difficult to avoid thinking that Anglophone Caribbean colonies constantly had the image of Haiti in mind[7] and therefore a deep desire to avoid a revolutionary break in which whites would lose their positions of privilege and dominance over all other groups.

The search for physical (land) space was perfectly rational. Land represented freedom, because previously slaves as property themselves were restricted in the scope of their ownership of commodities, particularly land. Of course, no social system operates in strict accordance with its formal rules and regulations, and consequently, many slaves did in fact enjoy the utility of land ('ground', for personal/domestic and sometimes market provisions). None the less, the land – the plantation – represented an absence of freedom and the presence of oppression for many in the region. When the opportunity came, therefore, ex-slaves wanted to distance themselves from the plantation.

In some accounts, it is suggested that the ex-slaves wanted to distance themselves from the land, but this was not strictly so. In Jamaica, for example, a protracted debate ensued between, on the one hand colonial administrators and planters and on the other, elementary schoolteachers, often supported by churchmen, over the purpose of education from the 1880s to the point when the independence process began in earnest in the 1940s (see Goulbourne, 1988a, ch. 5). The former group wanted to promote vocational training in the schools and argued, not unlike educationalists and politicians in the 1980s and 1990s in Britain, that the schools were too 'bookish' and too 'literary', when what was being taught were the three Rs. On the other hand, in the words of a leading spokesperson for the Jamaica Union of Teachers, schooling had the 'purpose of so developing the intellectual facilities of the child that it will be fully equipped on leaving school to be able to specialise in that branch of industry to which it has decided to devote its energies' (Goulbourne, 1988a, p. 140).

Whatever the avenue of escape, what the free Africans wanted was to place a safe distance between themselves and the plantation, which was owned by planters, managed by overseers and had alienated their total labour in providing value for others to enjoy. Their resistance to the plantation should not, therefore, be confused with their legitimate desire for land of their own. It was this desire that the Baptists, such as William Knibb and others in Jamaica, recognised and they provided assistance to the free people to acquire land and organise in communities independent of the plantation. Indeed, to again refer to the Jamaica Union of Teachers' long-running debate with the education authorities, in 1929 the JUT powerfully argued:

Let the boy feel certain that he will not share the fate of his father, whose acre of stone was forfeited by the Crown because he could not make enough from it to pay the taxes and support a family, or whose provision ground was destroyed by the landlord because the rent was seven days in arrears; let him feel satisfied that adequate measures for the encouragement and protection of agriculture are existent, and it will need no application of physical or verbal force to get him 'back to the land'. [Goulbourne, 1988a, pp. 140–1]

The urge on the part of free Africans to find land of their own was, of course, restricted in those islands where land was already a scarce commodity. Barbados was such an island. It is not, therefore, surprising that land acquisition and significant population movement within the island were relatively restricted and that the white population have continued to own, manage and dominate the economy. However, the point should not be stressed too far. After all, until recent decades, in places such as Jamaica or Guyana, where there was (in the words of one of Tolstoy's short stories) 'land enough for a man', the white population which had been dwindling since the middle of the nineteenth century continued to dominate nearly all public spheres until recently (see Johnson and Watson, 1998; Stone, 1983). Land ownership represented power, authority and freedom and in those islands and territories where it could be acquired at some distance from the plantation, Africans availed themselves of this opportunity (see Cumper, 1956). And in societies such as Jamaica, from as early as the 1860s, free Africans rapidly transformed the basis of the economy from largely monocultural king sugar to such diverse products as banana and coffee (see for example, Eisner, 1961; Post, 1978).

The second area in which self-improvement was manifested was, as implied so far, education. During slavery education was severely restricted. Some religious denominations had promoted the three Rs, because they felt that literacy was necessary or useful in the saving of souls and the reading of the Bible, that is, once slaves were deemed to have souls and therefore were recognised as humans. In the main, however, the major denominations, the state and planters/overseers believed that education of the slave could lead to an undermining of the social order. This reinforced their view that the African was, in any event, incapable of attaining the higher levels of the educated mind.

With Emancipation came the possibility to acquire numeracy, literacy, the skill of writing and, exceptionally, a secondary grammar school education. Barbados is often credited with having the best education system in the region, and it may be that the probable greater emphasis that Barbadians place on education has been a response to the severe restriction on land acquisition as an alternative or an additional avenue of self-improvement in a post-slavery social order. But to one degree or another this fact is true for the other islands and Guyana. Indeed, in Guyana where the colonial state and the planters pressured Africans off the land to accommodate Indian indentured labourers, there developed a situation that has not been conducive to racial peace since the early 1960s (see, for example, Greene, 1974; Baber and Jeffrey, 1986; Goulbourne, 1991a; Premdas, 1995). In Jamaica, the largest English-speaking society in the region, mass education has long been part of the state's remit, but has always been less than adequately funded. When, out of fear of black and brown (that is, people of black and white parentage) domination, the white plantocracy voluntarily surrendered the powers of the Free Assembly to Westminster following the Morant Bay Rebellion of 1865, white Jamaicans were taken aback when colonial administrators from Whitehall began to reform the education system in a manner beneficial to the children of free Africans. Though not as extensive as Forster's Act of 1870 in England establishing free primary education, the various education initiatives between 1865 and 1914, and particularly the Education Act of 1892, established an island-wide system for boys and girls. Under a generation of reformers from the late 1880s, including Sydney (later Lord) Olivier as colonial secretary for the island, Jamaican popular education was to be given a boost never to be seen again until the reforms of the 1970s under the radical government of Michael Manley (see Stephens and Stephens, 1986; Goulbourne, 1988a).

Despite severe limitations to the attainment of education, the English-speaking Caribbean people continued to place it at the top of their list of priorities. Thus, as noted, the Jamaica Union of Teachers – reputed to be the earliest such union in the region – struggled from its foundation in 1894 to the 1960s, when it merged with unions representing the elite secondary schools to form the Jamaica Teachers' Union, to maintain the distinction between education and training. But, because the West Indian plantocracy and the British colonial administration failed to establish tertiary institutions in the region before the eve of departure (1940s), primary schools and teacher training colleges, especially the Mico College in Kingston, became the sites or locations of the region's intellectuals before the establishment of the regional University of the West Indies in 1948. To be sure, there were intimations of tertiary education from the nineteenth century. For example, there was the College of Tropical Agriculture in Trinidad from the 1920s, which later formed the basis for the UWI at St Augustine; so, too, was there an attempt to establish a theological college in Barbados. In Jamaica, the demand for a tertiary institution, particularly following the very successful Jamaica Exhibition of 1891, met with limited success while for some years up to the turn of the century it appeared possible for students to take divinity degrees in Jamaica, under arrangements with Durham University.

Perhaps, however, the major obstacles to the realisation of universal primary education and the establishment of tertiary education in the region were economic as well as a shift of humanitarian concern from the region to new spheres of empire – India, particularly following the Mutiny of 1857, and Africa, especially from the 1880s. Whilst Eric Williams' point that slavery did not end simply because of the humanitarian movement in England in the first decades of the nineteenth century, this humanitarian urge was certainly needed and could have helped to provide the region with the wherewithal of a truly modern civic society such as characterised much of Victorian England: secondary schools to include sons and daughters of free Africans, and universities and specialised institutes to promote the emergent Creole culture of the region (such as museums, parks, civic patterns of social behaviour, and so on). To be sure, there were some such developments, but they were undertaken to meet the needs of a small administrative elite and the plantocracy. Instead, the Caribbean became a backwater, a kind of embarrassing left-over from the first British Empire. As Williams was later to put it, speaking of Trinidad & Tobago but in terms applicable to the region as a whole, after 1838:

> Trinidad and Tobago attracted metropolitan attention only in periods of riot and disorder (1903 and 1937), only when the discovery of oil made it an object of interest to the British Navy and British capitalism, only when its invaluable natural harbour, Chaguaramas, made it a useful pawn to be traded by Britain against American aid in the Second World War.
>
> These developments apart, Trinidad and Tobago was merely a crown colony, forgotten and forlorn. No British statesman of substance was ever distracted by it from larger and more important issues, unless it was Joseph Chamberlain, and his connection with

Trinidad and Tobago is probably the least reputable phase in his career. No British scholar found it worth his while to pay any attention to the history and potential of Trinidad and Tobago, unless it was Froude who came and went on a tourist visit leaving only froudacity[8] behind. [Williams, 1964, p. vii]

For all the work of a creative generation in the islands to develop and enhance cultural aspirations (see, for example, Nettleford, 1978, 1989), it is perhaps true to say that the independent governments and societies have not themselves excelled in making provisions for the development of civic culture.

Given the general neglect of the region, it is not surprising that emigration should became the third outlet it has long been for Caribbean people seeking to improve their lot. As already noted, during the last half-century we have experienced or seen the sizeable migration of people from the region, and their contribution to what the Phillips (1998) brothers have called 'the irresistible rise of a multi-racial' Britain is not seriously doubted. The BBC programmes in the summer of 1998 and the various celebrations commemorating the docking of SS *Empire Windrush* in 1948 should be enough to establish the significance of the Caribbean post-war presence on these shores. My point is a twofold one: first, this development was and remains part of the West Indian urge to improve; second, the intervening years between 1838 (end of slavery) and 1948 (when sizeable migration to Britain started) are a consistent whole in terms of the historical experiences of West Indians or Caribbeans in the Atlantic world. If the wherewithal to achieve improvement does not exist in the region, then outward movement is a legitimate route or instrument. Thus, from the first generation after slavery West Indians were emigrating: to Panama to find employment in the building of the Canal in the 1880s; to the opportunities offered in Cuba with the rejuvenation of sugar as a result of the shortage of beet-sugar in war-torn Europe after 1914; to the US in the booming 1920s, and so on. It is a paradox of Atlantic history that at the very time that Africans were leaving the West Indies, Asians (from China and India) were finding their way into the region to seize what they saw as an opportunity to improve their life chances. I would hazard a guess that today most Caribbean scholars are in agreement that migration has become an essential aspect of the West Indian or Caribbean psyche and this has been strongly expressed in the dynamic literature associated with the region over the last fifty years as well as in other art forms.

Finally, I want to suggest that the migration experience of Commonwealth Caribbeans is part of the continuing construction of African diasporic communities, and this is no more irrational than the African's appearance in the Americas through slavery. It was an accident of history that Africans established homes and sovereign territories in the Americas, particularly the Caribbean. Making homes in Europe is a continuation of that process, except that this aspect of the construction has been embarked upon with a degree of autonomy, unlike the construction in the Caribbean and the Americas. The slavery past continues, therefore, to be of great relevance to the present historical moment of diasporic relations across the Atlantic.

THE CONTINUING RELEVANCE OF THE SLAVERY PAST

There are several examples of how the slavery past continues to influence or condition our perceptions and present concerns, but I want briefly to mention three of these: first, the readiness in Britain to go back to slavery to explain present problems and concerns; second, the huge preoccupation in Caribbean historiography and social science with that past; and third, the new and increasing demand that there should be reparations for slavery. These are, of course, closely related and are not as disjointed as suggested here, but for the purposes of discussion they can sensibly be separated.

First, within the context of Britain there has long been a readiness to refer to the slavery past as explanation of present concerns. And this is sometimes done without regard to empirical evidence. Let me refer briefly to two simple examples from contemporary writings. First, writing about reggae, rastas and rudies in 1970s Britain (republished as recently as 1998) Hebdige states that the

> ... experience of slavery recapitulates itself perpetually in the everyday interactions of the Jamaican black. It is principally responsible for the unstable, familial structure (disrupting the traditionally strong kinship networks which even now survive among the peoples of West Africa) and obviously goes on determining patterns of work and relations with authority. It remains an invisible shaping presence which haunts the slums of Ghost Town and even now defies exorcism. In fact it is interpolated into

> every verbal exchange which takes place on the teeming streets of
> every Jamaican slum. [(Hebdige, 1998, p. 136]

The late Ken Pryce asserted a similarly strong connection between
slavery and contemporary Britain. In *Endless Pressure* (1979), based
on research in Bristol's St Paul's area, Pryce asserted that many of the
problems he witnessed here could be traced back to slavery in the
Caribbean. He stressed that the family structure of Caribbeans that
obtained in Britain in the years of entry and settlement, such as
female-headed households, families without men, and so forth were
practices that 'stem directly from slavery, which was responsible for
the total destruction of conventional family life among the slaves.
And today economic constraints are so persistent in the life of the
rural and urban poor that they cannot break out of the patterns laid
down under slavery' (Pryce, 1979, p. 16). This is a point in Caribbean
social science that Raymond Smith (2001) has consistently pointed
to: we cannot continue persistently to lay at the door of slavery all
the problems of today, as if human beings are completely at the
mercy of their pasts. It is true, of course, that Marx famously stated
that we make our own history, but we do so in the context of the
material conditions into which we are born, but this was meant as
a modifier of autonomy, and also written in one of Marx's more evo-
lutionary moods when considering the processes of social change.

A second example of the abiding relevance of the slavery
experience to an understanding of the present has been the
profound impact of slavery on Commonwealth Caribbean historiography and social theory. There is, of course, a rich historiography
of the post-Emancipation period, but on the whole historians in the
Commonwealth Caribbean have been remarkably focused on the
problematic bequeathed by slavery, as the impressive UNESCO four-
volume *General History of the Caribbean* reveals, particularly Higman's
contribution (1999, Vol. 4). In the main, whilst there are any
number of accounts on slavery in the region, work on the post-
slavery era, particularly from the 1880s or the turn of the century to
the present, is less impressive. Again, there are exceptions, such as
Carnegie (1973), Goulbourne (1988a) on Jamaica, and on Guyana
there is the celebrated work of the late Walter Rodney (1981), who
was himself trained in African history. Much of what we know about
the period from the 1880s come less from historians than from social
analysts, such as economists and demographers interested in
population movement; examples here would include the economists

Cumper (1956) and Beckford (1972), and political analysts such as Post (1978), Munroe (1972) and Ryan (1972) in the Caribbean. Needless to say, the monumental contribution to the understanding of Caribbean societies made by a generation of social anthropologists in the last fifty years, has been second to none. They tended to lead the debates about the nature of Caribbean societies, and included such giants as the late Michael Garfield Smith (see, for example, 1965), Raymond Smith (see, for example, 1963) and several others whose works constitutes the bedrock of Caribbean studies.

Similarly, Caribbean social and economic theories have necessarily been influenced by the wider concern with the slavery past. Indeed, even when their purpose was to understand contemporary society and economy, social and economic theorists have sought to relate their work to that past. An example or two of what I mean may be useful here. Orlando Patterson has been one of the most catholic and productive of Caribbean intellectuals, so let me use him as an example of this genre in social thinking about the Caribbean. Patterson's interest in slavery as part of the human condition over the last two and more millennia is well known and well articulated in his monumental and seminal work *Slavery and Social Death* (1982) and his earlier *The Sociology of Slavery* (1967). The Sartrean existential themes to be found in his novels help to reinforce a powerful view that slavery as a force in Western civilisation is a continuing presence to be reckoned with if we are properly to understand relations between different racial and ethnic groups in our contemporary social order. It goes without saying that the continuing shadow of the slavery past was transparent in the earlier debate which emerged from the seminal work of the social anthropologist, the late M. G. Smith, over social and cultural pluralism. But the point I wish to make about Patterson's *oeuvre* is that the slavery past dominates, and whilst this may be acceptable for a historical sociologist, I find it difficult to accept as a total explanation of the conditions of Africans in the Atlantic world. But let me turn to the economic scene.

To one degree or another, the two general theories of economic life in the region had the slavery past as explanatory backdrop. First, W. Arthur Lewis' (1958) model of the dual economy with its emphasis on economic development with 'unlimited supply of labour' appears to have the neglected West Indian colonies as a backdrop where labour supply was far greater than labour demand, and where capitalist development had been arrested since the middle of the nineteenth century. Some might think that I am stretching a point too far, but it might be borne in mind that in his Preface to Gisela Eisner's highly informative *Jamaica* (1961), Lewis stressed that in the middle of the nineteenth-century Jamaica was more part of the developed world than Russia or Japan, whereas by 1950, these countries could not be spoken of in the same breath because they belonged to very different worlds. Second, we should also bear in mind Lewis's earlier Fabian Society statement entitled *Labour in the West Indies*, published in 1939, demonstrating his familiarity with conditions in the region. The impact of the slavery past and its immediate aftermaths on the New World Group of economists – George Beckford, Norman Girvan, Clive Thomas and particularly Lloyd Best in his seminal essay, 'The model of a pure plantation economy' (1968), which was to be an inspiration to others of this school – was, of course, quite obvious.

Third, the question of reparations has arisen as an issue across the triangular world of the Atlantic, that is, the Atlantic world of Africa, Americo-Caribbean and Europe. But the question is not entirely new. Apart from other occasions when reparations may have been considered by free people in the continental Americas and the Caribbean islands, the notion of reparations may now be seen to have underscored the ventures undertaken to establish Sierra Leone by the British, and Monrovia and Liberia (later merging to form one state) on the African West Coast in the early nineteenth century. After all, the returnees were largely financed and supported by former slavers, the British and white Americans. Similarly, it may be assumed that the journeys and colonisation undertaken by Martin Delaney and Edward Blyden in the early 1860s implied questions about reparations to what was then perceived as the 'dark continent'. As the nineteenth century wore on, missionaries from North America and the Caribbean – many of whom were from the African diaspora – may also have been enthused by the general notion of 'paying back' or repairing the breach with Africa. Indeed, well into the latter decades of the last century it was not uncommon to meet well-intended and highly skilled individuals from North America, Europe and the Caribbean traversing Africa in search of opportunities to make amends and find salvation for themselves – all within the shadow of past wrongs, betrayals and losses.

But, in recent times and before the United Nations Durban conference on racism in September 2001, perhaps the most dramatic public airing of the reparation issue was in the 1960s when the Black

Panthers in California raised the question of the American state honouring what was believed to have been a promise to give the freedmen 'forty acres and a mule' in return for support for the Federal government's cause against the Confederate States a century earlier during the Civil War.

In its present form, the demand comes out of Africa, and was stated by the Organisation of African Unity in its Abuja Declaration in the rapidly changing last decade of the twentieth century. The then Nigerian opposition leader, the late Chief Moshood Abiola, the distinguished Kenyan academic, Ali Mazrui, and Jamaica's veteran politician and former High Commissioner to Lagos, Dudley Thompson, were charged with taking the idea forward. In Britain one notable supporter of this claim was the late Bernie Grant, MP for Tottenham, who sought to link the question of reparations with that of the British state funding the return of Caribbean families and individuals who wanted to leave Britain. Another powerful British voice was that of Linda Bellos, a former leader of Lambeth Council in South London. In the US, major figures in the African-American community, such Johnnie Cochran, J. L. Chestnutt and J. Pires have associated themselves with this demand (see, for example, the *Sunday Times*, 20 January 2001, p. 11). But perhaps the most influential figure in the US has been Randall Robinson whose book *The Debt: What America Owes to Blacks* (2000) explores the issue of black exploitation in the West and powerfully raises the question of reparation for this exploitation, particularly slavery.

If not the clearest then one of the more interesting explanations of the demand is to be found in the speeches of the late Chief Moshood Abiola published under the catch-all title *Reparations* (1992). This collection of 36 speeches delivered in Africa, Asia, Europe and North America display the range and depth of Abiola's pan-Africanist vision for a renascent Africa living in harmony with the rest of the world and Africa's far-flung diaspora, especially the US with which as a businessman he had strong links. Of particular interest is his speech called 'Reparations' in the collection, but originally entitled 'Reparations for Africans in the motherland and diaspora', and delivered at a meeting of the US Congressional Black Caucus in Washington, DC, in September 1990. In this speech, the late Chief spoke eloquently about the past wrongs inflicted by one group on another in the world community: the experiences of the Jews throughout the world, Japanese internment during the Second World War in the US, and the injustices done to the indigenous peoples of North America and Australasia. In each of these cases, he pointed out, reparations – which he defined as 'making whole again' or 'compensation made for damage done to a state or a people by another state' (Abiola, 1992, p. 233) – to France, Israel and communities in North America and Australia were made. He then went on to outline why Western Europe and North America should pay reparations to Africa by freeing the continent from the debilitating debts it cannot repay, and by implementing social programmes to lift African Americans out of the ghettos, and transform the lives of the young. On this last point Abiola interestingly posed the following challenge:

> Let us goad our brilliant young entrepreneurs, from the sordid classrooms of crack and cocaine into the panelled boardrooms of corporate America. Are we saying that our seventeen year old son or brother who runs a multimillion dollar business in crack, could not succeed in the far easier schedules of the Harvard Business School? [Abiola, 1992, p. 237]

The interdependence and interconnectedness of the world community – that is, globalisation – Abiola argued, are forces which should point towards considerations of reparations for 'Mother' Africa which would have maintained its comparative status in the comity of nations 'had it not been for the intervention of slave traders and colonialists' (ibid., p 237). Abiola foresaw and dismissed objections such as the fact that the states that presently exist in post-colonial Africa did not exist at the time of slavery; he also showed that the state of Israel did not exist during the holocaust in Nazi Germany in the early 1940s, but this has not hindered the payment of reparations to Israel. Abiola stressed that:

> While reparations to the indigenous Americans, the Japanese-American detainees or the State of Israel can never replace the millions of dead, the stolen lands or the separation and loss, compensation is an attempt to say *Sorry, I won't do it again, here's a little something to reduce your suffering, to right the symbolic imbalance.* [Abiola, 1992, p. 124; original emphasis]

For Abiola, slavery deprived African Americans in such a way that as a community they have 'never fully recovered from the damage done to the family in slavery and after and may never recover' (ibid.,

p. 235). This damage was mirrored in the motherland by depopulation, debasement of traditional values, trickery in the exchange of trinkets for valuable commodities, and so forth. The continuing underdevelopment of Africa both in terms of its material resources and its people are because of the slavery past. The case is that slavery depopulated Africa, massively contributed to the underdevelopment of the continent *vis-à-vis* Europe and other parts of the world, and inflicted unparalleled sufferings on one group of humanity. But perhaps the far more important sense of reparation with regard to Atlantic slavery, is the recognition of this historic injustice which needs to be recorded alongside the great injustices of modern history. The call, therefore, is for compensation to be made in material kind for the physical and moral wrongs inflicted on Africans on the continent and in the diaspora by West European states such as Britain, France, The Netherlands, Spain and Portugal, and they would be required to repay in material terms to Africa and the African diaspora.

The UN conference on racism in Durban was an occasion for raising other significant issues, such as the question of whether Zionism is racism and whether the scheduled castes in India are discriminated against on the basis of their race. The first of these issues very nearly undermined the success of the conference (the participation of the US Secretary of State Colin Powell was withdrawn and the UK sent a relatively low-level delegation), and the Indian government was successful in keeping the scheduled castes off the agenda. As a result, reporting of the conference turned therefore very much to the question of an apology and reparations for slavery, with individuals such as the Revd Jesse Jackson having their say, and some African presidents deferring from the majority position. In Britain itself, the media, particularly the newspapers, was dominated by the issue, and provided a fair hearing of the case for and against reparations (see, for example, *The Times*, 3 and 7 September 2001 and the *Guardian*, 3 and 4 September 2001). With the end of the conference and the highlighting of the call for apology and reparations, it is unlikely that they will disappear from public discussion in the near future.

To the extent that I understand the point being made, there are several important considerations not openly addressed by those who are making the demand, and I therefore share the reservations of those African leaders – such as presidents Thabo Mbeki of South Africa, Abdoulaye Wade of Senegal and Yoweri Museveni of Uganda

– who urged caution and sober thinking at Durban. In the first instance, no amount of apologies and material compensation can remove the ignominy of Atlantic slavery: this is an ignominy that has become a stigma for Africans in the overall African diaspora and demands recognition not only from Europeans but also from Africans in parts of the continent for their active participation and material gain from the trade.

In this reckoning there are therefore several parties to be brought on board. There are the Christian denominations which provided moral and ethical justifications for chattel slavery and for making the slave a dehumanised commodity. Of equal significance are the African chiefs and merchants who colluded in the trade and, like Marx's piratical capitalists, acquired capital but went on to squander it in much the same way as many post-colonial political leaders in Africa have squandered their country's assets in the decades from the 1960s. These participants were not innocents, but free human agents, as are those today who participate in the slave trade in West Africa. Moreover, it is to be wondered why the question of slavery on the Indian Ocean side of the continent – slaves to the Arabian Peninsula and the islands of Pemba, Zanzibar and Lamu – is not part of the discussion. Rounding up only 'the usual suspects' *à la* the film *Casablanca* (the usual culprits whose roles are well known, that is, the European traders and their governments) who were responsible for transforming the system into a mode of production (as Marx might have said) so that it provided needed capital for the Industrial Revolution, does not really address the questions involved about this large historical and contemporary issue.

It is not necessary to conflate the wrongs of slavery with the colonial and post-colonial exploitation of Africa and the continuing subordination of Africans in the diaspora. The inequitable structural relations that exist between states and countries can be addressed separately, as indeed has been done by radical Third World leaders and intellectuals. Whilst there have not been agreed solutions to unfavourable terms of trade and access to markets, and while Africa seems poised to continue to go in the opposite direction from development, the demand for fairer terms will continue.

Finally, there appears to be an obsession with apologies – Tony Blair's apology to the Irish people for the Great Hunger in the nineteenth century, the demand that the Australian state should apologise for European cruelty to Aborigines, Christian leaders' apology to Jews for past persecution, demands for Italy to acknowledge, apologise and pay reparations to Ethiopia for Benito Mussolini's atrocities in the late 1930s, and so on (see, for example, the *Guardian*, 25 June 2001). But the uttering of a few kind words cannot wipe away the great historic wrongs, and it may be wiser to leave the guilt and shame where it should be, than to encourage people to think that a few material things, the crumbs from the masters' table, and kind words can rectify the wrongs of the past. The support given to these demands by many radicals in the West may be more by way of clearing their consciences than by way of rectification to the victims.

Indeed, it is possible to argue that what the history of free Africans in the diaspora has consistently shown is that the only meaningful apology that can be made is for there to be a fair and level playing field in the competition over resources. This has been what Africans in the West have fought for and partially won, thereby extending and redefining the notion of democracy. This has required and will continue to require structural change which will in turn change the differential incorporation of Africans in Atlantic societies.

CONCLUSION

The slavery past has been and will no doubt continue to be employed in order to explain present conditions across the Atlantic. Social values, customs, cultural traits, lifestyles and so on have all been at one time or another traced back to the period of slavery. To corrupt T. S. Eliot, we live under the shadow of this great rock of the past. While not denying the relevance of the slavery past, I want to suggest that its deployment is not only sometimes unduly pessimistic and over-deterministic, but can also play a trick on us by sending us down a *cul-de-sac*, diverting our energies from demands for structural changes to the politics of gestures which assert preciousness and holiness, but has little or no impact on societal structures. Trying to explain present conditions by reference to slavery can unwittingly lock us into a historical determinism, and underplays the tremendous efforts Africans in the diaspora have undertaken to change the world that slavery bequeathed and to construct one better suited to their own purposes. However, while that slavery past does not entirely determine our present, that past will continue to be a very real force in the cross-Atlantic lives of Caribbeans as well as others who inhabit this part of the world, as subsequent chapters show.

3 Contemporary Social and Political Dimensions of British-Caribbean Transnationality

This chapter outlines some peculiarities of the political characteristics of the transnationality of Caribbean communities in Britain. In particular, the discussion focuses upon two aspects of these characteristics or features. The first of these is the formal structure of relations between the Commonwealth Caribbean countries and Britain, which provides a general context for understanding the political dimensions of the mixed national identities on the one hand, and on the other hand, the limited range and comparatively quiet nature of exilic and diasporic transnational politics involving the two regions locked within the perimeters of a common Atlantic heritage and potential future. The second aspect of these relations that this chapter focuses upon is the integration or incorporation of people with Caribbean backgrounds into political life in Britain in recent years. The notion of politics being discussed here is to be understood in the classical sense, namely, discussion about public things, the *res publica*, not what some cultural theorists call personal politics.

ELEMENTS OF BRITISH-CARIBBEAN RELATIONS AND DIASPORIC POLITICS

For convenience, the formal relations between the UK and the Commonwealth Caribbean may be separated into those that are of a bilateral nature and those that are established through regional or multilateral mechanisms. The former involve the exchange of High Commissioners (ambassadors) along with the usual officials and services that an embassy would provide for their nationals living, working or travelling abroad. Typically, these missions will have legal and trade attachés with specific tasks allocated. Antigua, Barbados, the Republic of Guyana, Grenada, Jamaica and the Republic of Trinidad & Tobago have High Commissioners in London, some with officials who pay regular visits to the provincial regions of the UK to service nationals and keep them informed about developments 'back home'. The Eastern Caribbean states of the

Commonwealth of Dominica, St Kitts, St Lucia and St Vincent have shared representation in London, but it was expected that from July 1998 each of these states would have their own High Commissions.[1]

These High Commissions act as focal points for nationals living and working in Britain who need information or help about affairs 'back home' and, during the period of migration and settlement, some affairs in the UK. Similarly, there have been UK High Commissioners in Bahamas, Barbados, Belize, Jamaica, Guyana and Trinidad; there have been British representatives in Antigua and St Lucia but below High Commissioner level and, like the other East Caribbean states, they came under the High Commissioner to Barbados. Montserrat, the Caymans, Turks and Caicos, and the British Virgin Islands enjoy internal autonomy, with Britain providing overall responsibility, particularly for security; the governors of these territories therefore exercise some executive power and a degree of control over the chief ministers who head the governments.

A second aspect of bilateral relations is the fact that the UK and nearly all Commonwealth Caribbean states share the serving British monarch as head of state. The exceptions to this are Guyana and Trinidad & Tobago, which are republics with their own heads of state: Guyana has an elected executive president and Trinidad & Tobago has a nominated ceremonial president as head of state. In the other Commonwealth Caribbean countries, the Queen is still the head of state, with a governor-general (usually an elder statesman or stateswoman who can command respect from their own as well as the opposition parties) representing the Queen. From time to time in the past it has been suggested that this arrangement should be ended to reflect the changes that have occurred since political independence in the 1960s. For example, P.J. Patterson made it clear at his last swearing-in as prime minister in December 1997 that this will be the last time that a Jamaican head of government will swear allegiance to the British monarch (see, for example, *Caribbean Insight*, February 1998, p. 3). It seemed likely that Patterson's government would take steps to establish a non-elected ceremonial president as head of state with executive power remaining in the hands of the prime minister.[2] It was not, however, until May 2001 that the prime minister, with the next elections in sight, decided to take the firm step of ending the constitutional links with the British crown (see *The Times*, 28 April 2001, p. 18). The report in *The Times* centred around the oath of office that civil servants and ministers of government in Jamaica have had to take under the independence constitution, and stressed that Patterson wanted to make the changes to coincide with Jamaica's fortieth anniversary of political severance from Britain to inaugurate a republican system.

As part of the overall constitutional package of having the British monarch as head of state, most Commonwealth Caribbean countries also accept the British Honours List, although slight variations are to be found. For example, during the 1970s, Jamaica under the radical leadership of Michael Manley's People's National Party did not accept British honours, but an exception was made by Edward Seaga's Jamaica Labour Party's ministry in the early 1980s for the then governor-general Florizel Glasspole, who was allowed to accept a knighthood from the British monarch. In the more conservative 1990s this seemed like one exception that the PNP under Patterson accepted for the serving governor-general, Howard Cooke, a veteran PNP politician, with an earlier career in the teaching occupation. In contrast, the British Honours List does not appear to have been ever questioned in traditionally conservative Barbados.

There is a third and more important dimension to bilateral relations between Britain and the Commonwealth Caribbean. State structures and functions in the region are direct replicas of those in England, established as they were mainly in the seventeenth and eighteenth centuries (sometimes before these were established in the North American colonies on the Atlantic seaboard), and, of course, many if not the majority of Britons today would find them not only anachronistic but also unfathomable. The legal and judicial system follows much the same pattern. Thus, in the same way as several states decided to retain the British monarch as ceremonial head of state, so have they, like New Zealand and several other Commonwealth members, voluntarily decided to invest certain legal powers in the British Privy Council Judicial Committee[3] comprised of Law Lords (see, for example, Ingman, 1996, pp. 87–9). Whilst there are courts of appeal in the region, the Privy Council acts as final court of appeal for the Commonwealth Caribbean states, and this is more than a mere formality. For example, for much of the 1990s and into the new millennium, a number of drug and murder cases have been brought to the Privy Council from the region. Implementation of death sentences continues to be a sore point between the Bahamas, Jamaica, Trinidad & Tobago and Britain, as expressed by the Privy Council and reflecting British parliamentary (though not necessarily public) opinion on the subject. For example, the Privy Council ruled in cases involving Earl Pratt and Ivan Morgan (see *Caribbean Insight,*

December 1993) that, after a stay of execution for five years, execution was inhumane, and therefore commuted their death sentences to life imprisonment. There have been, therefore, frequent discussions between British and Caribbean governments over cases which are overturned by the Privy Council Judicial Committee of the Lords. Presently, there is discussion between Commonwealth Caribbean governments to set up a regional court of final appeal to replace the British Privy Council, and it is expected that the new regional body will offset costs as well as achieve the desired distance between judges and parties to disputes in small, face-to-face, societies. In an increasingly globalised world this development will be a clear demonstration of the efficacy of regional solution to national problems, but also will respect a growing sense of national institutional maturity in the eyes of nationalists (see S. Goulbourne, 2001).

Finally, nationality status is undoubtedly the most immediately important aspect of bilateral relations between Caribbean states and Britain, which underpins the transnationality of Caribbean people across the Atlantic. This is most clearly expressed by the acceptance of dual nationality by both Britain and Commonwealth Caribbean states. It is possible, therefore, for an individual to be legally a Barbadian or Jamaican citizen as well as being a British citizen. Such a person may carry the passport of either country or both, own property,[4] vote and stand for office provided the usual residential qualifications under respective electoral laws are met.[5] The country's laws which apply to such an individual are those of the country in which they are, at a given time, resident or present. In the Commonwealth Caribbean citizenship is principally through birth but also can be acquired by descent, registration or naturalisation and, where migrants to Britain and their offspring are concerned, the issue of nationality does not appear to have been a political issue in any of these states. Two factors may explain this. First, most of these countries are points of departure in the migration process, and returnees are generally welcomed as will be explained in a later chapter. Indeed, the countries with the heaviest flow of returnees, Barbados and Jamaica, have not only set up units to help returnees, but have also been generous to dependent spouses and to those who may have had to renounce their Barbadian or Jamaican citizenship in order to live abroad. Second, increasingly governments in the region have come to see communities abroad as a resource upon which to draw, in terms of investment and during times of natural disasters such as volcanoes and hurricanes.

Prior to the British Nationality Act 1981 (which came into effect in 1983), British nationality was also transmitted principally through birth, irrespective of the national status of an individual's parents. Under the 1981 Act, British nationality is secured mainly by descent, but individuals may also attain citizenship by registration and naturalisation. The Act abolished the rule of *jus soli* whereby individuals acquired nationality simply by the fact of birth on British soil, or within space under British jurisdiction such as a ship or an aeroplane. In other words, the Act adopted the more widely common Continental European tradition of citizenship by descent as enshrined in the *jus sanguinis* principle. The Act also set out four new forms of British nationality: British citizenship, British Dependent Territories Citizens (BDTC), British Overseas Citizens (BOC), and British subject, but it has been pointed out that the 'question of who belongs to the four categories of citizenships ... cannot be determined simply by looking at that Act' (Supperstone and O'Dempsey, 1996, p. 6). Earlier laws, such as the British Nationality Act 1948, the Commonwealth Immigration Act 1962, the Immigration Act 1968 and the British Immigration Act 1971 may have to be consulted to determine an individual's citizenship. This has led to what Cohen correctly perceives as the 'fuzziness' of post-imperial British national identity (Cohen, 1994, ch. 1). But this fuzziness is not entirely absent from the definition of national identities in Commonwealth Caribbean states, which shares with Britain, but perhaps particularly England, a kind of ambivalence about 'the national' entity not present in, for instance, African Commonwealth states.

As Britain's colonies in the Caribbean gained their independence from 1962 onwards, Jamaicans, Barbadians and others – who had migrated to the UK from 1948 as colonials within imperial boundaries – found that they had lost their status as citizens of both the UK and colonies (usually referred to by immigration lawyers as the CUKC category). Depending on period of residence and other factors, individuals in the Caribbean community could acquire UK nationality if they so wished. In any event, their legal, political or social rights in the UK were not affected, but if they left the country and stayed beyond a certain period they were deemed to have lost their right to return. The Immigration Act 1971 required that former CUKCs whose country of birth had become independent from Britain should become UK citizens through a process of registration. This volume of laws governing immigration and defining nationality, taken together with anti-racist discrimination laws – namely, the Race Relations Acts of 1965, 1968, 1976 and 2000 – provides many lawyers in Britain with a good living. The British state has been concerned none the less that – the salutary work of non-governmental organisations such as the Joint Council for the Welfare of Immigrants and the state's own unit on immigration matters notwithstanding – there is a need for better-trained legal functionaries to work in this area (see Lord Chancellor's Advisory Committee on Legal Education and Conduct, 1997).

Whereas people with British Overseas Citizens (BOC) status may be found in such places as Hong Kong, other parts of Asia and in Africa, in the Caribbean British Dependent Territories Citizens (BDTC) are more likely because there are still a number of British dependent territories in the region. With the return of Hong Kong to China in July 1997, Britain has 13 remaining dependencies across the globe. In the Caribbean, Montserrat was much in the news because of the Soufriere Hills volcano eruption in 1999 and Clare Short's (the minister responsible for overseas development) unfortunate gaffe about aid to the islanders;[6] Bermuda with the largest population (60,000[7]) of any remaining dependency is, of course, in the Atlantic, but perhaps because there is an African majority population the dependency is sometimes thought of as being a Caribbean territory.

The term 'dependency' is, of course, something of a misnomer, because whilst they all depend on Britain for defence and representation abroad, apart from piracy there does not appear to be much that they require to be defended from. Some, such as Montserrat and St Helena (not a Caribbean island) may from time to time also require material help from Britain, but in the case of Bermuda the dependency has a higher per capita income than Britain itself; the Caymans are importers of labour and successful off-shore banking economies which have benefited from the return of Hong Kong to China as some transnational corporations relocated themselves. Hintjens (1997) has suggested that it would be desirable for the rights of persons with BDTC status to be changed, bringing them more into line with the similar cases in the Dutch dependencies of Aruba, Curaçao, Bonaire, Saba, St Eustatius and St Maarten or the French DOMs of Martinique and Guadeloupe in the Caribbean and French Guiana on the South American continent. This would mean that BDTCs would have rights in the UK, such as right of entry, residence and the vote as citizens in the French dependencies in the region have in France and the right of entry as citizens in the Dutch Antilles have with respect to The Netherlands. Following a Foreign Office meeting addressing the problems of the British dependencies in London in early February 1998, the *Guardian* newspaper strongly supported this position and urged the then Foreign Secretary, Robin Cook, and the then Home Secretary, Jack Straw, to extend such rights to the dependencies, particularly since it is thought that people in these territories would not wish to settle in Britain. Indeed, there appears to be more of a concern on the part of some spokespersons in these territories that the real problem would be people from Britain relocating to the dependencies if there were to be a situation of reciprocity.

Multilateral relations between Commonwealth Caribbean states and Britain have come to be structured through memberships of a number of international bodies. Undoubtedly, the two most important of such bodies are the Commonwealth and the European Union. As is well known, the Commonwealth or what used to be called the *British* Commonwealth, grew out of the close association that Britain sought to maintain between herself and the white Dominions or colonies with internal autonomy during the late nineteenth century and the first half of the present century – Canada, Australia, New Zealand, South Africa and, between the two World Wars, the Irish Republic. With the political independence of India and Pakistan in 1947 and the rapid constitutional decolonisation that followed from the 1950s in Africa (starting with highly visible and militant Ghana under the leadership of Kwame Nkrumah in 1957), the Caribbean and the Pacific, the Empire and Dominion gave way not just to an expanding world of nation-states but also to a voluntary British Commonwealth of independent nations. Some former colonies, on winning independence chose to cut their links clear of Britain. This was particularly so in the semi-colonial world of the Middle East (for example, Aden, Jordan, Egypt, Iraq, Israel) but also in parts of Asia (for example, Burma) and Africa (for example, the Sudan and Cameroon).[8] In the Caribbean, former colonies passed easily from this status to become members of the expanding Commonwealth, and provided one of the Secretariat's most dynamic secretary-generals to date in the person of Sir Sonny Ramphal, Guyana's former foreign minister. Though political, judicial, administrative, educational, professional and other institutions derive essentially from the UK, there are any number of practical connections and assumptions shared between the Commonwealth Caribbean and Britain. These are enhanced by the Commonwealth Secretariat to which members contribute, and states in the region have been able to maintain close links with the former imperial power, not least through the Commonwealth Fund for Technical Co-operation which provides assistance to less industrially developed members.

The Lomé Conventions, from the 1970s to the turn of the century, grew largely out of these relations and assumptions. As is well known, the Conventions represent perhaps the most favourable terms that Third World countries have been able to gain in negotiations with a bloc of advanced industrial states in world trade. The Conventions covered specific items of trade, particularly the agricultural and traditional manufactured goods (bananas, sugar, rum and so on) from the former tropical colonies to the imperial centres[9] of Britain, France and Holland. Britain's joining of the EEC in 1972 stimulated the coming together of ex-colonies in Africa, the Caribbean and the Pacific (ACP) to negotiate as a bloc with the EEC regarding the continuation of their common products finding secure markets in Europe. Whilst the agreements between these blocs of states and markets did not achieve the goals that radical Third World leaders such as the late Michael Manley and the former president of Tanzania, Julius Nyerere, wanted, the Conventions none the less went a long way in satisfying leaders that their countries' products would continue to find their way to their traditional markets within an integrating Europe.

The several Conventions agreed since the mid-1970s have held to this principle, but the ACP states have always had to make a strong case for the relatively privileged position they enjoyed. Indeed, in the discussions over the last agreement it was required that the ACP states broaden their membership to include other Third World states in each region.[10] It is also widely acknowledged that the original moving spirits behind the Conventions were chiefly P.J. Patterson, then finance minister of Jamaica and Sonny Ramphal, then foreign minister of Guyana (Talburt, forthcoming). This means that whilst a number of African and Pacific politicians played important roles in the formation of the ACP-EEC meetings which developed these Conventions, Caribbean leaders have had a particularly strong investment in these arrangements, and this is not unrelated to the conditions of Caribbean communities in the UK, although its relevance may not be immediately obvious.

Given this structure of relationship between Britain and the Commonwealth Caribbean, it is not surprising that there is comparatively little to be said about active transnational politics emanating from Caribbean communities in Britain. These kinds of politics are generally latent, becoming active and therefore observable during moments of crisis in the Caribbean (such as the various Guyana crises, the Grenada invasion, perennial violence in Jamaica, hurricanes in the region, and volcano eruptions). An additional reason for this general characterisation of Caribbean transnational politics is the fact that politically the sub-region is relatively stable and does not experience large-scale upheavals in its political arrangements. In particular, the question of national belongingness, whilst perhaps somewhat fuzzy, is not the issue it can become in several other parts of the contemporary world, nor is belongingness exclusivist in orientation. Subsequently, the relatively few specific moments of crisis which illustrate the nature of Caribbean transnational political relations can easily be identified.

First, whilst it should be noted that the process of migration from the Caribbean to Britain and the return migration that has been developing since the late 1960s (see Peach, 1991) involved relatively little active state intervention, there has been at least one instance when Caribbean leaders felt compelled to intervene. This was occasioned by the riots in Notting Hill, London in 1957 (see Pilkington, 1988), when young white men attacked black immigrants and the St Vincencian Kelso Cochrane was killed, triggering similar events in other British cities such as Nottingham in the East Midlands; these set the backdrop for the 1962 Commonwealth Immigration Act which drastically limited black and brown immigration. These events are properly described and analysed elsewhere (see, for example, Foot, 1969; Layton-Henry, 1992) and need not detain us here. Suffice it to say that the events led to Norman Manley, Premier of Jamaica (acting on the behalf of the short-lived West Indian Federation) visiting London and seeing for himself the reaction to West Indian entry. After holding discussions with relevant authorities about the conditions West Indian immigrants faced, a number of people on the liberal wing of British society collaborated with concerned West Indians to found the West Indian Standing Conference (WISC) whose main aims included representation of West Indian problems to the relevant authorities and promoting 'good race relations' between natives and newcomers. Thereafter, Caribbean governments tended not to involve themselves too closely with the lives of their nationals in Britain, and this may be because in general Caribbeans in the UK enjoy citizenship rights and their welfare is not, therefore, always the direct and exclusive responsibility of governments in the Caribbean. It is possible too that I would be stretching the point to suggest that this may also be due to a perception on the part of Commonwealth Caribbean governments that their people are simply moving around within a commonly shared world-in-formation on the rims of the Atlantic.

Whatever the case may be, the states in African-dominated countries in the Commonwealth Caribbean have not been entirely silent about the fate of nationals and their offspring in the UK. From time to time, there have been indications that governments, irrespective of which party was in office in the main islands, kept themselves aware of developments as these affected Caribbeans in the UK. There is also much that is not known about these states' responses to some of these major events in Britain. The responses of Caribbean governments to a wide range of problems faced by Caribbean people in Britain need to be researched: the dramatic negative effects of the late J. Enoch Powell's 1968 'rivers of blood' speech in Birmingham, the various immigration and nationality laws, the high incidence of brutal policing in black communities, disproportionately high unemployment and prison rates, poor schooling, increasingly poor mental and physical health are some of these problems. In recent years a number of other problems have, however, concerned Commonwealth Caribbean governments with respect to British authorities. These include the frequent stopping at ports of entry of legitimate tourists, relatives visiting family members in the UK, and the British customs and Home Office's concern about the mobility or entry of drug traffickers associated with Jamaican 'yardies' and other transnational criminal fraternities. As Castells (1996) noted, the growth of the network society not only facilitates ease of communication across the globe, it also promotes more rapid criminal networking.

On the other hand, moments of crisis in the Caribbean have from time to time elicited noticeable concern amongst the Caribbean population in Britain. Again, these need to be specifically researched, but a number of instances can be pointed to: the conflict symbolised by the African-dominated People's National Congress (PNC) and the East Indian-dominated People's Progressive Party (PPP) in Guyana led, respectively, by the late Forbes Burnham and the late Cheddi Jagan in Guyana; Maurice Bishop's 1979 New Jewel Revolution in

Grenada against 'uncle' Eric Gairy's uncharacteristically repressive Commonwealth Caribbean government; the invasion of Grenada (incidentally, a Commonwealth state) in 1983 by Ronald Reagan. In the same period of the early 1970s that the Tory government of Edward Heath was introducing a draconian industrial relations bill in the British Parliament, the radical Manley government in Jamaica was also introducing a similar measure, and the veteran Jamaican trade unionist and erstwhile politician, Richard Hart, led the Caribbean Labour Solidarity group in London in opposition not only to Heath but also in opposition to his former comrade Michael Manley. The impact of the US Black Power Movement in Britain and the Caribbean also involved Caribbean people in Britain. Not only did that movement stimulate political awareness and growth in Britain, but UK-based Caribbeans also responded to the impact in the Caribbean. The two main incidents include the Rodney riots (see, for example, Payne, 1994; Rodney, 1969) in Kingston in 1968 (part of the worldwide student-cum-academic revolt of that year), and the Black Power revolt in Trinidad in 1970. There are important connections between these events and the growth of political and national consciousness across the North Atlantic. And when the mysticism that surrounds Caribbean participation and belonging-ness in the Atlantic world is debunked, future research will no doubt elaborate and explain these connections. It is, however, now necessary to turn to some specifics about political participation in this Atlantic world that we are discussing.

POLITICAL INTEGRATION AND PARTICIPATION IN BRITISH POLITICS

In contrast to exilic politics, the political integration of people of Caribbean backgrounds in Britain is a dynamic process whose history, as Almond and Powell expressed the point, has been one of 'pressure from groups in the society for having a part in the decision making of the system' (1966, p. 35). If peacefully handled, the pressure to expand the limits of popular participation may enrich what Almond and Verba (1963) described as the civic culture, by developing negotiating skills and capacities, and greater competence in the management of conflict on the part of political leaders. The new issues that have arisen as a result of the presence of African-Caribbean and Asian communities in Britain have indeed expanded the capacity of the system, extended the notion of tolerance, and provided politicians with the opportunity to develop new skills absent or not displayed in the imperial age.

But whilst Caribbean and other new minority groups' political behaviour is usually situated within the context of the behaviour aspects of politics, it is a mistake to assume that political participation is limited to the periodic activity of casting a vote or being an active member in a political party. I have usually found it useful to employ Milbrath's (1965) distinction between what he called *gladiatorial activities* (holding public or party office, becoming a candidate for such office, seeking funds for the party, taking part in strategy meetings and spending time on campaigning), *transitional activities* (attendance at public meetings or rallies, contributing money and getting in touch with an official or party leader), and *spectator activities* (wearing a button or sticker, trying to influence others to vote in a particular way, starting a political discussion, voting, exposing oneself to political stimuli). It is interesting to note that voting is seen to be low in this ordering of participatory activities, and is described as a mere spectator activity. Of course, it is a paradox that although the right to vote is basic to democratic theory and practice, actual turn-outs at local and national elections in older democratic states are low for reasons that Birch describes as 'complex and somewhat contradictory' (1993, p. 94). His ordering of participatory activities appears to situate specific activities somewhat differently. Voting in local and national elections and referendums come fairly high on his list, followed by participation in organised group activities such as what political scientists call the interest, professional, promotional groups; cooperating with others in demonstrations, strikes and civil disobedience; and membership of a range of public committees and councils. The specific activities in both lists are sufficiently flexible to include any social action which might have an impact on any aspect of the political process, directly or indirectly. These descriptions of what constitutes political participation share the Lasswellian perception that has become popular, namely, that all human activity has a political aspect or dimension (see Lasswell, 1958; also, Lasswell and Kaplan, 1950). In this sense, political participation is not restricted, as an Aristotelian definition might suggest, to engagement in the formally established channels of a given political system.

These comments are relevant to an understanding of the participation of individuals and groups from Britain's new minority ethnic communities in the nation's political life. After all, as indicated earlier, the backgrounds of the vast majority of Britain's new minority ethnic communities, particularly Caribbeans, are not entirely exclusive to each other. They overlap in important ways and provide the historical and sociological bases for what has been a common set of concerns about social and political integration into the wider national community. More immediately relevant, particularly for the growing majority who have no direct experience of either colonial or post-colonial societies, these groups share experiences of discrimination in such vital areas as housing and employment and exclusion from important decision making and implementation in areas of national life. These bitter experiences have created the need to articulate jointly a number of common issues, but the political unity which characterised much of the period from the 1960s to the 1980s may have given way to a less aggregated political articulation which is specific to cultural communities.

It is useful to consider the overall or general patterns of the participation of these minorities in the political life of a traditional society which has also incorporated change over time. Developed over the better part of a thousand years to become the archetypal political system, through a largely non-written constitutional arrangement, the British political system has been able to incorporate different social groups and conflicting interests into a socio-political order that must appear to the post-eighteenth century rational mind to be nothing short of disorderly and illogical.[11] None the less, if British socio-political traditions exhibit a certain Burkean cautiousness towards deliberate and sudden change to the body politic, its tolerance and uncertainty ensure a modicum of controlled change. The changes that the presence of African Caribbeans and Asians have engendered, and their own desire to actively participate in British political life, have taken place within constraints historically defined and partly closed off from radical departures.

In order not to become involved in a lengthy descriptive account of African-Caribbean participation in British society, it may be worth reiterating my crude typology of their political behaviour according to welfare/cultural, broker and political kinds of activities. In doing so, I want to suggest, in opposition to a genre of writers such as Rex (see Rex and Tomlinson, 1979); and Dench (1986) who have done much to promote a false understanding of the Caribbean presence in Britain, that individuals and organised groups from African-Caribbean (and Asian) communities in Britain have engaged in a wide range of spontaneous, semi-structured as well as more formal kinds of political activities in British society.

Welfare/cultural activities are those which involve collective welfare needs and support. In these activities are concealed many latent political issues, some of which sometimes develop into big, actual political issues involving major political action at the level of either local or national governments. At this level, it is often enough for managers of services such as health, education or housing authorities to address them. No substantial changes in rules and regulations are required in order to satisfy demands. Indeed, more often than not, such welfare/cultural activities occur within the broadly accepted context of multicultural provisions and relatively little is required from the local or national state. In the main, the basis for collective action and organisation is the fact of shared common affinities, which themselves have become the basis of exclusion and discrimination, whether wittingly or unwittingly. The variety of West Indian or Caribbean social centres providing for the needs of the young, women or the elderly; the promotion of alternative education classes, training groups, and so on are examples of this kind of activity (see Hinds, 1992). So too are the many black-led churches which sprang up throughout British cities from the 1960s (see, for example, Edwards, 1992; Gerloff, 1992; Calley, 1965). In general, however, Caribbean groups are not best able to exploit ethnic solidarity as a resource in the competition for scarce resources, even in the so-called multicultural society.

Broker-type activities are involved when and where groups or individuals seek to mediate between official organs (of the local or national state, statutory bodies, employers and providers of services), and the community. As the word suggests, brokers stand at a point from which they can mediate between actual or potentially conflicting interests. Increasingly, brokers are private individuals or small groups providing services for needy clients, groups or individuals, sometimes with conflicting interests. In all communities, however, there have long been large umbrella-like organisations which have functioned as brokers between state bodies and communities. The best known of these has been the West Indian Standing Conference (WISC) mentioned earlier. Whilst WISC continues to be consulted by officials,[12] the organisation is no longer the force it was in the 1960s when it was at the forefront of several struggles in the black community, particularly in North London where leaders such as Jeff Crawford and John LaRose were active.

This is largely because with the integration of Caribbean people into British society, not only have they variously participated in established organisations, but they have also initiated a large number of organisations in London, Birmingham and other cities (see Hinds, 1992) where they have settled and negotiated their own relationships with the various High Commissions in London and local and national authorities. Moreover, these organisations have followed the broad patterns of those in the indigenous populations, representing for example youths, women, the elderly, and people with particular ailments such as sickle cell anaemia or mental illness.

There have also been various national or island associations of Barbadians, Jamaicans, and so on. Similar to the village associations organised by Greek Cypriots in London, several Caribbean communities have established village, educational (old schools, universities) and health support groups. At one time it was thought that these bodies would fade with the passing of the migrant generation, but they appear to be continuing amongst younger people who wish to retain close links with the lands of their parents' birth. These organisations sometimes participate in or even organise demonstrations around key issues, but in the main they have served as brokers with their respective High Commissions in London, and organise social events, thereby overlapping with welfare/cultural groups. They have also sometimes helped individuals to return 'home' after a period of settlement in Britain; some of them are now being linked with groups of returnees to continue giving mutual assistance on both sides of the Atlantic.

The most dramatic mass protest by people of Caribbean backgrounds in Britain was, as is well known, the Brixton disturbances during the weekend of 10–12 April 1981. From the 1950s Brixton had been regarded as a prime destination of Caribbean migrants, and streets such as Somerlayton, Railton, Mayall, Shakespeare and other roads had become familiar to many Caribbean people, particularly Jamaicans (see, for example, Patterson, 1965) who may have started life in Britain in the area or in nearby Clapham or shopped at the famous Brixton market with its colourful stalls run by Jews who had earlier migrated from the East End. Brixton also became the central site of excessive policing in London and black men the focus of such police attention (see Scarman, 1982; Humphry and John, 1971). The disturbances of that fateful April weekend are chronicled by Scarman and have been variously commented upon (see, for example, Keith, 1990, 1993). The events are usually seen as the entry of black youth into British public life (see, for example, Hall et al., 1978; Solomos, 1988), and they triggered similar events in other major British cities such as Liverpool, Manchester, Birmingham and Bristol. The importance of this kind of entry into the political system was not only that the events highlighted the problems of excessive policing and lack of police accountability but also the problems of high unemployment, poor housing and the general marginalisation of black people in British society. Like the commissions into urban disturbances in the great American cities in the 1960s, the Brixton events forced the British political elite and establishment to bring onto the national political agenda the question of the place of new minorities in a post-imperial society which claimed to be multicultural, fair and democratic. Islam's place in British society was to be similarly brought into question following the publication of Salman Rushdie's *The Satanic Verses* in 1988 (see, for example, Appignanesi and Maitland, 1989; CRE, 1990a, 1990b).

The integration of new minority ethnic communities into the political system is usually measured in terms of voting behaviour, membership of political parties and their election to Parliament. Consequently, a sizeable body of literature has developed since the mid-1970s around these observable forms of political participation (see, for example, Anwar, 1994; Messina, 1989; Saggar, 1992; Sewell, 1993; Fitzgerald, 1988, 1984). It is not, therefore, necessary to go into details here about these forms of participation; suffice it to highlight some salient aspects.

In the first place, it is generally agreed that whilst Asians attain the highest level of voting in elections, people of Caribbean backgrounds tend to have a lower turn-out at the polls than voters from the white majority population (see Anwar, 1994; Layton-Henry, 1992). In sharp contrast, however, voters of Caribbean backgrounds are usually seen to display a higher level of political awareness and political issues of the day than other groups (see, for example, Layton-Henry, 1992). The disparity between political awareness and voting behaviour may therefore suggest that voters of Caribbean backgrounds feel that they have little to gain from the political system, and low voter turn-out is not evidence of political apathy but paradoxically the opposite.

Second, whilst voters of Caribbean backgrounds register comparatively low turn-out at elections – thereby stimulating the activities of the Operation Black Vote group in London in the late 1990s and into the present century – in the 1980s and 1990s individual politicians from these backgrounds played the more prominent role in forcing the doors of public office open to new minorities generally. For example, in proportion to their numbers there has been a significant number of elected councillors in London boroughs (see Anwar, 1994) contributing to the 400 Asian and African-Caribbean councillors Anwar estimated in 1996. From the early 1980s, councillors of Caribbean backgrounds began to be appointed as mayors in places such as Lambeth and Southwark and by the end of the decade Bradford was boasting the country's first Muslim mayor. Not surprisingly, it was in the London boroughs that the most notable political successes were seen in the breakthrough years of the second half of the 1980s. First, Bernie Grant, a Guyanese with a militant trade union background, became the first person from a new minority ethnic background to become leader of a council, Haringay. This was followed by the election of Merle Emory to the leadership of Brent council and Linda Bellos as leader of Lambeth. In smaller cities, such as Coventry and Leicester in the English Midlands, it took much longer for new minority politicians to be elected to councils, but by the late 1980s Asian politicians became familiar figures on councils such as that of Coventry though it was as recently as 1994 before an African-Caribbean person was elected to that city's council.

The second significant point to note about the Thatcherite 1980s with regard to black and Asian participation in national politics is that the 1987 general election marked a breakthrough for politicians from these communities. Diane Abbot (of Jamaican background) and Bernie Grant were elected for London constituencies to Parliament, as was Paul Boateng (of Ghanaian background); Keith Vaz (of Goan background) was elected for Leicester East. These politicians were returned to Parliament in the 1992, 1997 and 2001 general elections, with Boateng becoming the first member of a new minority ethnic group to be appointed to a ministerial position in a British government.[13] In the years between 1987 and 1997, the careers of other individual politicians from new minority ethnic backgrounds, such as Ashok Kumar in Yorkshire, Piara Khabra and Nirj Deva in London, and John Taylor in Cheltenham prospered and waned with the fortunes of their respective parties, Labour and Conservative. Tony Blair's landslide at the polls on 1 May 1997 saw the election of all nine politicians from minority ethnic backgrounds fielded by the Labour Party. The other two major parties had fielded more candidates from new minority backgrounds – Conservatives 10, Liberal Democrats 15,[14] – but none were elected.

In the House of Lords, where membership is both hereditary and by nomination, the presence of individuals from new minority ethnic communities has also increased at the turn of the century. Each of the three major parties have nominated black and Asian supporters to the upper chamber, including individuals of Caribbean backgrounds, such as Baroness Patricia Scotland, a barrister, and Baroness Valerie Amos, former chairperson of the national Equal Opportunities Commission, on the Labour benches and John Taylor, a barrister, on the Tory benches. In the post-war years, Lord Constantine (the legendary Trinidadian cricketer) and Lord Pitt (a medical doctor and long-time Labour activist of Grenadian background) sat on the Labour benches.

New minority ethnic communities in Britain have consistently given their overwhelming support to the Labour Party, although there is growing, particularly Asian, support for the other two major parties, the Conservatives and Liberal Democrats. For example, over 70 per cent of Asian and African-Caribbean votes went to Labour in the 1983 general election. In 1987 there was a shift to the Conservatives in the Asian vote, but Labour still enjoyed 61 per cent of their votes, whilst 92 per cent of African-Caribbean votes remained with Labour (Anwar, 1994, p. 37). There are several factors behind this strong support for Labour. First, there has been the party's more liberal stance, particularly when in opposition, on immigration issues. Second, there is the fact that it has been Labour governments which have enacted legislation against racial discrimination and other equality measures with respect to women. Third, the party's activists on the left have been more receptive to the radical demands of black and Asian aspirant politicians who organised themselves in Black Sections in the 1980s in order to gain selection for seats where they had a sporting chance of winning (see Shukra, 1990). Whilst the other parties also took measures to encourage new minority membership and participation (see Sewell, 1993), up to now they have tended to be pusillanimous efforts by their leaderships rather than the dynamic movement from below that Black Sections represented in the momentous 1980s. With the new emphasis on youth and newness initiated by Blair in British politics and the Tories' attempts to copy this, there may be opportunity for greater participation by ambitious individuals from the new minorities to join the Conservatives where they may stand a better chance for promotion than in Blair's party with its unshakeable majority in middle England as well as in Scotland and Wales, in urban as in rural regions of the country.

CONCLUSION

Clearly, much remains to be explored about the nature of the relationship between Britain and the Commonwealth Caribbean not just at the level of state to state relations, but particularly at the level of relations and relationships between elements of civil society between these regions united by a common, but largely unacknowledged, Atlantic heritage. When Caribbean communities in Europe are looked at from this global perspective, a number of new horizons beckon, but it remains to be seen whether these will open new opportunities or new forms of closures and exclusions with respect to forms of political participation and therefore incorporation. The following chapter addresses the question of how Africa and the Caribbean have become part of Caribbean consciousness in Britain, as constructed by one radical community group in the 1970s.

4 Africa and the Caribbean in Caribbean Consciousness and Action in Britain in the 1970s

Of the various Caribbean groups in Britain which saw themselves as being essentially political in purpose, perhaps none was more consistently so in the formative years of the 1970s than the Black Unity and Freedom Party (BUFP). But, expectedly, the BUFP could not neatly separate political from welfare activities. However, with its radical agenda for change, it eschewed what it saw as cultural nationalist postures, but at the same time drew upon Caribbean and African heroes, icons and radical ideas, thereby playing a major part in the development of the consciousness of a wider Caribbean as well as reviewing the historic breach with Africa, themes that were to become fairly familiar by the 1980s.

This chapter analyses three aspects of the group's history in order to illustrate two important points: first, the sense of Africa and the Caribbean as parts of a general Atlantic diaspora; and second, the backdrop to active political participation of Caribbeans in mainstream British politics and society in the last decades of the last century and the beginning of the present one. The three aspects of the group's history are, first, the origins of the group; second, its beliefs or ideology, and third, the kinds of activities with which the group was involved in the emerging Caribbean communities of the 1970s. The account here draws on the group's publications, including minutes, memoranda, leaflets and its newspaper, *Black Voice*, coverage in the local press, and personal observations at meetings. While subsequent developments are not neglected, the emphasis here is on the early history of the group in the 1970s, when, not unlike other similar groups, BUFP was most active and relevant to the general articulation of radical politics in these new communities.

ORIGINS, CONTINUITY AND STRUCTURE

On Saturday 27 July 1991, the BUFP celebrated its twenty-first anniversary with an afternoon programme around the theme of 'self-defence and community organisation'. Held at the premises of the Simba Project at 239 Uxbridge Road in West London, the programme included an address by founding member Danny Morrell who spoke on 'The first year – 1970' followed by open discussion. There were two sessions of poetry readings by young writers, messages of solidarity from other groups in Britain and abroad, and open discussion sessions. During the course of the afternoon there were long presentations by BUFP spokespersons on 'From Aseta Simms to Rolan Adams (1970–1991),[1] and 'Self-defence and community organisation – the struggle for liberation today'. Crèches for babies and small children were provided; a 'collection' was made, a donation of £1 requested and a small charge made for some food items – all in order to help with the costs of the day. Book selling, the playing of music, the exchange of a variety of information, 'reasoning', and good cheer and humour punctuated the day. The event was billed for the afternoon, and everything went on in a well-organised, orderly manner, with the programme being kept within schedule. At no point did it appear that there might be police interference, as would have been the case in the 1970s, when one or more comrades would be tasked to keep an eye open for either *agents provocateurs* and/or the raiding police. Participants appeared to be perfectly at ease with themselves and their surroundings and many appeared to be conscious of the fact that the BUFP had played an important role in the development of black consciousness in Britain.

Indeed, there was something here of a happy family affair. True enough, Comrade Danny, Comrade Jerry and myself were present, but missing were most of the original founding members of the BUFP, and a different membership had command of affairs. George Joseph, the premier figure in the founding of the group, had returned to Trinidad in 1973, worked as a civil servant and came to an untimely death in the mid-1980s. His widow, Sonia Chang (from Jamaica) had accompanied him to Trinidad, but returned first to Jamaica and then to London with their son Che (named after Ernesto Che Guevara, the Argentinean turned Cuban revolutionary). Busy working in London with the Hackney West Indian Neighbourhood Association and caring for her son, Sonia was also absent at the BUFP meeting on 27 July. Also absent were Emil Chang (a cousin of Sonia's), who had come to Britain to play cricket in the 1940s, returned to Jamaica in the 1970s and then returned to live in north-east London (where he died in the mid-1990s) There was a noticeable absence of the kinds of young, critical, intellectuals who would have been present in the early years.

Typical of this last group was Alrick (Ricky) Xavier Cambridge, undoubtedly the second moving spirit behind the formation of the group in the summer of 1970; he was also absent at the twenty-first anniversary celebrations. He and the BUFP had parted company in late 1971. A dynamic and creative personality, Ricky had gone on to found the *Black Liberator* journal which sought to pull together a number of themes about revolution and change in the Caribbean and in Britain. Indeed, for the few years of its existence the *Black Liberator* became the leading black and Caribbean journal in Britain, but apart from Hall et al. (1978), the work of this publication has attracted no attention in the academic literature. With the demise of the journal Cambridge went on to realise a long ambition of completing a degree. Following well-established middle-class West Indian tradition, he went to Oxford, where he later registered for a doctorate in philosophy, studying the Trinidadian historian and intellectual, C.L.R. James, and publishing on issues such as identity and belongingness.

George Joseph on the other hand, of a less intellectual bent than Cambridge but with perhaps a more practical mind, had studied sociology at university and held an MA. The first years of the BUFP were very much a credit to him, moving between south-east and north-east London and Manchester (Moss Side and Oldham) in the north-west of England. He exuded quiet confidence and optimism among both the majority younger, as well as the older, members of the group. Of the generation of middle-class West Indians who came to Britain primarily to study, he was one of the first of the relatively few who established a meaningful and practical relationship with working-class West Indian immigrants and their offspring. The fact that he ended up teaching/training the Trinidad police is part of the irony of class, race and the migration process. The story for a number of the group's members was to be similar, that is to say, some would end up in professional (medicine, law, academic work, etc.) or semi-professional (teaching, social and youth work, etc.) occupations in Britain or elsewhere.

The family atmosphere of the twenty-first anniversary celebrations was also reflected in the sense of forgiveness, the irrelevance of past differences and quarrels. Danny Morrell, for example, had for a while been regarded as 'Daft Danny', due to his enthusiasm over some now forgotten matters. Two decades on, he proved to be one of the most faithful and consistent of the group of 1970–71, and he clearly appreciated the respect the younger people were paying him. Comrade

Jerry had gone on to establish a happy family, with children doing well at school and one about to go to university (the bourgeois institution he would have condemned in the early 1970s). He looked as young as he did in 1971, but he was now a great deal more tolerant and appeared a wiser man.

In many respects, the agenda in 1991 was not very different from what it would have been in the early 1970s. There would have been much the same mix of social provision and care, entertainment and general social mixing reminiscent of the church, the family and the social club in Caribbean communities in Britain. Political discussion, however, formed the central concern of the day. Earlier, there would have been a stronger emphasis on constitutionality, and procedures would have been more formal; dogmatism and certainty, verbal intolerance and adherence to purity of doctrine, with frequent references to Marx and Engels, Lenin, Stalin, Mao and Fanon would have been stronger, or at least less subtle in 1970 than in 1991.

But perhaps the noticeable difference between the founding members of the BUFP in 1970 and those who met to celebrate its twenty-first anniversary in 1991 was the gender dimension of the leadership. In 1970 all the leading speakers were men, with women aplenty playing supportive but less prominent roles. On 27 July 1991 the main players were women. Now, a number of men played supporting roles, and thereby reflected one of the major social shifts in Caribbean communities in the UK, that is, the greater prominence of women in the public sphere.

Thus, whilst the invitation to the occasion went under the signature of a male, Kimathi (name of a Kenyan Mau Mau leader who fought against settler colonialism), the chairperson for the day was Julietta Joseph (no relation to George), and women dominated the occasion. It was as if the men had come to recognise or accept their broader subordinate role to the women (where active participation and responsibilities are concerned), but there was no sign of resentment, disrespect or competition. The situation seemed natural enough to all present. Nor was there any reference to gender issues in order to justify the situation. The group had obviously either achieved something important here or was reflecting the sad state in the community whereby the absence of men or their less than active leadership roles are becoming more pronounced.

In terms of age distribution, the membership of the group appeared to be much the same as in 1970. In general, the BUFP had been an organisation of young people in their late teens or early adulthood to their thirties. The re-migration of many of its members in the 1970s, and the moving on of some to other concerns, had helped to keep the age profile of the group more or less constant. Spawned by the protest of youths in the 1970s, the BUFP in the 1990s sought to renew its original inspiration; it appeared as if one generation was passing on responsibility for the organisation to the next. This youthful profile did not conform to the general description of most groups where there is usually the tendency for the membership either to remain constant or decline, the membership ageing with the organisation. This is certainly a major problem for what may still be the main Caribbean umbrella organisation in the country, the West Indian Standing Conference (WISC) which has been both a broker and a protest group from its inception in 1957 following the Notting Hill white riots (see Goulbourne, 1990).

The constantly renewing membership of the BUFP did, however, have its weakness. If older members were inaccessible, then the accumulation of useful experience could disappear all too rapidly, and younger people were then forced to start afresh the process of learning. The continued existence of the BUFP beyond the early 1990s was therefore in question. One mitigating factor was the prospect of there being more elderly Caribbean folks spending their retirement years in Britain instead of returning to the Caribbean or re-migrating to North America. Another mitigating factor was the fact that the organisation had relatively clear ideas about its work: it kept records, published, and members were deeply committed to what they saw as their work. The group was also rooted within local communities. The ups and downs of state and other forms of public funding did not affect the group, because it did not depend on such resources, but on its own membership.

It was not surprising, therefore, that the publications announcing the group's activities in 1991 would appear familiar to anyone from a meeting in 1970. One poster called upon supporters to celebrate the two-hundredth anniversary of the emergence of Toussaint L'Ouverture, the Haitian liberator, who led the only successful slave rebellion in history; the Haitian Revolution was being interpreted as 'black history for action' in the 1990s. Another leaflet called for support of the family while others protested against the racist killing of Rolan Adams on 21 February 1991 in Thamesmead, and was to trigger a London-wide protest with the famous Revd Al Sharpton of New York participating at one point, thereby continuing to make links between black struggles and concerns across the Atlantic. The group called for support at the Old Bailey on 7 October 1991, when the case would be heard, and at the British National Party head-quarters in Welling (East London) on 2 November 1991. Not surprisingly, another pamphlet was concerned with the 'black community against women's oppression'. There was information about developments in the Asian communities in Britain, events in the Caribbean, Africa and elsewhere. The group reaffirmed its basic principles, which were first set out in 1970, and although modified over the years, remained consistent.

It may be useful, therefore, to consider the circumstances which brought the group about, circumstances which would have, to one degree or another, most likely informed the formation of similar groups in and around London and a number of large cities in Britain such as Birmingham, Bristol, Liverpool, Manchester and Southampton. London was, however, the centre of these activities not only by virtue of being the nation's capital, but more importantly because the vast majority of people from the Caribbean between 1948 and 1962 had settled in one or the other of the inner boroughs such as Lambeth, Haringey and Southwark.

Three closely related sets of developments may be said to contribute to, and set the context for, the emergence of the BUFP and similar groups such as the Croydon Collective, the Black Liberation Front, the Black Panther Movement, and the South East London Black People's Organisation, which sprang up throughout the city in the early 1970s.

BLACK CONSCIOUSNESS AND GROUP FORMATION

Perhaps the first development which formed the backdrop for the emergence of these community-based groups was the breakup of the Universal Coloured Peoples' Alliance (UCPA). This had been formed by the Nigerian playwright Ebi Egbuna in 1967 (Egbuna, 1971), and some leading lights included the Guyanese Ron Phillips who later played a major role in community politics in Manchester,[2] and Roy Sawh, later of Black Rights UK. As the UCPA explained in one of its leaflets in 1970, the word 'coloured' was widely accepted at the time, and the name also reflected that of Marcus Mosiah Garvey's Universal Negro Improvement Organisation of the 1920s (see Lewis and Warner, 1986; Lewis and Bryan, 1988). The formation of the UCPA followed the dramatic visit of Kwame Toure (at the time, Stokeley Carmichael) to London and his talk at the Roundhouse in Chalk Farm.[3] Just as the earlier visit in 1964 by Martin Luther King

– en route from Stockholm after receiving the Nobel Peace Prize –
had stimulated the founding of the Campaign Against Racial Discrimination (CARD), so Kwame Toure's visit stimulated the birth of
a new body. CARD had been an umbrella organisation, bringing
together existing Asian groups – such as the Federation of Pakistani
Organisations, the Indian Workers Association and Caribbean
groups such as WISC themselves umbrella bodies – under its aegis.
CARD sought to influence government to legislate against racial discrimination in housing, employment and public places such as clubs
and restaurants, much as civil rights groups in the US had done,
resulting in Lyndon Johnson's momentous 1963 Civil Rights Act (see
Heineman, 1972).

It would appear that just as CARD broke up into its previous con-
stituent parts and in the process stimulated the birth of new groups
– such as the Joint Council for the Welfare of Immigrants (JCWI)[4]
and the Runnymede Trust and the UCPA itself – so too the collapse
of the UCPA spawned new groups in black communities in England's
inner cities. With respect to Caribbean groups, the two main organisations which emerged during these years were the Black Panther
Movement (BPM) and the BUFP.[5] The BPM was initially led by David
Udah, a Church of England clergyman, who later went on to play
an important role in opening the established church to issues of
colour and inequality in the Diocese of Southwark. Another leader
was Darcus Howe, a nephew of the late C.L.R. James and a then col-
laborator with John LaRose of New Beacon Publishers. Howe later
went on to lead the Race Today Collective with Leila Hussain
(originally from Zanzibar and a former member of the BUFP) and
the poet Linton Kwesi Johnson, who became, and has remained, a
symbol of the fusion of black poetry and music movement in Britain.
Later still, Howe became a programme producer and journalist with
the television network Channel 4, working closely with the former
student radical, the Trotskyist Tariq Ali, and Channel 4's programme
commissioner, Farouk Dhondi, who was himself a former member of
the BPM. Others included Eddie Leconte and Althea Jones (later
Leconte), who was at the centre of the famous Mangrove Nine trials
in 1970–71 in Notting Hill.[6]

The BUFP founders claimed that they were the legitimate
inheritors of the UCPA. Indeed, the build-up to the formation of the
BUFP occurred under the umbrella of the UCPA, and the pre-launch
documents as well as early BUFP letters, were written on UCPA-
headed paper, and UCPA addresses in London and Manchester were

taken over by the BUFP. One of the earliest BUFP letterheads read 'Black Unity and Freedom Party (Formerly the UCPA)', and two addresses were given: 45 Fairmount Road, London SW2, and 22 Monton Street, Moss Side, Manchester 14. One of the major documents prepared for the launch of the BUFP with 'confidential' written at the top and the bottom of the front page reads, 'UCPA for members only, draft reorganisation document'. This document, almost certainly written by Cambridge and Joseph, sets out the group's reasons for the need of a new organisation which would pursue both short- and long-term goals in the interest of the 'masses', or 'black humanity'; it hailed 'Marxism-Leninism-Mao Tse Tung Thought' as the relevant ideology which would guide the new organisation, whilst practical examples would be drawn from the Chinese and Cuban revolutions. But it proclaimed that the 'best example today' of how to avoid slipping into a totally reformist ideology and programme was declared to be 'the breakfast programme being carried out by the Black Panther Party, while at the same time revolution is on the agenda' (BUFP, p. 4, n.d., but presumably 1970).

The founders of the BUFP, principally led by George Joseph and Alrick Cambridge, saw the BPM and themselves to be divided along fundamental ideological lines. In brief, these lines of difference involved their understanding of the notion or concept of Black Power and the place of the class struggle in the fight for equality in Britain and elsewhere. It would appear that the BPM placed the emphasis on cultural awareness and the unity of all blacks, and were therefore regarded – using the American term popular at the time – as 'cultural nationalists'. This meant that African history, culture, dress, hairstyle and so on were of predominant importance to them. So too were events in the Caribbean and elsewhere in the Third World. These were also important for the BUFP, but as will be noted, the BUFP tended to place the class struggle at the forefront of their concerns, and cultural matters as relatively less important. Indeed, for the BUFP, events in Britain, the Caribbean, Africa and elsewhere were properly to be understood in class terms. The group condemned the black bourgeoisie as 'Uncle Toms'[7] as vehemently as it condemned capitalism and imperialism. The BUFP also sought more actively to work with white radical groups than most black groups did, not because they were white but because these groups shared or had similar ideological orientations as the group, that is to say, they placed the emphasis on class, not colour/race or gender.

The ideological hegemony of feminism and cultural studies as well as the demise of collective politics in the 1980s and 1990s were to vindicate the position taken by the BPM and marginalise the BUFP's more uncompromising political position.[8]

Yet, in several ways the BUFP and the BPM were not so very different from each other as their members thought. Their differences might have been as much about personality as about ideology, although both groups would have denied this. They were physically located close to each other in the Peckham, New Cross and Brixton areas in South London, and again in North London in Hackney, King's Cross and the Angel. To a degree they both drew upon local communities for their memberships. For example, Linton Kwesi Johnson was a pupil at Tulse Hill Comprehensive School a mile or so from Shakespeare Road in Brixton where the BPM had its South London headquarters. Probably half of the BUFP membership in Peckham, New Cross (such as Garfield James, Philip Murphy,[9] Joan and Roger Lofters[10] and several others) had been at comprehensive schools in the area such as the then Peckham Manor, Peckham Girls', Dick Shepherd's and so forth. Members of the groups knew each other, and shared similar experiences. George Joseph, Althea Jones and a number of the BPM members were from Trinidad and had come to England to attend university. Memberships were, however, spread across the continents for both groups, because black (a crucial criterion for membership in both groups) was understood to mean any person who hailed from Africa, Asia, the Caribbean or South America; black or blackness pointed as much to a person's experience as to his or her pigmentation. The largest membership was in both cases African-Caribbean, because these were primarily Caribbean groups responding to and also shaping the radical challenge of young black people to their status in English society.

The second factor which influenced the formation of the BUFP the BPM, and other groups was the coming of age of a relatively small number of individuals who were neither part of what are usually called the 'first' nor the 'second' generations of immigrants by migration scholars. Typically, the leaders of these groups, such as Joseph, Cambridge, Howe, Leconte and others were individuals born and brought up in the Caribbean. Some, like Howe, had had direct experience of political life before coming to Britain, and were close to individuals such as C.L.R. James and John LaRose who, between them, had considerable Caribbean, North and Latin American experiences. Most members, however, were individuals born in the

Caribbean but almost entirely brought up in Britain in the late 1950s and early 1960s. Some had graduated from colleges and universities, others had just left school and were entering the world of work. Here was a mix of factors which spawned a radical questioning of the socioeconomic structures of a Britain which was barely beginning to adjust to its post-imperial position in the world.

The memberships of these groups represented, therefore, a creative cross-fertilisation of youthful aspirations, and these young people were able to draw upon British as well as wider international experience. Perhaps for the first time a dynamic link was being forged between immigrant communities and those who had come to Britain primarily to study. In these years, Caribbean communities in Britain lacked a recognisable elite; middle-class migration had been relatively small, and in any event the relatively few who had come from that class did not necessarily share the experiences of the majority of black workers and their offspring. The progressive Caribbean Artists Movement (CAM) – documented by Anne Walmsley (1992), one of its English participants – was the major outlet for the Caribbean intellectual elite in Britain but was coming to an end in 1970. This was just at the point when new groups, new voices representing different experiences, were about to begin to articulate new demands and new issues bred largely of the immigrant workers' experience as well as the exclusionary experiences of their disaffected children in the school system and the employment market. CAM was not, however, an elite with particularly strong connections with the immigrant communities; it was a Caribbean elite of young scholars and artists temporarily away from the Caribbean – or in 'exile' as some were wont to say.[11] Their production was important in portraying and structuring the Caribbean across the Atlantic, but the vast majority of its members returned to the region rather than become intellectuals in Britain.

This was a time for the coming of age of a neglected group in the migration process – those who had accompanied immigrant parents to Britain and were not prepared to face the prospects of replacing their parents in lowly, marginal, jobs. It was the loss of innocence about the nature of British society on the part of older folks who had been schooled in the Caribbean about fair play and equality in the 'Mother Country' (see, for example, Carter, 1986). The new assertion also marked the decline of groups such as WISC, which had carried the banner for Caribbean protest in Britain since 1957.

The third aspect of the period which provided the general context for the emergence of radical and black Caribbean groups was, of course, the prevailing social and political situation of the years 1968–71. Enoch Powell, MP for Wolverhampton and member of the Conservative shadow cabinet, had given his infamous 'rivers of blood' speech in Birmingham in 1968, at a time when US cities were in flames as black America protested on the streets about their centuries-old repressed and marginalised conditions. These scenes were on television for everyone to see. Also, in the summer of 1970 the Tories under Edward Heath unexpectedly won the general election, and although Powell had been sacked from the shadow cabinet in 1968, his influence in the country and indeed within the Conservative Party was paradoxically on the increase, not in decline (Goulbourne, 1991a).

Moreover, the new government soon made clear where it stood on domestic and international issues pertaining to Africa and Britain's new black minorities. The foreign secretary, Sir Alec Douglas-Home, the former prime minister who had accompanied Halifax to appease Hitler in the late 1930s, visited South Africa and agreed the sale of arms from Britain to the apartheid regime at a time when all South Africa's neighbours were prosecuting wars of liberation against Salazar's Portuguese colonies and South Africa itself. Nothing significant would be done about the illegal white minority regime of Ian Smith in the then colony of Southern Rhodesia (now Zimbabwe). Not that Labour, in office when UDI was declared in 1964–65, had demonstrated any greater willingness to bring the regime to heel. Indeed, whilst Harold Wilson's government had been quick to dispatch Metropolitan police officers to the tiny islet of Anguilla to squash Webster's attempt at self-government, Smith was made to understand that the British would not use troops against kith and kin in the colony of Rhodesia.

To Britain's black population these clear signals of support for whites at home and abroad seemed to fit perfectly into a more general pattern of international affairs. From North America to the Caribbean to Southern Africa (including South Africa, Zimbabwe, Mozambique, Angola, Namibia), using NATO, multinational corporations and police forces, white power appeared to be mobilised against the very existence of black populations in Africa and its diaspora.

Discussions in Britain over control of immigrants soon led to the Immigration Bill which in 1971 became an Act virtually barring black immigration into Britain by resurrecting from Reconstruction America the 'grandfather clause' as the 'patrial clause'. Individuals with no personal connections with the country but whose grandfathers had been born in Britain could gain entry, but individuals with origins outside Britain currently living in the UK would be restricted in their rights to invite members of their families to join them. Coupled with the policy of repatriation which Powell and the Tory right-wing Monday Club were trying to get their party to adopt, these measures amounted to a very nasty signal from the government to people from Asia, Africa and the Caribbean that they were unwelcome in Britain. Moreover, these were years when the US under Richard Nixon and Henry Kissinger was making a desperate attempt to defeat by any means necessary the Vietnamese people, and expected Britain's political support. In Britain, the anti-Vietnam war movement was petering out after the dramatic demonstrations outside the American Embassy in Grosvenor Square in 1969, and the Vietnam Solidarity Campaign appeared to be at a loss over what should be done to assist the peoples of East Asia in their struggles against imperialism.

Of these developments none seemed more relevant to a settling British black population than those in black America. The slogan of Black Power, the news about the Black Panther Party in Oakland, California founded and led by Bobby Seale and Huey P. Newton, ex-prisoner and celebrated essayist Eldridge Cleaver and others, the militancy and fluency of Stokeley Carmichael, the flamboyance of H. Rap Brown, the bravery of Angela Davis, the courage of the Soledad Brothers[12] and a number of similar developments throughout the US (in politics, the arts, sports, etc.) fired the imagination of radicals throughout Britain's new minority ethnic communities. The Americans' books and popular publications, particularly the *Black Panthers Speak*, were avidly read. The fact that the youth of Caribbean backgrounds shared a common history of slavery and a diasporic African culture with black America meant that their activities would be more immediately received by this section of the new communities in Britain. Moreover, in the late 1960s and early 1970s, before Idi Amin's expulsion of British Asians from Uganda, black youths with a Caribbean background constituted the majority of young people in the ethnic minority communities. It is a mistake however to assume – as it has become fashionable to do since the mid-1980s (see Modood, 1988) – that the black explosion in America did not affect people in the British Asian communities; it did (see Sivanandan,

1986). And it was also to have a major impact on most areas of community life in Britain for the next two decades, thereby forming – for better or for worse – part of the link between British and American race relations issues and perspectives (see Hiro, 1971).

The militant radicalism of the American Black Panthers was also to influence the formal structure of the BUFP. The Panthers had deliberately set themselves up as an organisation mirroring the governmental structure of a state, even though they did not formally demand territorial separation and the establishment of a black state in North America. There was a prime minister (Stokeley Carmichael), a minister of information (Eldridge Cleaver), a minister of defence (Huey Newton), and as in Mao's China, a chairman (Bobby Seale), and a chief of staff. These titles demonstrated the group's seriousness and the main problems they faced. The BUFP did not seek to import wholesale this structure to the British context, but the general tone could be felt within the organisation as reflected in the emphases the group gave to the functions these 'ministers' would be expected to perform in the US. Information and propaganda were important, but of greater significance was the role of the general secretary.

The influence here came from an entirely different source – Leninism. The BUFP's proclaimed adherence to Marxism-Leninism meant that many of the titles used by the American Panthers had to be subordinated to those of the Leninist theory of organisation. This not only involved having a general secretary of the party, but also a commitment to what Lenin called democratic-centralism, the fusing of the dual or contradictory principles of democracy and central control. In practice, central control has proven to be the stronger principle in Leninist organisations, as Rosa Luxemburg had foreseen in the states where such parties came to achieve control of power – the former state socialist systems of East Europe and the former USSR. In the BUFP, Joseph and his successor general secretaries never came to exercise the power or control expected of a Marxist-Leninist group. For several years discussion took place over the appointment of a full-time national organiser, but this was never achieved. Instead, the work of the organisation was conducted by members themselves, with their own internal resources. Unlike the BPM the BUFP never came to own their own premises, but used rented accommodation. This meant that the group did not go through lengthy disputes over ownership of property when some members left the organisation, due to differences, or remigration or return to the Caribbean. However, again, this difference between the groups was to be reflected in later developments, with the BPM being vindicated; the more idealistically orientated BUFP, which eschewed private ownership of property, was proven to be mistaken.

There would be several reasons for this, for instance, the BUFP had never been the clandestine, underground organisation Lenin had in mind; nor was it really a political party as its name would suggest – it never contested elected seats either at national or local levels of the state. The principal reasons for the failure or irrelevance of the Leninist principle, however, are that membership (entry and exit) had been voluntary, and the socio-political culture of members was deeply rooted in the liberal individualism that was characteristic of the social and political ideologies and values of the Commonwealth Caribbean. As I have suggested elsewhere (Goulbourne, 1991b, 1998) and have implied in the discussion so far, this is one of the most important underlying principles within the value system of English-speaking Caribbeans; it is in sharp contradiction with the extreme collectivism the Leninist principle takes for granted.

AIMS, OBJECTIVES AND IDEOLOGY

What then were the aims and objectives of the BUFP in 1970, which were still considered to be relevant in the significantly different early years of the 1990s? These were clearly set out in the group's manifesto dated 26 July 1970 (the precise date of the BUFP's founding[13]) repeated in one form or another in the group's newspaper, *Black Voice*, and in various documents. The manifesto is divided into two parts.

The first is a general statement of BUFP's ideological predisposition. It proffers a radical prognosis of British society, and the international context of imperialism and capitalism, and in 1970 its central principles were set out in six points (seven in later years). The differences between the original and the revised later statements are perhaps more significant in this part of the manifesto than in the second part about demands. There is a shift here in ideological tone away from the Maoism of the early years. These principles also set out more forcefully the aims and objectives of the group. It is interesting that the first principle stated by the 1970 document is that it recognised 'the class nature' of British society; the second point was the recognition of the usual Marxist consequence of class and class struggle, resulting in the Leninist commitment to 'the seizure of state power by the working class and the bringing about of socialism'. The later document commences with the 'aim to build a unified and principled organisation capable of serving the needs of Black people'; the statement about socialism and class struggle comes second. Both documents are clear about the class nature of British society, the need to unite against capitalism and imperialism, and bringing an end to the exploitation of 'man by man' (changed to 'people by people' in the later version). In 1970, however, the group's leaders drew heavily upon Mao's essay 'On contradiction' in stating these points. The contradiction, following Mao, between the working class and the capitalists is fundamental (of 'primary importance' in the later version), whilst the contradiction between the white and black working classes is a contradiction among the people (and therefore presumably, in Mao's terms, non-antagonistic). The later statement does not employ Maoist thought.[14]

On the other hand, racism continued to be seen as a major factor in the lives of Britain's black population. Additionally, in line with the changing times, the manifesto firmly addresses the need to overcome misconceptions among 'oppressed peoples of different cultures', and to promote good understanding among them. Clearly, the multiculturalist theme had worked its way into the group's thinking about British society, because the major ideology embraced by both left and right along the political spectrum had become multiculturalism, as noted in Chapter 2. Even so, the later statement, like that of 1970, ended with a commitment to the 'complete overthrow of capitalism/imperialism', bringing to an end exploitation, and forging unity with all who share common goals against inequality and are committed to equality and social justice for all.

The second part of the manifesto is a list of immediate demands patterned on the platform of the US Black Panther Party. This part of the manifesto later came to be called the group's 'short term demands', and later still they were condensed from eleven to nine points. The demands were modified, in most cases, to meet British conditions. The first of these remained over the years an end to police brutality against black people, and a call for a public enquiry into the activities of the police against this section of the community.[15] Official racist hostility at ports of entry into the country; abolition of the Race Relations Acts of 1967 and later 1976, the Race Relations Board and later the Commission for Racial Equality, because these measures and bodies were perceived to be used against black people or were tools 'for the purpose of maintaining the status quo', not changing it. The demands included, further, full employment, trial by peers, an end to racist education of children, representation of black people on school boards, and 'decent housing, bread, peace and social justice for all people', following the Panthers of Oakland, California.

Whilst the list of demands had remained consistent over 21 years, they had also undergone subtle modifications, reflecting change as well as closer engagement and knowledge of the situation. For example, the fifth demand of 1970 which spoke about returning superannuation and national insurance contributions to black people who return to their homelands was later omitted, no doubt because it was recognised that people returning to the Caribbean were indeed able to repatriate their contributions. Again, the later version of the demand to be tried by peers does not specify as the 1970 statement does that this means trial by black magistrates, judges and jurists. It is not clear whether this was because by the 1980s the point had been well made and partly accepted, or because the group's leaders had come to recognise that having black magistrates did not necessarily alleviate injustice and that their own emphasis on class as the major determinant factor was indeed the more powerful and relevant consideration in such matters. The later statement is also concerned about 'the discrepancy of sentences passed on Black/White "offenders"', reflecting how the debate over the judicial system had moved on. By the 1990s the demand for full employment was no longer the bland, abstract statement it had been; the group now called for an 'end to all forms of discriminatory practices in employment', thereby reflecting change and development in its understanding of the complex employment market situation for black workers (see Modood and Berthoud, 1997).

The later statement contains two new important demands: first, 'an immediate repeal of the Immigration Act 1971, the repeal of the 1988 [sic] British Nationality Act'. The second new demand is for an 'end to all types of sexual discrimination and the ending of the exploitation of women by men'. These clearly reflected crucial developments since 1970, for although the group was deeply concerned about the status of women from its very beginning, the gender question was less sharply focused upon in British society in the early 1970s than it came to be in the late 1980s and the 1990s. From its very first issue the *Black Voice* carried specific articles on black women; some were about black women of historical significance in America and the Caribbean, such as Harriet Tubman who organised the underground escape route for runaway slaves to Canada, and

Nanny of the Maroons in seventeenth-century Jamaica. Contemporary women in sports, such as Marilyn Neufville, the Jamaican Olympic gold medalist, and political figures, such as Angela Davis who was being prosecuted by the US authorities for her part in the black movement in that country, were also featured. The paper also carried pieces on women in Vietnam, and other places where wars of liberation were being waged.

Apart from its formal statement of aims, objectives and broad principles, the BUFP articulated its ideology at its discussions, through its publications and in the causes it espoused. The next section considers some examples of the last of these. But for the remainder of this section I want to look at some of the main questions which the BUFP addressed and in doing so elaborate more generally its beliefs and principles.

The first of these was the question of the revolutionary potential of the working classes in advanced capitalism. This was, of course, a long-standing question within Marxism. Marx had argued that the world proletarian revolution would first occur in the advanced capitalist West where the proletariat was being transformed from a class-in-itself into a class-for-itself through class consciousness. In later life he became less certain of this by admitting that the revolution could start in Russia where German capital was making rapid progress in capitalising production and relations of production. It was the debate between Lenin's Bolsheviks and the Mensheviks, leading to the breakup of the Russian Social Democratic and Labour Party at the end of the nineteenth century, which clarified this issue. Lenin and his supporters held that capitalism had reached a new stage where it needed to export capital in order to continue to create surplus, and to defeat capitalism in the present age it was easier to break it at its weakest link. This would be in the periphery of capitalism, in the imperial hinterlands, not in the centres of capitalism. The revolution's success would, however, depend on the eventual revolution in these heartlands by the proletariat. The Bolshevik Revolution of 1917–18 came, but with the defeat of the Spartacists in Germany, Syndicalism in France, and Fabianism in England no revolution occurred in the West.

But revolution occurred in China, a farther hinterland from the centre of capital in Western Europe and North America. Moreover, the Chinese Communist Party, whilst preaching Marxism, had come to hold state power in 1949 after abandoning the cities following the debacle of 1927 at the hands of the nationalist Koumintang, two decades of fighting in the rural areas and eventually taking this fight to the cities. Fidel Castro's successful seizure of state power in Cuba in 1958 further demonstrated the seeming validity of the Leninist-Maoist principle of organised insurrection from outside the advanced centres of capitalism.

BUFP leaders were convinced that contemporary history revealed that revolutionary change could not be realistically expected to come from the workers of Europe and America. Lenin's thesis of the 'labour aristocracy'[16] in the West seemed to be about right with respect to the behaviour of workers, particularly their leaders. Moreover, the working classes had imbibed the racism of the capitalists; workers, organised or otherwise, had allowed themselves to become divided, seeing colour or race or culture as being more important than objective class interests. In Maoist terms, they had allowed secondary, non-antagonistic contradictions to override the fundamental contradiction between capital and labour. This fundamental basis for organised opposition to, and resistance of, exploitation and the divide-and-rule tactics of capitalists, was seen to be frustrated, and revolutionary action by white workers and their organisations was not to be expected in the foreseeable future.

With migration, however, black workers from the neo-colonial world had come to the centre of capitalism. Racism had become a further tool of divide and rule. Whiteness united white workers with their white capitalist bosses against black workers. There were few black capitalists to speak of; and the black *petite bourgeoisie* (intellectuals, bureaucrats, small capitalists, etc.) would vacillate between support for the working classes and support for the capitalists and the oppressors of black people. In these circumstances, black workers were placed at the forefront of revolutionary politics in Britain. They constituted the most exploited, the most marginalised and therefore the most class-conscious element within the wider working classes. A particular historical responsibility, therefore, fell to the black worker. This position pitched the BUFP against those who held firmly to a Eurocentric view derived from Marx, the Mensheviks and particularly Trotsky whose followers felt that they were carrying forward the authentic principles against heretics such as Stalin, Mao, Castro and others.

A second question over which the BUFP's position was very clear, if unorthodox amongst black groups, was colonial wars of liberation. The group agreed that these must be situated within the broader context of the class struggles, and not be seen as essentially a struggle between black and white people. This was particularly relevant and important with respect to Africa. In the contention for supremacy between different radical groups in Angola, Mozambique, Zimbabwe and South Africa, the BUFP sought to support those groups which presented a class position coupled with the notion of 'people's' struggle for national liberation as the first step towards emancipation from capitalism and imperialism. Thus, the BUFP supported the ANC in South Africa, SWAPO in Namibia and MPLA in Angola, because these were groups which sought to organise the 'whole people' irrespective of class, colour or creed against the common enemy of colonialism. But these were also groups which sought to see things in class, not racial, terms; imperialism was being opposed, not the colour of the oppressors.

Third, the BUFP sought to impress on its members and the black community that the just hunger for a closer knowledge of the history of blacks in Africa and the West and the promotion of black culture was not enough to put an end to capitalist and racist oppression and exploitation. At the same time, it was important for the BUFP to emphasise that given the history of white working-class organisations which marginalised black workers' interests, it was important for blacks to organise themselves autonomously. This view was also supported by the observation that where white liberals joined black organisations their superior resources usually result in whites controlling the agenda. Additionally, to maintain its independence of thought and action, the BUFP was consistent in refusing to accept funding from national or local government departments, or foundations. Although it supported the socialist bloc of countries, it maintained its independent political position from them by not aligning itself to any national or international group, and therefore unwittingly, reflected the healthy scepticism of radical Third World leaders such as Abdul Nasser of Egypt, Jawaharlal Nehru of India and Kwame Nkrumah of Ghana who, with other radicals, founded the Non-Aligned Movement in response to the Cold War.

COMMUNITY ASPECTS OF THE GROUP'S ACTIVITIES

Whilst it is important to look at a group's stated aims and objectives, and to take into consideration their ideological orientation, it is their activities which best help us to define them. This may be particularly true with respect to Commonwealth Caribbean groups, which, as noted in the last chapter, are prone to establish elaborate constitutional devices without doing the necessary practical work to make their organisations the living and dynamic bodies they sometimes appear to be from the outside. Following the schema of group types and activities outlined in the last chapter, it should be noted that most of the activities in which the BUFP engaged were essentially of a community welfare nature. This does not negate the fact that the intended purpose was mainly to raise political consciousness in order to better struggle against what the group saw as exploitation and oppression.

From its very beginning, the group engaged itself in a number of social or community welfare activities. Such activities varied from the organising and running of a summer and alternative school for black children, to defending black youngsters against attacks on the streets. Activities ranged from defending black workers, to critically assessing women's roles in the workplace and the household. These issues were raised at meetings and discussion groups, and in publications such as leaflets and the *Black Voice*. The group adopted a tough line against what was described as 'male chauvinism', and drug taking; for these offences members could be suspended or expelled. Like most Marxist-Leninist groups, the BUFP advocated what amounted to a late Victorian bourgeois morality which eschewed excess of any kind such as heavy drinking, promoted the strict utilisation of time, and displayed what Max Weber described as the Calvinist Protestant ethic of hard work, discipline and accountability for individual action underpinned by a this-worldly asceticism (see Weber 1930). 'Good manners', exemplary and orderly behaviour, cleanliness were all virtues to adhere to, particularly when out on the streets selling newspapers, distributing leaflets, and at public demonstrations.

Although not the first to raise the question, the BUFP was perhaps the first group in the country to organise alternative schooling for black children who had been marginalised by local education authorities and schools.[17] The publication of Bernard Coard's (1971) *How the British education system underdeveloped the black child* by New Beacon Books had an immediate impact on the founders of the BUFP. In 1971, the group organised a summer school for black children who were placed in educationally subnormal schools. These children were drawn mainly from the boroughs of Southwark, Lambeth and Lewisham. The school was held mainly in Deptford, on premises provided by the Church of England, when a number of local schools refused to help with what was then perceived by many as a subversive action by hotheads. Again, in 1972 the BUFP organised another summer school for these children, and with the help of Sybil Phoenix, the veteran Guyanese community worker, premises were provided at 77 Pagnell Street, New Cross. During the year classes in maths, English and history were conducted in members' homes for a smaller group of children. The summer schools had about fifty children, and outings to zoos and other places of interests were organised as well as a one-week holiday by the sea in 1972. The subjects offered were deliberately limited to English, history (black, Caribbean, US and African), and maths (subjects neglected in their schooling), art and drama. Table-tennis, badminton, football, chess, draughts and swimming were also offered at break times and for specific periods, with teachers and helpers actively participating.

The teaching and summer school experiences were intended to achieve three principal aims and objectives: first, developing the children's skills in the traditional 'three Rs' of reading, writing and arithmetic. In several cases the children had to be taught these rudimentary skills which their schools had claimed these children could not be taught because they were educationally subnormal. It was important to teach English in a manner that would properly situate, and not ignore or marginalise, the creole the children spoke at home with their parents and spoke in groups at school. The second aim was to redress the imbalance in the regular school curriculum by teaching the children about their own neglected backgrounds in Africa and the Caribbean; to acquaint them with names, events, places and achievements of black people; to help develop a framework within which they would understand their own and their parents' presence and position in British society and how they, like others before, could help to change the situation. These helped, thirdly, to develop their confidence in themselves as young black people in a world almost entirely owned, controlled and defined by the white majority society in which they lived. In the wider black world the Afro hairstyle, the musicians, sportsmen and sportswomen, politicians and artists of black America were recreating an environment of black worth and value to which British blacks could relate across the Atlantic. The teaching of specific subjects could help to fill in the details missing in the collective knowledge of a people experiencing the loss of their illusions (see Carter, 1986; Cross and Entzinger, 1988).

It was hoped that the total experience would result in the children not only having a stronger sense of self and history or background, but that they would also develop a deep commitment to their own communities. It was therefore important that the children gained confidence in their teachers, experienced the caring environment their parents would have enjoyed at schools in the Caribbean, and for them to realise that although nearly all their schoolteachers were white people, black people were also capable of imparting the knowledge they would need for forging their own individual paths through life in a competitive society.

Thus, whilst small grants and support were secured from public bodies in order to help with this specific project, the initiative, organisation, work, teaching and so on were conducted by black schoolteachers, sixth-formers and undergraduates as well as other BUFP members with relevant experience.

In 1972 the BUFP was joined by the Croydon Collective in mounting the summer project. The alternative school experience was a challenge not only for the children, but also for the teachers and helpers, because they themselves had to learn some of what they were teaching. Whilst they were able to draw on black American experience, there was nothing comparable in Britain from which to learn. This was because Caribbean groups in Britain had not yet developed the institutions they required for survival in a society based on (white) ethnicity which automatically excluded the black 'other'. The black-led churches were both an exception to this and also partly a symptom of British exclusivity. Paradoxically, however, the black churches' proximity to white churches and the sharing of a common faith by black and white practising Christians, prevented the black churches being active participants in the youths' radical protest against marginalisation. The churches' message seemed too quietist in the face of massive police brutality and state repression; to the churches, the radicalism of black youths was simply bewildering. Yet, in the longer view, the different forms of social action in which black radicalism and the conservative churches were respectively involved, were largely responses to more general processes of exclusion in British society. Both responses – of conservative quietism and militant radicalism – were also deeply rooted in Caribbean social and political traditions and these were being established in the emergent Caribbean diaspora in England.

The BUFP's concern with the young in the black community in South London and elsewhere brought them into conflict not only with the education authorities (which were initially hostile to the alternative school initiative because they did not control it), but also with the police and the courts. There were several dramatic instances of such confrontations throughout the period which was marked by community activism. Demonstrations against legislation, such as the 1971 Immigration Act in specific localities with significant black settlement involved sharp confrontation with the police, and were covered in the *South London Press*. Attacks on members of the group by the police in the early 1970s led to several confrontations and locally celebrated court cases. The group's support, for example, of the struggles of others such as the Irish against the 1971 Internment Act, or the trades unions' demonstrations against the 1971 Industrial Relations Act, again led the BUFP into confrontation with the authorities. As the decade drew to a close, the group became deeply involved with what came to be known as the New Cross Massacre on its doorsteps. With respect to the black community and the police and the courts, two well-documented events will suffice to make this general point.

The Peckham Rye Confrontation of 1971

During the second and third weeks of September 1971, Peckham Rye Park had its long-standing traditional summer fair. According to the proprietor of the travelling fair, the company had been coming to the Rye since 1946 and before handing over the usual cheque (£900 that year) to the mayor of Southwark he expressed the hope that they would be continuing to do so for the years ahead. The remark regarding the future was occasioned by the tumultuous events of the week which took Peckham by storm and occupied much of the *South London Press* (hereafter, the *SLP* or the *Press*) for the week 14–21 September with headline stories, opinion/editorial, and letters from the public. The events they described involved the BUFP in its work as protector of vulnerable black youths – many of them school-children – against the police. These events reflected the growing confrontation between black youth and the police, which was to explode in the early 1980s in Brixton in Lambeth, Toxteth in Liverpool and St Paul's in Bristol (see Scarman, 1981). Indeed, at the very time of these events a House of Commons select committee was hearing evidence on the deteriorating relations between the police and the black community.

On 14 September, the *Press*'s main front-page story read: 'Gangs of youths roam Peckham Rye, MOBS AT FAIRGROUND BATTLE WITH POLICE'. The paper reported that angry traders and residents were calling for an end to the fair:

... following a week of trouble from mobs of youths, mostly coloured and frequently as many as 200 strong, congregating in the grounds and providing a big headache for local police who were out in force backed by men of Scotland Yard's special patrol squad, for the last four nights until the fair closed on Saturday evening. [*SLP*, 14 September 1971, p. 1]

These dramatic events were triggered on the evening of Tuesday, 7 September, when, according to this account, a stall-holder was stabbed and 'several youths arrested'. A 'full-scale anti-violence campaign was mounted with police in pairs and groups of three, together with dogs, patrolling the fair ground'. The dramatic clash between the police and the youths first occurred, however, on Friday night after the fair closed at 10.30, and some two hundred youths surrounded the bumper cars area of the grounds. The lights were dimmed, and the youths moved to the corner of East Dulwich Road where the special squad police in two large vans awaited them. After ten minutes the youths walked along Rye Lane towards the centre of Peckham. The windows of a laundrette, a furniture store, a hair-dresser's saloon and a greeting cards shop were broken. The following evening, the fair was closed early at 9.45 in the evening 'on the advice of the police', and the evening went on peacefully, according to the *Press*. Even so, there were eleven arrests made by the police. These included young people ranging in age from 17 to 28; they had come from Peckham and the surrounding areas of Lewisham, Dulwich, Forest Hill, New Cross and even faraway Tooting, and were charged with damage to property, and various counts of assaults on police officers.

On Friday, 17 September, the *Press* continued the story under the front page headline 'Hooligan gangs threaten the fairs'. The London secretary of the Showmen's Guild, a Mr Bill Bailey, was reported as saying that the incident of black youths and police confrontation at the fair grounds 'is a new menace we are facing all round, but par-ticularly in the past year at places like Reading where there are large immigrant populations' (*SLP*, 17 September 1971, p. 1). In his view these events were taking place all over the country, and fair managers were losing money as the violence kept people away from the grounds. Earlier in the year, he said, in June when the fair was on the Rye there had been minor incidents, and while he did not say whether those events were caused by black youths there was the implication that these youths were responsible. Of particular concern to Mr Bailey, however, was the fear that the disturbances at fair grounds were politically motivated. He stated 'We find usually that these gangs have their own photographers around to take pictures whenever the police are forced to grab hold of them and it seems they are deliberately provoking the police' (ibid.).[18]

The main headline on the same page read 'Immigrant dispersal crucial, RACE COMMITTEE BACKS LAMBETH ALL THE WAY'. The housing problems of the neighbouring borough of Lambeth were leading to poor living conditions for blacks and this was fuelling militancy among teenagers, which in turn was 'straining the previously tolerant attitude of the white community' (ibid.).

'Black Unity hit at police, RYE-La. PROTEST MARCH AGAINST ARRESTS AT FAIR', was the main headline on the front page of the *Press* on Tuesday, 21 September. It described the march of about a hundred protesters '70 of them black, chanting slogans alleging police brutality at last week's fair' (*SLP*, 21 September 1971, p. 1) along Rye Lane in the afternoon of Saturday 17 September. The chants included 'down with the police pigs', 'no more racist attacks on black youths', and so on. There were leaflets describing the action of the police at the fair, and the police's attempts to 'frighten, harass and brutalise black people as individuals and the black community as a whole' (ibid.). The leaflets called for unity, and pointed to the high incidence of black people in prisons. The event passed without incident, and the police community liaison officer, Chief Inspector Douglas Turner, expressed pleasure and confidence that it would not damage community relations 'because the white population were not interested in the demonstration or the leaflets that were being handed out' (ibid.). The report stated that black shoppers also 'ignored' the marchers, and that many of the marchers came from North London.

The BUFP had, however, planned a short, effective and peaceful demonstration during the shopping hours along Rye Lane. As noted, whilst it was organised by blacks, many of the protesters were whites who were also concerned about the behaviour of the police. Contrary to police reports, the group never went out to cause disturbances. Indeed, it was the BUFP's view that the police should have been congratulated for not causing a disturbance. These were, after all, protests against the police, not 'race riots'. The officers of the community relations councils of Lewisham and Southwark, Asquith Gibbes and David Asphat respectively, told the press how members of the public had reported to them that the police had simply rounded up youths who were not involved in any of the incidents during the week, and that the CRCs were convening conferences between the police, local community workers and the BUFP. From the police report too it is clear that the BUFP informed them of the march, and the group controlled the events of the day.

For the first time in these reports there is mention of involvement by an organised group, although there is still the view that there were 'gangs' at work. These 'gangs' were never named, and no one was ever found to be a member. The BUFP's leaflets informed the public that the events at the fair and subsequent developments started when on the Tuesday evening fair attendants beat unconscious a black schoolboy, Radcliff Carr, while the police looked on without intervening. The paper quoted a BUFP spokesperson, Garfield James (a teacher at one of the local schools), as saying that reports had only given one side of the story, ignoring what black youths themselves had been saying. There had been no trouble at the fair at the beginning, but the heavy police presence and intimidation after refusing to stop a child being beaten to a state of unconsciousness necessitated that the young people organise themselves to prevent further intimidation and arrests. James concluded, 'While I do not justify the breaking of windows which took place in Rye Lane, it is fair to say that the youths had been forced to walk down the lane regardless of where they came from – and not everyone lives in Peckham – and they were pushed by the police' (ibid.).

The *Press*'s editorial for the day was headed 'Not all fun at Peckham's fair', and it argued that the traditional fun occasioned by such events was being turned upside down by

> ... the mass hooliganism of teenagers, nearly all of them black, who not only tried to intimidate the showmen, alarmed the general public by rowdily walking en masse down the approach roads, but also seemed hell-bent on testing their emergent manhood against the scores of police who had to be drafted to the fair to break up the gangs before trouble flared in [*sic*] a large scale. [ibid.]

The police and fair managers were exonerated, and black male teenagers were seen to be the cause of the disturbances: 'the fair was made the target for a hooligan demonstration and an uncomfortable feeling is left that it was not unpremeditated' (ibid.). However, the fair had moved on to Bermondsey 'an area not very near the recognised immigrant centres in South London' (ibid.).

The BUFP's *Black Voice* gave a somewhat different account of events. Under the heading 'BLACK YOUTHS TERRORIZED BY POLICE IN PECKHAM' the paper argued that between 7 and 11 September 'was a week of terror for all the Black youths in the Peckham area. It was impossible for any youth to walk in the streets without being harassed by the police' (*Black Voice*, vol. 2, no. 4, n.d. but presumably September 1971, p. 6).

The paper reported that 14-year-old Radcliff had been beaten by eight fair attendants; the attackers used hammers, iron-bars and spanners. One eye was dislodged from its socket, and not only did the police not intervene but prevented anyone administering first aid; the Red Cross unit which was at the scene also failed to give any aid. The white attackers, still brandishing their weapons went free while the police set about attacking witnesses, mainly young black people. Carr was hospitalised for seven days and received 30 stitches to his head; his left eye had to be pushed back into its socket, and his body was badly bruised and swollen.

The following evening the police increased their numbers, brought in dogs and surrounded groups of black people at the fair. One black man who opened his door to see what the commotion was about was beaten and arrested by the police; a white man who witnessed the action of the police and who went to the station to make a report was beaten and thrown out; a young white woman who on witnessing ten policemen beating one black youth went to protest, was herself thrown into the police van and beaten. The report is a catalogue of similar individual cases. At the police station legal representatives were denied access, and parents and other relatives ill treated.

The only organisation of the crowd was provided on the Friday night by the BUFP, encouraging the young people to stay together in a disciplined fashion and not respond to the provocation of the police as they deliberately attacked individuals and hurled racist insults at individuals. On the last night of the fair, an estimated four hundred police officers were on duty, and immediately on closure of the fair, all lights went off and the police attacked any black person they came across in the vicinity. Desperately trying to escape, small groups of black youths found themselves miles from their homes, taking circuitous routes in order to evade the police cordon thrown around the Peckham area.

The BUFP charged the police with assault, riotous assembly and causing an affray, and fabrication of charges against black citizens. Like the Black Panthers in the US, the group called for the police to be put on trial for their crimes against the people. But it was not until the McPherson Report into the Stephen Lawrence Case in 1998–99 that the London Metropolitan Police admitted that as a force they were guilty of 'institutional racism' (McPherson, 1999). The earlier Scarman Report (1981) into the Brixton disturbances discussed the issue but studiously avoided using the concept to describe the behaviour of the police in England.

At a more general level of community, the BUFP worked closely with groups similar to itself in the area to highlight such increasing incidence of police attacks on individual black men and women as distinct from what the police had come to regard as the rowdy black youth. Before the early 1970s police attacks on blacks were not infrequent but these appeared to be restricted in the main to young, active men out for a good time at fairs, outside cinemas or at club and house parties. Close watch had long been kept on groups of black workers from the early 1950s, and was not something new in the early 1970s. After the first years of the 1970s, police brutality against black communities in the inner cities was to become so commonplace that it was widely believed in the black communities that there was hardly a black family in Britain which had not had a nasty experience with the police. In the 1990s this continued to be the focus of much public attention, with a disproportionately high number of individuals of African-Caribbean backgrounds housed in the nation's prisons, and an even higher proportion seeing the inside of courts and police cells. The beginning of the decade of the 1970s, however, marked the watershed in the generalisation of poor police–black community relations. As we now know, the subsequent confrontations between the black community and the police have led to a generalised questioning of the nature of the police force, policing and accountability in the country as a whole.

Central to this process was the Brixton disturbance of 1981, and subsequent events in leading British cities in that year and again in 1985. It may be suggested, however, that the basic attitudes of Britain's black communities to the police were formed in the early 1970s, when for the first time the authorities confronted Britain's first generation of black youths. These were young men and women who had been either born or brought up in these cities, with little or no practical knowledge of the Caribbean, and certainly none of

Africa which featured prominently in their rhetoric. A deep-rooted legacy from those days is the view that blacks should not join the police force, because it is inherently racist, and black recruits would tacitly be supporting the brutalisation of their communities. Campaigns mounted by police authorities in several English cities to attract recruits from new minority ethnic communities, particularly black communities, in subsequent years have met with relatively little success.

There were several incidents between the black community at large and the police and the courts during these years, as a perusal of the files of the BUFP shows. As noted, the *South London Press* is also an invaluable source of wider public confirmation of police–community relations during these crucial years. The Joshua Francis story, which follows here, is a case in point.

The Joshua Francis Case

Joshua Francis's case must first be situated within the general local context of South London. On Wednesday, 5 April 1972 the *Press* featured three short articles on the same page entitled, 'W. INDIANS OPEN FIGHT FOR JAILED JAMAICAN', 'National Front demand: Sack this Communist', and 'Stresses between black and white focus on police relations'. The last of these commented on a report commissioned by the Bishop of Woolwich into police–community relations. The working group comprised Canon Eric James who had been vicar of St Giles's in Camberwell and St George's in Peckham, the treasurer of Southwark Diocesan Council for Social Aid, a member of Southwark Council's Welfare Department, and a member of the National Institute for Social Work Training. The report covered problems of housing, mental health, alcoholism, drug addiction, and homelessness and 'immigrants'. The group's concern about relations between whites and blacks led them to conclude that these were focused in the relations between young black people and the police. Quoting the report the article stated that, 'It is alleged, rightly or wrongly, that the police discriminate against coloured immigrants', which not surprisingly was denied by the police. White families were perceived to be afraid of people with black skins, because whites felt that blacks would take by force school places, homes and jobs which belonged to whites. The article went on to say the report warned that 'Black Power feeds on this because it gives the movement a very euphoric sensation and enables the participants to reject the often pathetic and patronising attitudes of the white intellectual liberals' (*SLP*, 5 April 1972). Black communities in South London, the report warned, were turning inward, becoming hostile towards white society, and mistrustful of officialdom. The various black political organisations would have the 'capacity to act violently against white society', because of the growing number of unemployed youths with little or no education. At the same time the report asserted that 'Black leadership is scarce' (ibid.).

The second article reported the circulation of 11,000 leaflets by the National Front against Asquith Gibbes, Lewisham's Community Relations Officer, whom the Front claimed was a member of the Communist Party and therefore too biased to occupy his sensitive position. The Front pointed out that Gibbes was attacked because he was a 'red-hot communist', not because he was black. Gibbes, naturally enough, defended his political freedom. The fact of his blackness remained, however, the unstated main interest in the Front's attack on his integrity.

As will be noted from the large typeface of the first article, the case of Joshua Francis was by far the most important of the three features on 5 April 1972. The events it reported marked a turning-point in the developing story of community–police relations in the black communities in South London. The article opened with the statement that 'Brixton's black community last week mobilized a massive action campaign to raise funds for an appeal against the conviction of West Indian Joshua Francis who is now serving a nine-month jail sentence for assaulting two policemen'. The occasion was the launching of an appeal at Lambeth Town Hall in Brixton which several hundred people attended.[19] Speakers included the legal attaché at the Jamaican High Commission, Alan Alberga, representatives from the Association of Jamaicans (AOJ), Lambeth Council for Community Relations, WISC, the BPM, Revd Robert Nind of St Matthew's Church,[20] the BUFP and other organisations in South London. The coverage of the event stressed the points made by Alberga and Revd Nind, and little was said about the BUFP, the BPM and other community-based groups. It was, however, these groups which had played the major part in organising the event under the aegis of Joshua Francis Defence Committee (JFDC), which attracted a number of groups and individuals.

The committee was formed around the case of Joshua Francis, a 38-year-old Jamaican who worked at London Transport garage at Thornton Heath. Early on Sunday morning, 22 November 1970, an off-duty police officer and three other men from an all-night garage chased a man to Francis's backyard. Francis, who had been in bed suffering from a broken jaw as a result of an industrial accident, became involved in the ensuing struggle. He was severely beaten, dragged over broken glass and taken to a cell half-naked by the other officers who arrived on the scene. At King's College Hospital in Camberwell he received three stitches in the forehead, two on the left index finger, and three in the left shin; he had cuts on both hips and right buttock, grazes on the right calf and the left knee, bruises on the left foot, and was tender in the genitals, kidneys, neck, right arm and over his rib cage. After a 23-day trial at Croydon Crown Court on 7 March 1972, he was found guilty on three counts of assaults on the police officers by Judge S. A. Morton and sentenced to nine months' imprisonment. The *Black Voice* and the group's leaflets published pictures of a beaten Francis in hospital.

A deeply religious man and part-time preacher in his local church, Joshua was widely known to live (in biblical terms) in fear of God and the law. His experience alerted many throughout London to what appeared to be a new turn in police–black community relations. He was no party-going young man out for the fun of an evening; he was a solid family and community person, who though ill felt secure in his home before being dragged into court and made a criminal for assaulting a number of fit policemen who violently intruded into his quiet life. If a person such as he was not safe from the police, then who in the black community was safe from the long arm of injustice, which had the sanction of the state's legal instruments?

At the meeting in Lambeth Town Hall in Brixton, Alan Alberga stressed that the Jamaican Commission was finding the behaviour of the British police to be so unwarranted in a number of cases that the High Commission no longer regarded this as 'a problem. I call it an illness and we who are here on behalf of the Government of Jamaica find it extremely difficult to cure' (*SLP*, ibid.). Although the black community in Britain looked to their High Commissions for representation to the British authorities, Alberga confirmed the view of many that community action would have a much greater impact on the attitudes and behaviour of the police and the courts, than anything others such as Commonwealth governments could do.

Founded in February, the Joshua Francis Defence Committee changed its name to the Black People's Defence Committee after Francis's conviction was upheld on 3 July, though he himself was released from prison. The Committee held its first and all its subsequent meetings at 1 Mayall Road, Brixton, at the offices of the

Brixton Neighbourhood Centre under the leadership of the late community veteran campaigner, Courtney Laws. Meeting early on Saturday mornings, the committee brought together activists and members from a wide range of groups, including those mentioned above as well as the Croydon Collective from Selhurst led by Lloyd Blake. The chairman, Cliff Lynch, was the public relations officer of WISC, and the BUFP provided two representatives who acted as secretary and legal adviser respectively to the committee. At one point or another, individuals such as the late Dr David (later Lord) Pitt, Cecil Collier (Association of Jamaicans), Len Dyke (Dyke & Dryden and WISC), Joe Hunte (WISC), David Asphat (CRC), the late Rudy Narayan, the radical Guyanese barrister, and several other individuals became involved with the case or the campaign. Planned activities ranged from public demonstrations in Brixton (within the Town Hall, Library and St Matthew's Church triangle) to social events to raise funds for Francis's case and others which were later taken on by the committee.

The change of name from JFDC to BPDC was due both to the successful campaign to release Francis, and the recognition that his case was no longer an exception, but was, rather, becoming a familiar part of the experience of many ordinary black men and women lawfully going about their business. The committee's campaign led to many individuals from black and Asian communities writing in to offer their support and to make donations of money. The BPDC organised, with local groups, a number of meetings throughout London, and planned meetings in Liverpool and elsewhere, which were addressed by individuals such as Len Dyke, Francis himself, Farouk Dhondi, and others. An appeal fund was established, leaflets distributed, prisoners and their families visited and solicitors contacted. The committee's successes included not only helping to free Francis, and highlighting the cases of others such as Edward Cole,[21] but demonstrating that the various groups in the area, irrespective of their ideological bent, were able to unite over specific forms of action necessary to defend the community.

CONCLUSION

The events described here were to become increasingly common as police–black community relations deteriorated in the face of massive police brutality against black youths and then the community as a whole. Police behaviour, coupled with an effective non-education for young black people by schools and education authorities, large-scale unemployment, etc., fuelled black protest on the streets from the 1970s. Groups such as the BUFP worked to control and channel such protest, but by the late 1970s it was clear that organised groups had failed to galvanise and control such powerful social forces. Thus, although groups such as the BUFP would see themselves as being primarily political, in essence their work was one of community building, but their community work was guided by well-thought-out and deeply committed political perspectives. While not strictly of a political nature, that is, competing for public office on a general platform, such work none the less prepared the community for the more radical direct political participation of Britain's black population in the late 1970s and throughout the 1980s to the turn of the century, as outlined in the last chapter. Of equal significance, however, was the use made of Africa and the Caribbean as sources of strength for the emerging communities in Britain. The issues raised and the sources of inspiration were to become central pillars in the consciousness of these communities.

5 Black America in Caribbean Public Discourse in Britain: Uncle Tom, Frank Bruno and Lennox Lewis

The epithet 'Uncle Tom' is generally applied to a black man occupying a position of formal power or influence who is perceived by other black people to behave in a manner that is not an apparent threat to the existing white structural and cultural dominance over black people in the North Atlantic world. The black man daubed with the epithet 'Uncle Tom' is, therefore, perceived to sublimate his personality or humanity and cultural autonomy to the spirituality and aesthetics of the dominant values shared in the main by white people across the North Atlantic. It is also a masculine term. Whilst there is no good reason why the term may not apply to successful females, in general and historically the term has, with one exception as we will see, applied to black men. The individuals to whom the term is most often applied are prominent in one field or another, particularly music, sports, and highly visible areas of public life in which black people have actively participated. Increasingly, as more black people gain access to elected political or nominated public office, and senior positions in the traditional professions, the term has been applied more widely. In general, individuals in the various fields of entertainment are more vulnerable to the accusation of being labelled an Uncle Tom because they have been perceived by white society to be representatives of the black community as a whole. Additionally, such individuals are perceived by black society to be role models for members of the community to which they are restricted.

There are several other negative phrases or terms used to describe individuals in the African diaspora in the Western world. But the unique feature of the Uncle Tom epithet is that, unlike other negative terms used against black people, 'Uncle Tom' is employed almost entirely within the black community itself and not in the wider white society. It may be acceptable for black people to use the epithet but not for white people to do so.

The epithet reflects the perception of particular individuals in their communities across the African diaspora in the Atlantic world and its use by Caribbeans reflects the growing similarities between African groups in the North Atlantic. What then is at issue, when the epithet is used to describe the behaviour and values of a person, is the black public perception of a prominent individual in his general relationship with a majority white society by members of their own minority community or group. This public perception which informs social action functions to remind the prominent individual that he is part of a dominated group and that his individual achievements do not allow him to transcend the structured differential incorporation of the community as a whole.

THE MEANING OF THE UNCLE TOM EPITHET

The Uncle Tom epithet is used mainly in the US and Britain, but would most likely also be understood in black communities in the Caribbean, and elsewhere such as parts of continental Europe where the relations between black and white is one of antagonism bred of competition, domination and subordination in an inequitable situation. The US and Britain are societies in which white people are in the demographic majority and exercise overwhelming control of social, economic, cultural and political power. Like all human communities, Britain and the US are societies in which populations are divided not only along such natural lines as gender, generation, colour, geography, aesthetics, etc., but also by social divisions of class, religion, culture, customs and so on. In both societies a fundamental division is that between people of white and black pigmentation. Through diverse but intertwined histories of colonisation and settlement, slavery, plantation life, imperialism, war, migration and cultural hybridism, a great deal of what we may wish to describe as either black or white has become a complex web in both societies during the past three to four centuries. This fact is evident in several layers of popular culture such as sports, music, drama and the visual arts, as well as in the physical types which we now crudely describe as being either black or white. Irrespective, however, of the greyness of the divide between black and white, it cannot be denied that peoples of African descent in what we call the West and people of European backgrounds or descent stand in sharp contrast in the two societies under discussion in this chapter.

Essential aspects of the relationship between these two, in themselves diverse, groups are the historical fact of slavery, the continuing significance of its aftermaths, and the seemingly perpetual subordination of black to white or their differential incorporation into these societies. The struggles of black people in these societies who share a common origin in Africa, the Atlantic crossing, and subordination in contemporary society, have significantly modified the terms and conditions in which they live. In the US, as in the Caribbean and throughout Central and South America, rebellion by slaves contributed to the abolition of slavery; struggles for social justice and equality – essential principles which first became generalised in white Western societies – in the last two centuries have placed black people at the forefront of the defence of these principles. Specific events in Britain, the Caribbean and the US punctuate this development: the emancipation of slaves in the British West Indies in 1834–38; President Abraham Lincoln's Emancipation Act in 1863, and President Lyndon Johnson's Civil Rights Act exactly a century later in 1963 (widely regarded as a second Emancipation Act); the winning of political independence in the present century after a process of reform which commenced in the 1880s in the Anglophone Caribbean; and in Britain the establishment of a Commission for Racial Equality under the 1976 Race Relations Act. In addition, there have been the election of black politicians to the US Senate and House of Representatives, and the British House of Commons, and nomination to the House of Lords over the last three or so decades.

In both Britain and the US these decades have witnessed the election and nomination of several black persons to prominent positions in public life at both local and national levels. More significantly, in both countries the broad principles of equality and justice for all irrespective of the colour or 'race' of the individual, has been more formally if not generally accepted. Although, therefore, W.E.B. DuBois' prediction at the beginning of the last century that the 'colour line' would be the dominant divide in the twentieth century has been vindicated, none the less this fundamental divide has not meant that there has not been progress towards equality between black and white. But the main point here is that this change has come about largely because of the struggles of black, oppressed, marginalised people in both societies.

Both the African-American and African-Caribbean populations in the US and Britain share experiences of New World, post-Columbian slavery, migration from more agrarian to more industrial-based societies, and subordination based on colour, and so-called racial difference. In the US, African Americans have generally constituted the largest single minority group at around 12 per cent of the total population, that is, over 30 million people in a land mass covering almost half of the third largest continent on the planet. Whilst there has been migration, this has been internal migration from the South to the North. In Britain, however, whilst there have been pockets of blacks in such places as London, Cardiff and Liverpool, the vast majority of people of African backgrounds were either born during the last three decades or came from the Caribbean, principally Jamaica and Barbados. As indicated in an earlier chapter, the relatively small size of the Caribbean-derived population in the UK does not explain the generally high profile of black people in this important European Union country. The relevance or visibility of Caribbeans in Britain is partly accounted for by such factors as the continuing relevance of colour, their high participation in some areas of national life such as sports and entertainment, the visibility due to institutional exclusion and subsequent active protest, and the priority that European societies have placed on the value of equality.

Whatever differences there may be between Britain and the US, the black population of both countries share a common understanding of the Uncle Tom epithet, and it is important that this is so. In my view this is due largely to the impact of the black American experience on black Britain since the 1960s, as discussed in the last chapter. Not only is the black population in the US the largest in the industrialised Western world, it is also located in the largest and most powerful country in the post-Second World War international community. The concerns of white American society have impacts on society elsewhere, particularly Europe. Similarly, the concerns of black America in the 1950s, but especially from the 1960s, over discrimination, social justice, equal treatment for all, resistance to physical, economic, spiritual repression and humiliation became the concerns of black people who had fought much the same struggles in the Caribbean and colonial Africa – but with the notable exceptions that in these regions black people enjoyed demographic majorities, and in Africa direct historic links with a dynamic and continuous past. In the more complex situation of Britain where oppressed peoples from colonies and newly independent countries in Africa, Asia and the Caribbean met on former imperial/metropolitan ground, the black American model of struggle and universalised justice helped to unite rather than divide for the better part of a generation in the 1960s and the 1970s as they struggled for fairness and an end to discrimination based on perceived or self-defined racial affinity.

During this period, the vocabulary, symbols, icons of struggles of black America became those of people from Africa, Asia and the Caribbean in Britain (see for example, Sivanandan, 1986; also Goulbourne, 1990, 1988a, 1988b). This was true not only for radicals and liberals who wished to change aspects of British society. It was true too for the British establishment. Whenever there was a need for an institution – the police, the teaching occupation or the fire service – to formulate a policy which included rejection of racial discrimination, there was a tendency to organise a visit to the US to learn from their experience. This became particularly noticeable after the Brixton disturbances and the Scarman Report of 1981.

In these situations, the Uncle Tom epithet became a common one across the Atlantic. In order better to understand the manifestations of this shared perception and prolongation of Tom's career in the lived experiences of the Caribbean variant of the wider African diaspora it is in order to look briefly at aspects of the epithet's origins in the US and its continuing significance in both countries. The controversy between Frank Bruno and Lennox Lewis in 1993–94 forms the background to this discussion. In brief, the controversy arose from the bantering between competitors that has become familiar in boxing since its heyday in the days of Sonny Liston and Floyd Patterson, but more significantly since the appearance of the sportsman of the last century, Muhammad Ali and his confrontations with Liston and a generation of other black boxers. These were situations in which much of the antagonism between black and white America were symbolised and played out in public through non-fatal physical confrontations, rather like jousting in medieval Europe. The boxing ring became the jousting field in which the black people's champion faced the champion of dominant white society; while the champion of the black community is himself black, the 'white hope' may be black or may be white. This kind of confrontation came to be represented in Britain in a dramatic way, resembling the US in the 1950s to the 1980s, through the personalities of Bruno and Lewis, Britain's two most successful boxers in the second half of the last century and currently. The highlight of the confrontation occurred when Lewis described Bruno as an 'Uncle Tom' and this was published by the *Observer* newspaper in September 1993. Frank Bruno claimed that this was defamatory, and sought redress in the courts against the *Observer* and their owner the *Guardian*. The defence was not whether it was true that Bruno behaved like an 'Uncle Tom', but rather that this is a situation that can arise when a black person is successful, particularly in the performing fields, that such successful persons run the risk of being so perceived and described by their community, and therefore the issue is a proper one for public, including the press, discussion. The case was eventually settled between the parties out of court, but for a while it generated much discussion in the national as well as the Caribbean press. Its significance here is not the legal issues involved, but how the controversy reflected the increasing links between black America and Caribbean Britain across the Atlantic.

DERIVATION AND SIGNIFICANCE OF THE UNCLE TOM EPITHET

Popular black diasporic perceptions are at the very heart of the matter. After all, Uncle Tom's creator never intended him to be perceived in the negative and derogatory ways in which the epithet is generally used. Published in 1852, *Uncle Tom's Cabin* was written by the New England abolitionist pamphleteer Harriet Beecher Stowe as a condemnation of slavery, which after independence and establishment of the Union between 1783 and 1787 had continued in the states south of the Mason–Dixon Line. The book became a major intervention in the debate over slavery, particularly with respect to whether 'the peculiar institution' should accompany the expansion of free labour to the newly conquered territories in the West following President Polk's successful war in 1846 against Mexico and the acceptance of Texas into the Union. *Uncle Tom's Cabin* was quickly established as a classic. It is reputed to have been the first American novel to sell over a million copies. And its central character, Uncle Tom, already in the first decade of his creation, was the subject of poems, songs, plays and musicals. But Uncle Tom was destined to become perhaps the most derogatory and widely used epithet in black communities not only in the US but also in Britain. His meek Christian character resonated with the experiences of Caribbeans in Britain where they were being forced to forge their own identity in the way that black Americans had to do almost two centuries earlier. It is, therefore, important to have a firm grasp of Stowe's Uncle Tom.

Stowe's Uncle Tom embodies in his person and social action the upright man, firm in the conviction that his action adheres to a higher law than the laws of those who enslave him and his people. He is a deeply religious man, who takes his lot in this world rather like Job of the Old Testament, because his faith tells him that there is a better life to come. The pains and sufferings of this world can therefore be endured. Thus, Tom strives to realise his talents as a good manager of his master's property, and his competence and trustworthiness are not in doubt; indeed they are taken for granted. When urged to escape from his bondage because, unusually for a slave, he has 'a pass to come and go any time' Tom pointed out that 'Mas'r always found me on the spot – he always will' (p. 31). He prefers to be sold to a wicked master in order to save the other slaves from being dispersed. Tom encourages Eliza and her child to escape, and he willingly faces death rather than betray the plans of Cassy and Emmeline to escape. The figure of Tom that Stowe wishes to implant on the minds of her readers is rather like that of the Christian martyr to be found in Fox's *Book of Martyrs*, and there are echoes of John Bunyan's Pilgrim in his search for salvation and the endurance he displays in his journey. Indeed, the intentions of Fox, Bunyan and Stowe are much the same: to persuade the reader of a particular viewpoint regarding existing conditions in their respective time and of the relevance of the Christian message in attaining certain social goals through individual determination and faith. As William Berry pointed out, *Uncle Tom's Cabin* has one 'underlying but unmistakable accusation: by tolerating the brutal enslavement of an Uncle Tom, readers vicariously crucified Christ' (Berry, 1989, p. 592). And in *Good-bye to Uncle Tom*, J.C. Furnas argued that Stowe's 'Uncle Tom would be a credit to any race in any context' (1956, p. 9).

These virtues of Uncle Tom were intended, therefore, to point to the evils of the 'peculiar institution' which symbolised the difference between the North and the South in the Union, the difference between free and enslaved labour, the difference between good and evil. Stowe intended her readers to confront the moral dilemma the system of slavery presented to the nation which prided itself on being an advance on the old Europe. Slavery was contrary to the law of God. Tom's interest in the other world, his spirituality, his trustworthiness and moral rectitude were exemplary to both blacks and whites. So too was his application to hard work. As James Weldon Johnson's perplexing character expresses the point in *The Autobiography of an Ex-Coloured Man*, critics are wont to 'brush it [*Uncle Tom's Cabin*] aside with the remark that there never was a negro as good as Uncle Tom' (1990, p. 29).

As archetype of his race, Tom answered many of the fears and concerns of majority white society which feared that the abolition of slavery would result in black people posing a violent threat to white society. In particular, Tom contrasted with what Eldridge

Cleaver was later to call the 'supermasculine' black man (Cleaver, 1968), who posed a threat to the institution of family and the pristine and forbidden white woman, and who had little or no feelings for the declared human values such as love, care and sensitivity, which were perceived to be exclusively white. Through Uncle Tom, Stowe sought to assure an ostensibly Christian community that abolition would not result in the black man posing a threat to white society. His virtues are that he is other-worldly, long-suffering and altruistic. Tom is asexual but, as Ann Douglas pointed out in her Introduction to the Penguin edition of the book, 'he is so only in the way St Paul chose to be and urged others to be' (Douglas, 1981, p. 27), that is, through abstinence. Although away from his family, Tom transcends loneliness and tribulations to become a caring and responsible family man. Indeed, it is his wicked white master who destroys the family, and whose social action breaches Christian moral codes.

The use of Uncle Tom as an epithet in black communities in the US and Britain deliberately negates the virtues Stowe invested in him as one kind of protest and rejection, not of values but of attitude and behaviour. Indeed, the reading of the character is the direct opposite to what his creator intended. Thus, Tom's saintliness becomes cowardice, and an unwillingness to confront the inequities meted out by white society to black people; given the importance of the position Tom occupied on the plantation, his altruism demonstrates a lack of self-pride in improving himself and his community with whom his own fate is intertwined; his concern over his master's interests and the white child Eva – perhaps the most angelic child in Anglo-American literature – replaces a natural concern for his own family who are placed at the mercy of white society. Similarly, his Christian faith and practice amplifies the abandonment of his own culture, and signifies an unforgivable naïveté, which has cruel consequences for his own people.

Expectedly, the use of Uncle Tom as a negative and derogatory epithet has changed emphasis over time, as its usage has been made to adapt to changing circumstances in the lives of minority black communities particularly in the US, but also in Britain. One way to see this change is to consider how from time to time since the 1850s, both fictional and real-life characters have been perceived in terms of their replication of, or their contrast with, Uncle Tom.

An example of this in African-American literature is Bigger Thomas in Richard Wright's *Native Son*. Bigger violates the codes governing contacts between black and white America by raping and murdering a white woman. Unlike Tom, Bigger is not an asexual character; he is not a well-behaved, predictable Tom, he is not an uncle, but a young black man caught in the intricate contradictions of a plural society dominated by whites in which actual or perceived sexual contact with a white woman can mean certain death for a black man. The 1993 Nobel Prize winner for literature, the African-American Toni Morrison, picks up this powerful theme in her 1977 novel, *Song of Solomon*, when she depicts a young black man from the North travelling in the South, who admits that he has had sexual relationships with white girls. He seems not to realise that he could not do so in the South, or he wishes to defy time-honoured folk custom. He defies the prohibited code of the white South, and experiences the ultimate penalty – sudden, brutal and humiliating death.

James Baldwin, a major figure in the American and the African-American literary traditions, in his essay 'Everybody's protest novel' describes *Uncle Tom's Cabin* as 'a very bad novel' with its exaggerated self-righteousness, and 'virtuous sentimentality' (1990, p. 14). Displaying his own predilections which had deep roots in the European Romantic movement of the nineteenth century, Baldwin goes on to rage against 'a devotion to the human being, his freedom and fulfilment; freedom which cannot be legislated, fulfilment which cannot be charted' (ibid., p. 15). For Baldwin, Tom's divestment of his sexuality is more like what St Paul demanded of the man of carnality who is of the flesh and not of the spirit. Bigger Thomas, for Baldwin, affirms his manhood by acting out the drama that is Tom:

> Bigger is Uncle Tom's descendant, flesh of his flesh, so exactly opposite a portrait that, when the books are placed together, it seems that the contemporary Negro novelist and the dead New England woman are locked together in a deadly, timeless battle; the one uttering merciless exhortations, the other shouting curses. [Baldwin, 1990, p. 22][1]

An example of the continuing dilemma faced by blacks and whites in a society dominated by the latter, was more recently dramatised in a telling scene in Spike Lee's controversial film *Jungle Fever*. The main character, Flipper, and his Italian-American lover Angie, romp on the bonnet of his car in an act of joy and frivolity between generic man and woman. A neighbour (whom we must assume is white, but may have been black) rings for the police. When they appear with lights flashing, sirens blaring, and guns pointed at the black man we have perhaps the most dramatic scene of the film. Flipper is pushed against the wall, a gun at his temple, and roughed about for allegedly attempting to rape, not just a woman, but a white woman. In panic, Angie barks at the two white policemen that Flipper is her lover. This both panics and incenses Flipper, because, with the policemen's departure, we learn that Angie's declaration that he was her lover is tantamount to his death sentence by the white policemen (the apparently less malevolent of whom had said to the more malevolent, 'better luck next time!').

Angie's reaction is perfectly natural. But it is naïve. And herein lies the dilemma and pathos of the human condition in a society divided by social race, of society in the West which has become both black and white, both European and African. But these are also societies which, as the Jamaican social anthropologist M. G. Smith argued, integrated diverse groups of people differentially, so that different groups had different levels of rights, access and share of power. In stating the truth about their relationship, Angie does not appreciate the danger into which she placed Flipper. Lee, the director, wants us to believe that Flipper's salvation is that he avoids the fate of both Uncle Tom (asexuality and martyrdom) and Bigger (violent sexual satisfaction followed by death) by acknowledging his (natural?) fascination with the white woman, his lust for her, and his physical satisfaction, but also makes the deliberate decision to end the relationship, because he wants to reaffirm his love for his black wife. Moreover, although Angie says she is darker than some blacks (certainly visibly more so than Flipper's black wife), Angie is ill equipped by experience to cope with the differential status between whites and blacks. Angie is not herself a member of the dominant white, Anglo-Saxon, Protestant (WASP) community: she is of Italian background, is Catholic in religion, and she leans in the direction of the dark side of the colour line. In Britain, where there is comparatively little racial segregation where Caribbeans and whites are concerned, the relevance of the scene would not have the same intense dramatic effect as in America. However, given the colonial/imperial background to black settlement in Britain, the point would be easily understood by both black and white viewers in both societies.

UNCLE TOM AND THE WORLD OF POLITICS

The adage that life is stranger than fiction also holds true for the career of Uncle Tom. From his very birth, Uncle Tom might have been set against real-life political characters, and their relevance to the continuing moral imperatives of black and white in modern Western society. Contemporary readers of *Uncle Tom's Cabin* would have been at the very least acquainted with the anti-slavery activities of Frederick Douglass, the outstanding black abolitionist born in slavery, who escaped and campaigned actively in America and across the Atlantic to destroy the system. Many, if not most, would also have been aware of the activities of Sojourner Truth and her effective organisation of the Underground Railway for runaway slaves to the North and beyond to Canada. Some would have been aware of the British concern about post-slavery society in the British Caribbean, as Sewell's *The ordeal of free labour in the West Indies* suggests; Sewell's work was first published in New York in 1861, two years before President Abraham Lincoln's Emancipation Act. In Britain too, the worry about post-slavery society in the Caribbean was an ongoing concern from the 1840s to around the 1890s, as Thomas Carlyle's *An Occasional Discourse on the Nigger Question* (see Williams, 1963) and Anthony Froude's *The English in the West Indies, or the Bow of Ulysses*, (1888) reveal. Indeed, British workers' positive response to Lincoln's appeal for support against the Confederacy during the Civil War also hints at the wider Atlantic involvement with these issues.

The late nineteenth and early twentieth centuries in black America were dominated by the figures of Booker T. Washington and W.E.B. DuBois (see Lewis, 1993; Haskins, 1988; DuBois, 1965). Washington, an ex-slave who in good American style had pulled himself up by his own bootstraps, assumed leadership of black America at a time when the victories associated with the Civil War, Emancipation and Black Reconstruction in the former Confederate states of the South had been reversed, following the Compromise of 1877 between the northern Yankees and the defeated white Confederates. The Compromise led to the disenfranchisement of black men, to the growth and respectability of the Ku Klux Klan, and the rise of discriminatory practices known as 'Jim Crow laws' (named after another major archetype who appeared in the first pages of *Uncle Tom's Cabin*) which enforced in daily life the inequality between blacks and whites. In 1896 the US Supreme Court's judgment in *Plessy* v *Ferguson* formalised this inequality by upholding the principle of 'separate but equal' treatment of blacks and whites. Although the judgment was defended on a supposed natural distinction between black and white people, and claimed not to have destroyed 'the legal equality of the two races, or re-establish a state of involuntary servitude' (Ringer, 1983, p. 221) it none the less came to symbolise the legal recognition of inequality in post-Emancipation America. *Plessy* v *Ferguson* was not to be overruled until 1954 when Chief Justice Warren ruled in *Brown* v *Board of Education* that the principle of 'separate but equal' was contrary to the protection afforded all citizens under the Fourteenth Amendment to the Constitution.

In this situation, which lasted until the 1950s, black leadership could either actively oppose Jim Crow laws, or accommodate itself with these laws. Whilst emphasising the need for blacks to educate themselves, acquire skills, and thereby improve their status, Booker T. Washington decided on accommodation. This period was the height of so-called scientific racism, supported by the scientific communities in Britain and the US. W.E.B. DuBois, a scholar and founder of the Pan-Africanist movement, which organised its first congress under the Trinidadian Sylvester Williams in 1902 in Britain, argued strongly against what became known as the Atlanta Compromise in which Washington formally gave notice that he would not oppose Jim Crowism directly by fighting for civil and political equality, but would rather seek to work within its confines to gain education and skills.

Here then were two major leaders who came under the shadow of Uncle Tom: later generations were to see Washington as an Uncle Tom figure, and DuBois (who became a major figure in the Pan-Africanist movement, in the international struggle against imperialism and colonialism in Africa and elsewhere, eventually migrating to the newly independent Ghana under Kwame Nkrumah after 1957) has been seen as Tom's antithesis. A sophisticated, Harvard-[2] and Heidelberg-educated academic and intellectual from a not so very comfortable New England background (as Lewis (1993) shows), DuBois' commitment to the cause of equality and justice has been unquestioned amongst African Americans and people of African backgrounds everywhere. Washington's more cautious, accommodating, leadership has been less widely acclaimed, although in his own lifetime Washington was far more widely recognised as a great Negro leader, and he is likely to continue to have his supporters on both sides of the Atlantic (see, for example, Haskins, 1988).

In subsequent years other major African-American leaders were to be seen in much the same light as Washington and DuBois. One example was the non-violent Ghandian civil disobedience form of leadership offered by Dr Martin Luther King in the Civil Rights movement in the 1950s and 1960s, and the militant leadership provided by Malcolm X who urged African Americans to free themselves 'by any means necessary' from majority white oppression and exclusion. By the late 1960s, the radical Student National Co-ordinating Committee led by a young generation of militants such as Stokeley Carmichael (later Kwame Toure), and the Black Panthers in Oakland led by Huey P. Newton and Bobby Seale, came to see themselves as being within a radical tradition of black resistance to oppression, and against Uncle Tomism. This defiance of white power and apparent rejection of white values was symbolised by the figure of the uncompromising Black Panther, the Afro hairstyle, pride in blackness as beauty and resistance, and a passion to acquire and disseminate knowledge about Africa. This influenced, and continue to have an impact on, generations of young black people throughout the English-speaking African diaspora. Frustration with moderate leadership such as that provided by the middle-class National Association for the Advancement of Coloured People (NAACP) founded by DuBois in 1909, and the Urban League, as well as King's leadership, gave way to a political and cultural radicalism which in turn provided a new dimension to the negative image and meaning of Uncle Tom in black communities in the US and Britain.

THE CONTINUING SIGNIFICANCE OF UNCLE TOM

In the highly charged and radicalised atmosphere of the late 1960s and early 1970s, Uncle Tom came to mean not merely a servile black man who always agrees with whites,[3] but also someone who was perceived to be actively willing to take the side of white society against the interests of his own community. Such a man usually occupies a sufficiently important position to be able to act with a degree of autonomy. Thus, in 1993, *The African American Encyclopaedia* defined the Uncle Tom stereotype as 'an African American male who subordinates himself in order to achieve a more favourable status within the dominant society' (Williams, 1993, p. 1601).

Thus, as indicated earlier, the term is generally used to describe the perceived behaviour of black men of considerable standing in a white majority and dominant US society. Understandably, the use of the epithet has not been nearly as widespread in the black community in Britain as in the US. One or two examples from both societies will serve to illustrate the point. In early 1994, critics of the NAACP executive director Benjamin Chavis (who was charged with sexual harassment and the improper use of the organisation's funds) 'have been branded as "traitors and Uncle Toms" by Gibson (NAACP chairman) and Chavis' (*Time*, 8 August 1994, p. 28). Earlier, in 1992, the *New York Times* carried a piece entitled 'Canonizing a slave: Saint or Uncle Tom?' by Deborah Sontag who reported that many African-American Catholics were opposed to the Church making Pierre Toussaint a saint. Born a slave in Haiti, Toussaint fled the country with his white master and family at the beginning of the nineteenth century during the only successful revolt by slaves in recorded history. A brilliant hairdresser and stylist, he earned a reputation and good money but used this to keep his invalid owner who appears to have fallen on bad times, instead of purchasing his freedom. After the death of his owners, Toussaint dedicated his life and money to New York's poor, performing outstanding feats during an outbreak of cholera. Whilst early in the 1990s some Americans felt that he was an outstanding example to follow, others felt that he was unnecessarily servile to his white masters; one argument was that Toussaint 'was an Uncle Tom and a poor model for modern blacks'. Revd L.E. Lucas of Harlem saw Toussaint as a 'perfect creature of his times' who was 'a good boy, a namby-pamby, who kept the place assigned to him' by white society (*New York Times*, 23 February 1992, p. 1).

Perhaps the most riveting instance of a public figure being perceived as an Uncle Tom in the 1990s in the US was the Senate Judicial confirmation of Judge Clarence Thomas, President George Bush's nominee for the Supreme Court in 1991. The confirmation became a startling admixture of sex (Anita Hill's accusation of sexual harassment), race and class issues. Thomas was being nominated by a deeply conservative Republican president to replace the distinguished liberal jurist, Thurgood Marshall, on his retirement from the bench. An African American of conservative persuasion, Thomas cut a poor contrast with Marshall, one of the most outstanding African Americans in an age of distinguished leaders. Where Marshall had been deeply involved with the Civil Rights Movement, Thomas was seen as the least sensitive of the judges of the Supreme Court, all of whom enjoy security of tenure in a court which constitutes Montesquieu's third effective arm of the State. Following his confirmation by the Senate, Thomas has been consistent in his conservative judgments, and has alienated many who had supported his nomination in the view that since he is a black man from very humble background he would support the struggles of his community for equality in an inequitable society. The disappointment led the film director Spike Lee to say of Thomas that 'Malcolm X, if he were alive today, would call Thomas a handkerchief head, a chicken-and-biscuit-eating Uncle Tom' (Coleman, 1993). W.T. Coleman, Jr a leading African-American lawyer and former Secretary of Transport under President Gerald Ford is reported to have said:

> It is sad. Justice Thurgood Marshall was a tremendous justice and made a tremendous contribution, and people would have hoped that this particular person who went through the doors he opened, would act differently. Whatever Thomas got in life, he got because Marshall fought like hell to get him in the doors and you would think some people would have respect for those traditions. [Colemen, 1994 p. 42]

As Donald Suggs wrote in his editorial in *Crisis*:

> It is not any principled stand on politics held by Thomas that infuriates African-Americans: it is the self-righteous, self-serving whining of a person who owes more to his willingness to ingratiate himself to powerful white individuals mostly on the far right of the political spectrum than he does to personal merit. It is his history of reckless attacks on individuals and institutions that have struggled and suffered for increased access to opportunity for all African-Americans including justice Thomas. [*Crisis*, November/December 1993, p. 4]

Thomas seems to confirm for Jacqueline Johnson-Jackson her view, expressed in *The Black Scholar*, that the 'historical record clearly shows that most black racially integrated appointees, hirings, *et cetera*, have always been "safe niggers" or "Uncle Toms and Aunt Thomasinas" (which is how I see Hill)' (Johnson-Jackson, 1991, p. 20).

In Britain too, people of Caribbean background are very much alive to the continuing usage and meaning of the Uncle Tom epithet. For example, in 1971 the radical black community-based publication, *Black Voice*, condemned as an Uncle Tom a young Nigerian who wrote a book about the racism he experienced as a pupil at Eton. The group felt that a black man who was conscious of his position in white society would not be complaining about racism at Eton because he would avoid such ostensibly obvious racist institutions. As noted in the last chapter, the Black Unity and Freedom Party (BUFP) tended like many others to condemn members of what they saw as the black bourgeoisie as 'Uncle Toms'. In the late 1960s and early 1970s, the Uncle Tom epithet was widely used, but mainly within radical groups and in political debates, often behind closed doors or unreported. Although not as readily used in Britain as in the US, the Uncle Tom epithet is widely understood in the black communities in Britain in much the same way as it is understood in the US. Thus, even if prominent black men in Britain are less likely than in the US to be called an Uncle Tom by members of their community, the epithet is available and its use is not unusual.

BLACK ENTERTAINERS AND THE UNCLE TOM STEREOTYPE

Black individual entertainers, such as sportspeople and musicians, are particularly vulnerable to being called Uncle Tom. Perhaps elected officials are less vulnerable, because the fact that they are elected makes them dependent on their electorates for their tenure in office, and they have therefore to be seen to support members of their community or constituency. Not so individuals who depend on patronage and distinctively personal qualities for the positions of power or influence they occupy in predominantly white society. Entertainers are such individuals: their success depends largely on support from sponsors and patrons. At the same time these individuals are highly visible, and are perceived as models for large communities of young people, particularly young black men who, in the US as in the UK, are generally perceived as under-achievers and a drain on society's resources. Apart from this investment of symbolic leadership in entertainers and sportspeople, outstanding black individuals exposed to public scrutiny carry a heavy burden to behave in ways which conform to preconceived patterns.[4]

Although different, such preconceived patterns are held by members of the white majority as well as by members of the black minority communities. In very general terms, the two sets of expectations stand in sharp contradistinction with each other. For the white majority society the prominent black sportsman should be inarticulate, but physically superb, whilst the black community takes for granted his physical supremacy, but expects him to be intellectually rounded and articulate. The former exaggerates his physical prowess so that the sportsman becomes a supermasculine being, but harmless; he poses no threat, he is a gentle giant. The black community expects this man to be seen as a threat, dangerous, unpredictable. For whites the black sportsman should reflect a flat, uniform sense of national consciousness, a consciousness which abolishes divisions between 'the races' – he should be a nice man who takes white insults in his stride because he knows, like all whites, that these are exceptional not the norm. For the black community which experiences white racism every day and in most aspects of their lives, the successful black sportsman as a highly visible achiever should be critical of society, should be a champion of the community's struggles for social justice, and must therefore be keenly aware of society's inequality and of his own differential incorporation into the social fabric. In his personal behaviour the black sportsman should be quiet about his culture, and show appreciation for the majority white values; the black community, however, expects him to be a living manifestation of personal black pride in a society which has tried to destroy and then deny black, African culture. Whilst white folks may elevate the black sportsman to the level of national hero, as for all other black people, there are boundaries set by the majority society around him, and the black community would expect him to be aware of these and express his anger; in the eyes of the black community such a black man should be seen by white society to be unpredictable, and he is expected to give his support to popular causes for social justice and equality for his community. While most white people would expect him to underplay his individuality and his membership of a specific dominated community, the prominent black man's community would want him to be seen as a zealot for his culture and a champion for justice.

These juxtaposed expectations should be seen as end points on a spectrum, rather than as expectations which could always be empirically proven. For example, it is not at all the case that all whites would hold these expectations of black sportsmen; similarly, it is not the case that whole black communities have uniform expectations of their sportsmen. These expectations are more likely to be implicit than explicit in general commentaries about specific individuals. The general point, however holds: in white-dominated societies such as the US and Britain, members of the black communities are likely to have different expectations of black sportsmen from those shared by the larger white population:

> ... some black athletes perceive themselves as marginal persons because they are not fully accepted by either the white or black communities. Thus, they may feel forced to live by the white man's rules and to 'make it' in the establishment world lest they be viewed as 'radicals' or 'ungrateful blacks', yet among blacks they might be called 'Uncle Toms'. [Snyder and Spreitzer, 1983, p. 191]

The pressures experienced by black athletes have led a number of commentators in the US to 'wonder about the long range physical and mental health consequences' (ibid.) on these individuals.

There is a general view that sports are an avenue for upward social mobility for black people in both the US and Britain. With the desegregation of sports in the US in 1947, and the visibility and apparent success of black men and women in sports in both the US and Britain since the Second World War, it is not difficult to understand why such a view may be held. But whilst this may be exceptionally so, it is unlikely that individual upward social mobility is of the level that it changes the overall situation of inequality and subordination. Moreover, the high visibility of black people in sports may hide the fact that sport has been one of the most difficult occupations for black people of talent to enter in both the US and Britain (see, for example, Madison and Landers, 1976, p. 150; Cashmore, 1982; Lyons, 1991). It is still the case that black sportsmen and women in both countries suffer discrimination: only slowly have they been allowed to enter each individual sport; they tend to be concentrated in some sports (football, boxing, basketball, sprints) and to be nearly or entirely absent from others (swimming, tennis, golf, hockey, skating); within some sports (football, baseball) they tend to be 'stacked' or restricted to supporting rather than given leadership positions. In Britain just over a decade ago David Miller reported that the 'areas of administration, sports medicine, coaching and management appear, certainly to the blacks, to be quite out of bounds' (*The Times*, 16 August 1985, p. 8). It does not appear that this situation has significantly changed in the intervening years (Lyons, 1991, p. 75). In general, therefore, the success of black sports men and women has been achieved despite considerable barriers.

The reasons given for black success in sports have fallen into two broad categories. First, there is the argument from nature: black people are supposed to have a natural physical superiority over white people in some areas of competition. The law of the 'survival of the fittest' in nature selected only the fittest of Africans after the Atlantic journey and slavery. One of the most persuasive proponents of the argument from nature, Steven Goldberg, argues that blacks originating from West Africa have a genetic superiority over whites in certain sports, particularly sprints and high jump, where 'fast-twitch' fibres provide them with an advantage over white athletes with 'slow-twitch' fibres (Goldberg, 1990). Where greater endurance is required for longer distance, the 'slow-twitch', and more fat, white athlete will have the advantage. As another writer points out, however, the theory does not explain why East Africans sometimes dominate the longer distances. Similar reasons are sometimes given for the relative absence of black swimmers and black skiers; but as one commentator has quipped, it is most unlikely that there will be many first-class Alpine skiers found in Somalia. The biological explanation breaks down with respect to black people in the US and Britain, because black people in both countries are highly mixed, and as Harry Edwards pointed out

> ... inbreeding between whites and blacks in America has been extensive, not to speak of the influences of inbreeding with various other so-called racial groupings. Therefore to assert that Afro-Americans are superior athletes due to the genetic makeup of the original slaves would be as naive as the assertion that the determining factor in the demonstrated excellence of white pole vaulters from California over pole vaulters from other states is the physical strength and stamina of whites who settled in California. [quoted in Snyder and Spreitzer, 1983, p.187]

Edwards and others have also pointed to the unfortunate corollary of the biological argument: because blacks are physically superior to whites, it follows that blacks are intellectually inferior, and this view is time and again shown to be a guiding principle for teachers in British schools (see, for example, Carrington and Wood, 1983; Carrington, 1986).

The second category of explanations for the black athlete's success, stresses environmental or social factors. The main factors for black success in sports that environmentalists point to are perceived opportunities for self-improvement, family, peer and neighbourhood encouragement, the opportunity to participate in certain individualised sports, and the presence of role models for younger aspirants.

Whilst we cannot entirely ignore the fact of physiology, it would seem to me that the argument from nature is the weaker of the two perspectives. In addition to the points made by those who stress the environment, I have long been of the view that black men and women are perhaps more likely to succeed in sports than in most other professional occupations, not only because the wider society in both the US and Britain places a high priority on sports and winning is important, but especially because once access to participate is gained to a sport, winning in an event cannot be easily denied. In other occupations, access to participate does not so easily guarantee success. In other words, in most occupations reward for work done can be easily denied by arbitrarily changing the rules after the work has been done. In openly displayed events such as sports, only an Adolf Hitler can deliberately turn his back on a Jesse Owen and walk away. The openness of sports is the single most important factor for black success in this field of human endeavour in a racially differentiated society. This openness attracts young people, both men and women, because not only are they likely to achieve fame and fortune, but perhaps far more significantly, once entry into the event has been gained, the other agencies in the arena cannot deny the success of the socially dominated. The openness of sports also vindicates the democratic claims of societies across the North Atlantic where liberalism proclaims that each individual has an equal opportunity to enter, participate and enjoy the rewards of their labour in an open, free and level social space. Black athletes, therefore, are perhaps more assured of acknowledgement and reward than if they were to be equally successful in other areas of work in a white-dominated and inequitable society (Goulbourne, 1988a). Competitive sports, particularly individual events as contrasted with team events, are likely to continue to be a measure of black perception of fairness in white-dominated societies across the Atlantic. As such, black participation in sports is likely to continue to be visible and remarkable.

Whatever, however, are perceived to be the reasons for success by black sports men and women in Anglo-America (and also increasingly on the European continental rim such as The Netherlands and France) and whatever may be the reasons for going into sports, the fact of their success in this highly competitive occupation is always a matter of general interest, and therefore a matter for comment. This is so in the majority white society as well as in the minority black community. The case of Frank Bruno and Lennox Lewis in 1993–94 was a very apt illustration of the drawing together of black America and Caribbean Britain.

THE BLACK PRESS AND FRANK BRUNO

Frank Bruno is a highly respected black man who occupies a prominent place in the British nation's esteem. He has been honoured with an MBE; he is readily recognizable as the big man who helped to promote HP sauce; he is known as a devoted family man, a churchgoer, and a supporter of charities. A proud man, he is devoted to his fans, and cherishes his popularity with the general public. A reading of the British black press in the early 1990s depicts a Frank Bruno who is widely admired by the British people as a whole. As one reporter stated, 'Being British is something Bruno does extraordinarily well' (*Voice*, 21 April 1992, p. 14). Bruno also commands a good deal of respect in the black community, precisely because he is a big black man with a definite public presence. In the first part of the decade Bruno was, so to speak, bigger than Bigger Thomas, yet not a 'bad nigger' bent on destroying white society; rather, he was a gentle giant loved by all.

But when looked at more closely, his assumed community of black Britons appear less comfortable with the image Bruno projects of himself, and by extension, of black people in general. For example, in his fight with Lennox Lewis in Cardiff in the autumn of 1993, Bruno entered the ring to the tune of 'Land of Hope and Glory', while Lewis entered with Bob Marley's 'Crazy Baldheads' (*Voice*, 10 May 1994, p. 13). There are references to Bruno saying 'I feel as strong as a baboon' (*Caribbean Times*, 28 April 1992, p. 31) after beating the South African Gerrie Coetzee in a controversial fight in which Bruno ran the risk of being banned by the World Boxing Council which was still awaiting full reforms before recognising South Africa (*Weekly Journal*, 24 September 1992, p. 20). Reviewing Bruno's autobiography, *The Eye of the Tiger* (1992), Nigel Carter writing in one black newspaper pointed out that 'Bruno's standing in the black community and criticisms of his alleged "uncle tom" image is not addressed' (*Caribbean Times*, 28 April 1992, p. 31). The same writer noted that Bruno's considerable achievements have earned him '... the mantle of Britain's most popular fighter since Henry Cooper, a major coup for a black fighter' (ibid.). Ron Shilling-

ford writing in *Voice* about the book also speaks of Bruno's achievements, but expresses an unease about his attitude to questions of
race and discrimination in Britain, following an interview with
Bruno: 'I decide to broach Bruno on the subject of being a Black role
model. As I finish the question, his quiet, polite demeanour alters
considerably' (*Voice*, 21 April 1992, p.19). Shillingford reported how
Bruno's trainer entered the room where the interview was being held
and told the reporter that '"Frank doesn't get involved in discussing
those sort of subjects, son. He doesn't want to upset anybody"'
(ibid.). It would appear that the image Bruno cultivated is that of a
man standing above daily concerns about racism, and that his
actions are guided by a naïveté about this major division in society
which affects black people as a collectivity, although the negative
aspects of such differentiation do not necessarily affect the
individual black person.

A most penetrating analysis of the Bruno–Lewis antagonism was
provided by Onyekachi Wambu, a film-maker and journalist
involved with a television series in the mid-1990s about black
athletes entitled *The Will to Win*. Writing in the *Voice*, Wambu
argued:

> Bruno has been a difficult character for Black people. We cannot
> ignore him. He has been projected back to us as a symbol of
> success; the most popular Black person and one of the richest. But
> many (not all) Black people have found him inadequate. We
> cringe at his jokes, his apparently limited intellect and at his
> various forms. Everyone has their particular Bruno tale. [*Voice*, 10
> May 1994, p. 13]

Wambu goes on to show how the Bruno–Lewis confrontation stands
in a long tradition of prominent black men this century representing conflicting values in Britain and the US. On one side Wambu
sets Jackie Robinson (the first black man allowed into professional
baseball), Muhammad Ali, the athletes who took the Black Power
salute at the Mexico Olympics in 1968, and Lewis. Bruno is depicted
as a black man siding with and representing a declining Britain:
taking pride in defeat the way that white British sportspeople do;
displaying the stiff upper lip in traditional English determination.
Bruno tries to portray Lewis as being non-British because Lewis once
represented Canada. For Wambu, Bruno is symbolic of the forces of

continuity while Lewis represents change in Britain during the last decade of the millennium. He concluded his piece thus:

> While it could, to be fair, be said in Frank's defence that his success and popularity by themselves represent a positive role model for other young Black people, he was loved by White English people because he did not unsettle them; he reassured them that everything was all right. Their way of perceiving the world would not have to change ...
>
> There is nothing wrong with this in itself, apart from the fact that everything is not all right, and White English people need to understand that everything is not all right! [ibid.]

As for Bruno's lawsuit against Lewis and the *Guardian* newspaper for being called an Uncle Tom, Wambu asked 'Who would be the jury?' if it went to court. His answer was that this could not be twelve white people, but the black community itself.

CONCLUSION

It is hard to think of another image that more closely links the black communities of Britain and America than that of the Uncle Tom epithet. Uncle Tom is a complex character: he is proud, caring, sensitive, strong; he is also perceived to be fawning, insufficiently concerned about his own people in a society fundamentally divided between those who control social and economic resources and those who are deprived or excluded simply because of their colour – the hero's own colour. While we are admonished to be careful about how and when we apply the epithet to a particular person (Anderson, 1991; Berry, 1989), it is widely used within these communities, and successful black men, particularly those in sports, are likely to be accused of being Uncle Toms. This is because their communities as well as the majority white community project these men as models for the young, and whatever these sportsmen do or do not do is seen as a matter for public comment. It is therefore clearly understood in the relevant community on both sides of the Atlantic that public comment on how models are perceived is a necessity, because the welfare of the community is involved. Indeed, it may be argued that the use of the epithet is a means of reminding prominent individuals that they are part of a distinct but dominated community within a wider racially differentiated social order. Thus, the Uncle Tom epithet is often used in public debates to depict the behaviour of prominent public black men, and this is perhaps part of the occupational hazard, or the rough and tumble, that a public role model must expect. As a prominent boxer on constant display before the nation and the black community, Frank Bruno, like any other prominent black sportsman, could not avoid this risk in the transatlantic world that made him the popular hero he is.

6 Having a Public Voice: Caribbean Publishers and Diasporic Communication

This chapter advances the analysis of the Caribbean transnational experience by focusing on the work of two black publishing houses, and the major contributions they have made to the emergence and development of Caribbean publishing presence in Britain from the late 1960s. These are the New Beacon Books (NBB) situated in North London, founded by John LaRose from Trinidad and run with his partner Sarah White from Wales, and Bogle L'Ouverture Publications (BLP) in West London, founded by Jessica and Eric Huntley from Guyana. Both NBB and BLP have been far more than publishing concerns, and have been involved with British as well as world events. Moreover, they have been intricately wrapped up with specific forms of community action and have reflected as well as developed the Caribbean transnational experience in their practices. Before, however, exploring these aspects of the groups' activities, it is useful to make a broad observation about the publications scene in Britain and how they relate to the intellectual and community life of Caribbeans in Britain and relate to the wider Caribbean and African diasporas.

CARIBBEAN COMMUNITIES AND PUBLISHING

Publishing is important in its own right in all communities, but it has been particularly so in the process of Caribbean communities being established in Britain. However, comparatively little is known about this dimension of Caribbean life in Britain although it is generally taken for granted within the diaspora.

First, the weekly newspapers have played the crucial role of keeping people informed about events 'back home', introducing readers in Britain to a wider perspective of the Caribbean and African diaspora, and Africa itself than is the case 'back home' in the Caribbean where, in general, middle-class hegemony is still in a kind of colonial time warp regarding Africa and the Caribbean diaspora in Europe. Of course, there have been different kinds of newspapers over the years. For example, as seen in Chapter 4, in the 1970s papers such as *Black Voice* and *The Panther* were published by particular community-based groups in specific localities in the urban centres of Caribbean settlement. Earlier, in the 1960s, there was the far more professionally managed and produced *West Indian Gazette* run by Claudia Jones, one of the major figures who linked the Caribbean where she was born, the US where she was brought up and commenced her radical work, and Britain where she spent her last years and stimulated the birth of radical black journalism within the community (see Sherwood, 1999; Boyce Davis, 2001). What these publications shared was an emphasis on public concern over problems that faced the new Caribbean communities, and they were parts of a wider British activist agitprop (radical agitation and propaganda) literature characteristic of the years from the late 1960s to the early 1980s. Whilst Claudia Jones brought to Brixton and the emerging Caribbean communities springing up in England her immense experience from the US, the other publications were largely experimental, produced on extraordinarily messy Gestetner printing machines in often damp and unhealthy basements and terraced houses both north and south of the Thames.

With the consolidation of Caribbean communities in Britain, new popular publications emerged to meet a number of easily identified needs. The *Weekly Gleaner*, its headquarters in the Elephant and Castle, and offices in Brixton and Birmingham, established a recognisable place for itself in the UK market; it resonates particularly with Jamaicans, some of whom will still have memories of the legendary *Gleaner* in Jamaica. Regarded as one of the oldest newspapers in the English-speaking world after *The Times*, Jamaicans have long perceived the *Gleaner* as their eponymous newspaper. Clearly, the *Gleaner* company in Kingston, Jamaica, recognised the potential of a British market, and it is now well over 2,500 volumes in publication. The weekly paper, around 35 pages in length, carries news about Jamaica and the wider English-speaking Caribbean that may be of interest to communities in Britain; it also carries specific items about Africa that may be relevant to Caribbeans, and the same with respect to North America. Not surprisingly, music, general culture, activities by the region's leaders and sportspeople feature prominently, as does the Commonwealth Caribbean preoccupation with the ritual of ceremonies around all kinds of celebrity figures and trivia around fashion, gossip, and mediocre non-achievements by sons and daughters of relatively unknown individuals in the region whom few in Britain would know or particularly care about.

Of course, the same is true for the other papers that sprung up over the years since the 1960s. Such was the *West Indian World* edited by Aubrey Baines, which is no longer in existence, but helped to blaze a path. Such is the *Voice*, which at the turn of the millennium was nearing its second decade and was becoming more available in regular newsagents in some of the main cities of England where Caribbeans have settled. Where the *Weekly Gleaner* claims to be 'the top Caribbean newspaper', the *Voice*, with offices in Brixton, Birmingham and Bristol, asserts that it is 'Britain's best black paper'. Certainly, the latter is almost twice the length of the former, although their contents are not dissimilar.

Perhaps more than the *Weekly Gleaner*, the *Voice* and the *New Nation* – which started later in East London and boasts that it is 'Britain's no. 1 black newspaper' – would appear to cover more news of the kind found in any local newspaper in England: crime, injustice, racism, sometimes overlooked achievements by black individuals, and so on, and perhaps less coverage about the Caribbean, Africa and the US. Items which are apparently of considerable concern to people of Caribbean backgrounds in Britain feature significantly in both papers, and they all carry advertisements about hair and skin care, music and cosmetics, food and beverage, and holidays in the Caribbean – all are apparently items of considerable interests to Caribbeans. Nostalgia or concern to maintain close links with consumer aspects of culture appear to combine with an obsession over appearance and keeping up with style to provide a basis for such advertisements. As more Caribbean companies – banks, insurance, real estate agencies, legal firms dealing with such matters as immigration law, forwarding companies – became active in England offering services to nationals and their offspring, the papers have also carried advertisements reflecting the varied needs of members who live within a transnational Atlantic world.

Increasingly too these papers carry advertisements and general coverage about the activities of the various Christian denominations, particularly evangelical gatherings such as American preachers visiting the UK in search of souls for Jesus and money for their pockets. As in the Caribbean, these papers have all performed the task of what may be seen as admonition to improvement: education, achievement in private and public life, telling the story of individual achievement as well as group attainment. These papers, therefore, provide for the Caribbean communities in London, Birmingham and other English cities where the majority national and local papers do not. Of course, these functions or services are also provided by niche newspapers in Britain's other new minority ethnic communities and therefore Caribbean newspapers are not unique.

A second kind of publication that was vitally important in the process of establishing a Caribbean presence in Britain was, of course, books about the region and its people's experiences which were closely linked to England's past, but also distinctive. This was to occur at two levels. First, the decades of immigration from the region and steady settlement in Britain coincided with the great strides in Caribbean creative writing. Edgar Mittleholzer, Wilson Harris, V.S. Naipaul, Eddie Brathwaite, E.E. Braithwaite, Andrew Salkey, Sam Selvon and others became familiar names amongst those in the majority national and the new minority communities attuned with literary creativity. While, however, these writers may have been familiar to many readers, they sometimes tended to merge into a wider collectivity of writers from the former colonial world, and had little to do with the new Caribbean communities with children born and/or brought up in England. Much of what writers from the Caribbean expressed was primarily of concern to people in the Caribbean experiencing the transition from colonialism to self-recognition. There was clearly therefore a need for writers who shared the new experiences of emergent Caribbean communities in Britain. It was in this context that the new publishers in these communities were to make a definite contribution by introducing new writers such as Linton Kwesi Johnson to the British community and encouraging established writers, such as Salkey, to make more easily accessible his novels for children in the Caribbean relevant to a wider Caribbean diasporic readership.

The remainder of the discussion here focuses on the work of two key contributors to this important enterprise in the Caribbean communities, which is too often overlooked. The focus on New Beacon Books and Bogle L'Ouverture Publications in no way belittles similar contributions rendered by small bookshops and publishing enterprises in several English cities. In the first place, it is important to recognise that there have been other publishers, such as Saba Sakana's Karnak House, Buzz Johnson's Karia Press, Rudolph Kizerman's Blackbird Books and Len Garrison's Black Star Publisher. These ventures performed valuable services to the Caribbean communities, but for one reason or another folded after a few years and a limited number of new titles or re-publications.

Second, the Caribbean communities owe much to those many individuals who have long and consistently ensured that they find themselves at a range of public meetings with their suitcase of books and pamphlets from the US, the Caribbean, Africa and Britain about the perceptions and experiences of life in the Atlantic world. Veteran observers such as the Huntleys have noted that the presence of such individuals diminished in the late 1980s and early 1990s. However, by the turn of the century a return to the habits of the radical 1970s appeared to be on the increase, and here and there outside London small bookshops emerged. Whatever the reasons for such fluctuation in publishing and in the number of men and women with their suitcase of literature over the last three decades or so, it may be suggested that together these activities constitute an area of Caribbean enterprise in Britain that deserves more attention in much the same way as Caribbean participation in business enterprises and the management and ownership of companies which benefit from Caribbean sporting, musical and other artistic creativity deserve critical inquiry, assessment and advancement. After all, much of the access that many Caribbean intellectuals enjoy with major commercial publishers has come about subsequent to the early and dynamic contributions by unrecognised entrepreneurs in their communities.

BOGLE L'OUVERTURE PUBLICATIONS

As suggested earlier, both BLP and NBB had their origins in developments which took place in the Caribbean, but which had direct relevance to the emerging Caribbean communities in Britain. Perhaps the more dramatic, and at the same time less deliberate, was the founding of the Bogle L'Ouverture Publications in 1969 at 110 Windermere Road, South Ealing, which was the home of Eric and Jessica Huntley, who moved there from North London earlier in the 1960s. While the founding of BLP may be well known to the small group of individuals who were involved and who may now live in Britain, the US and the Caribbean, the story is far less well known to the wider community and the academic world. This story deserves telling as part of the process of the Caribbean communities' articulation of a public voice in print.

BLP, Walter Rodney and Jamaica

The dramatic occasion or catalyst of the founding of BLP was the banning by the Jamaican government in October, 1968 of a 26-year-old Guyanese historian, the late Walter Rodney, from returning to Jamaica (see Payne, 1994, ch. 1; Lewis, 1998, ch. 5). In 1963, Rodney had graduated with a brilliant first-class honours in history from the University of the West Indies, and gone on successfully to submit a doctoral thesis on the slave trade in West Africa[1] for London University's School of Oriental and African Studies in 1966. He had lectured at the University of Dar es Salaam, Tanzania for two years before returning to the Mona campus of the regional University of the West Indies in 1968 as a lecturer in his *alma mater* department of history. But Rodney soon attracted the attention of the government. He offered a series of open lectures to students at the campus and to a variety of groups in Kingston – in churches, school rooms, sports clubs and the gullies frequented by such social outcasts as the Rastafarians and the urban poor. In these talks he stressed the relevance of African history to the black majority of Jamaica. This simple activity in an overwhelmingly black country was perceived to be subversive and highly dangerous for the status quo taken wholesale from the colonial past. As the then minister of home affairs, Roy McNeill, stated in the Jamaican lower house, the House of Representatives, 'I have never come across a man who offers a greater threat to the security of this land than does Walter Rodney' (Payne, 1994, p 23). McNeill's statement was mere political hyperbole, or as would be recognised today, political 'spin'.

But Rodney's history lectures touched a very raw nerve in post-colonial Jamaica's national psyche. While the majority of Jamaicans were black, the wealth of the country was almost entirely owned by minorities such as the white Europeans, the Chinese and the Lebanese; political office was held mainly by the mulattos, even though they had to gain legitimacy from a black electorate. This situation arose from the history of African slavery, and the reconstruction of the history of the islands and of Africa. After the Haitian Revolution and the successful end to slavery in Haiti at the turn of the nineteenth century, there was the constant fear before Emancipation that Jamaica would follow the example of that island. Slave rebellions in the 1830s and the Morant Bay Rebellion of 1865 gave substance to the fear of disorder, that is, a threat to the social order established for and by white settlers. At the beginning of the independence period in the early 1960s the retreat into the hills around Kingston by Claudius Henry and his followers seemed to be giving further proof that Jamaican society was never far from this kind of disruption. The proximity of Cuba and the revolution of 1958 along with the Cold War and the Cuban crisis of 1960 all appeared to point in the same direction.

In August and again in October 1968 Roy McNeill (a brown man) and the prime minister, Hugh Shearer (a black man), discussed the matter of Rodney's lectures with the vice-chancellor, Sir Philip Sherlock[2] (a white man), who refused to take any action, even under pressure, against a member of his staff who had not committed any professional misconduct. Rodney's absence from the country at a conference of radical black writers in Toronto, Canada was seized upon by the government to ban him from re-entering the country when he landed at the international airport in Kingston on 15 October. Although a Commonwealth citizen, Rodney was a national of Guyana, not Jamaica and the authorities took the view that he was a serious threat to national security. The following day, Wednesday, 16 October, students and ordinary citizens in Kingston took to the streets in protest against the ban, and the rest of the week witnessed widespread disturbances in the capital city. But these events, known as the Rodney Riots, should be set within the context of other developments during the 1960s.

First, although Jamaica had won independence from Britain as late as 1962, this post-colonial state did not represent a new socioeconomic order, and its basic structures remained much the same as before, particularly as they had been since the return to self-government in 1944.[3] Indeed, the first post-colonial government was determined to defend the state structure established and slightly modified from the seventeenth century. It was, therefore, something of a paradox that the government of independence was formed by the Jamaica Labour Party (JLP), which had been hurriedly founded by the charismatic Alexander Bustamante on the eve of the first government to be elected under the universal adult suffrage in 1944 and was opposed to total political independence. The JLP's was a government supported by an amalgam of the old plantocratic, mercantile and the emergent manufacturing elements of the dominant classes in the country as well as the traditional external social elements who had economic interests in Jamaica. This was not an unrecognised story in other parts of the decolonising empire.

Members of the professions, the trade unions, and other *petit-bourgeois* elements who formed the government or administration naturally feared any talk about the racial and class dimensions of Jamaican society and its implications for the socio-political elite. In reality, whilst independence had come, in Jamaica as in much of the rest of the English-speaking Caribbean (as a result of the protests in the region from 1934 to 1938), the essential aspects of the colonial order continued relatively intact. It must be borne in mind that, unlike political independence in Africa and Asia, independence in the Commonwealth Caribbean was not only a relatively mild, constitutional affair, but it posed no fundamental questions about the ownership and control of the economy. Like the struggle for Emancipation a century earlier, the fight for political independence from the 1930s to the 1960s revolved around a valid but rather narrow appreciation of political democracy. Radical questions about economic matters in Jamaica were to come a decade later under Michael Manley, the son as well as political heir of Norman Manley, the father of modern Jamaican nationalism. But Manley the Younger's radicalism was in the post-Rodney years between 1972–80 (see, for example, Manley, 1974; Girvan, 1971; Beckford and Witter, 1984; Stephens and Stephens, 1986) and was crushed in the 1980s when the JLP returned to office under Edward Seaga. This was hardly surprising, given an international environment dominated by Ronald Reagan and Margaret Thatcher's monetary policies and prescriptions, which closed the space that existed in the 1970s for radical Third Worldism (see Talburt, forthcoming).

Second, at the end of the 1960s in the English-speaking Caribbean, as elsewhere in the Western world, students were at the forefront of a challenge to the established post-Second World War social and political order. Opposition to the Vietnam War, support for the liberation forces in Southern Africa, sympathy for Fidel Castro's revolution in Cuba at an international level, and within specific countries the questioning of oppressive regimes or seemingly impenetrable ruling elites, led to mass student unrest. The Rodney Riots combined elements of both opposition to exploitation by racial minorities without there being any hint of a 'race war', and the opposition of a new intelligentsia against the conservative post-colonial status quo. Although this was taking place in Jamaica, the protest that the Rodney Riots articulated had something of a Commonwealth Caribbean dimension to it. Mona was, after all, the oldest and largest of the regional university's campuses, with students from several contributing territories in the region. The concerns of students, as Payne and other commentators noted, coalesced around representation in the governance of the university. But the interests of the unemployed youths in Kingston were largely about jobs; accordingly, their anger was vented against property, not against persons. Like several other places in 1968, protest might have been expressed in the vocabulary of revolution, but the protesters' concerns were more limited; they wanted to participate in the running of affairs that apparently concerned them, and to see their interests forming part of the legitimate process of institutional or public affairs.

The Rodney affair in Kingston had an immediate and powerful impact on black communities in Britain. And it is surprising that the emerging scholarship around Rodney is failing or refusing to recognise this aspect of his influence. Perhaps the best example of this neglect or refusal is to be found in Rupert Lewis's (1998) otherwise widely researched and interesting treatment of Rodney's intellectual life in the Caribbean and Africa. Lewis correctly pinpoints Rodney's Dar es Salaam days as perhaps his most important in an all-too-short career; Rodney was only 38 years old when he was killed in a car bomb in his native Georgetown, Guyana – both the region and the world lost an intellectual and activist whom C.L.R. James (1982) later described as 'the brightest spark' to have been produced in the post-Second World War Caribbean.

Lewis's work is the latest and perhaps the most serious treatment of Rodney's life and work, but while Lewis touches upon Rodney's London years (1963–66) little or nothing is said about the pivotal importance of his London connections. It was in London that Rodney's most influential books, *The Grounding With My Brothers* and *How Europe Underdeveloped Africa* were first published. But London is more important than for just the publication of Rodney's books. And it is this story that needs to be told alongside the story of Rodney's overall place within the Caribbean and African diasporas.

Whilst a student at SOAS, Rodney had been close to a wide range of Caribbean fellow-students and intellectuals, but he was particularly close to his compatriots Jessica and Eric Huntley – a fact which is curiously ignored by a scholar as thorough as Lewis, and this weakens his account and analysis of Rodney's life and work. Rodney had sought out the Huntleys and often stayed at their home. He knew of their uncompromising non-racist principles and active participation in Guyanese politics during the 1950s, when the joint leadership of Cheddi Jagan and Forbes Burnham in the People's Progressive Party (PPP) appeared to be on the path to forge a prosperous future for both the African and East Indian populations in the physically largest English-speaking country in the region. Developments in Guyana (then British Guiana) – race riots, suspension of the 1950 Constitution, suspicions about US involvement, etc. – were of general interest to all Caribbean communities in Britain, and intellectuals, students and activists sought to make their views known to the Labour government of Harold Wilson as well as to inform the general public. Meetings were organised by the Huntleys, John LaRose, Richard Small and others and Rodney was a major voice and presence in these activities. In October 1965, Rodney presented a paper on the situation in Guyana at a symposium organised by LaRose and the Huntleys at the then centre of Caribbean attraction, the West Indian Students Centre in Earls Court. In the process, Rodney and the Huntleys became socially close, Jessica sometimes typing his work and also helping to find a typist for Walter's doctoral thesis; with others they frequented weekend dancing parties, for which he had a legendary liking.

It was not surprising, therefore, that on having news of Rodney's banning from Jamaica, the Huntleys, LaRose and others picketed the Jamaica Tourist Board (the Jamaica High Commission had not yet been established for them to target), where a number of protesters were arrested. Rodney, passing through London en route to Dar es Salaam, where he had worked and was again offered a post at the history department, expectedly called on the Huntleys. As Eric Huntley later recalled 'so then when he went to Jamaica and he was banned, it was the natural place for him to come back to Jessica', the central figure in the group he had known in London (interview with Eric and Jessica Huntley, 22 October 1992). A meeting was arranged and on leaving for Dar es Salaam, Rodney left with Jessica for safe-keeping the notes of a set of lectures he gave in Jamaica. Jessica in turn showed these to other individuals concerned about developments in Jamaica as well as the wider Atlantic world, including Earl Greenwood, Fitzroy Griffiths, Barbara Joseph, Chris LeMaitre, Dale Saunders, Richard Small and Ewart Thomas. With Jessica and Eric, these individuals quickly formed a committee to inform the Caribbean communities in Britain and abroad about Rodney's case and the repressive developments in Jamaica. Initially, the idea was to duplicate, using a Gestetner machine, some of these lectures and, following what was happening in black communities in the US, entitle them *Walter Rodney Speaks*. As various possibilities about effective dissemination occurred to the group, the idea came from either Jessica Huntley or Ewart Thomas that the whole series of lectures could be published under the title *The Groundings With My Brothers*; Thomas offered to edit them while Small offered to contribute an introduction to the collection and they agreed to go for immediate publication. But the group faced the problem of how to finance the venture. As Jessica explained:

> ... of course, the whole question is where are we going to get the money from? That was everybody's response. And I said, 'I will ask my friend, what about you asking your friend?' ... and right there I picked up the phone and I start ringing people and people promise a, b, c, d pounds. And Barbara Joseph who was at the meeting said she will give £50, in those days that was a lot money. [Interview with Eric and Jessica Huntley, 22 October 1992]

After much discussion it was decided not to approach white people or their agencies for financial support, but to depend on the group's own resources. Barbara Joseph, a Trinidadian student of architecture, and other individuals played a part in the publication by holding fund-raising parties. Apart from editing Rodney's notes and providing an Introduction to the text, Ewart Thomas went with Jessica Huntley to discuss the matter with John LaRose who already had more experience of publishing in Britain. John was supportive and introduced them to his printer, John Sankey of Villiers Press who was 'very concerned as to where we are going to get the money from, but I was so convinced we would get the money' (ibid.). Over two decades later, by which time both she and Eric had naturally become less than certain about the exact cost of printing, Jessica recollected that it would have been between £300 and £500. The publication was a campaigning document which highlighted the situation in Jamaica, and while the first edition was sold for six shillings and six pence, most copies were given away in the cause of raising consciousness of the post-colonial order that was emerging in the region.

But if the group's financial resource was meagre, they certainly possessed considerable social capital. For example, Richard Small[4] was from a prominent Jamaican family of lawyers, and while a law student in London had also been one of the leading figures in the Campaign Against Racial Discrimination (CARD) (see Heineman, 1972); in the late 1970s and the early 1980s Small was a member of the legal team representing Rodney and his comrades in the Working People's Alliance (WPA) in Guyana when President Forbes Burnham accused Rodney and his associates of anti-government activities. Ewart Thomas,[5] who had been at school in Georgetown with Rodney had, like him, come to England (Cambridge in Thomas' case) after UWI to do his doctorate in mathematics; he went on to a successful career at Stanford University. In other words, while material resources were limited, the group had considerable human capital at its disposal, and individuals undertook different tasks. Eric had been editor of his post office trade union newsletter and contributor to *Thunder*, the organ of the PPP in Georgetown, and therefore contributed his skills and experience.

The Groundings With My Brothers (1969) quickly became a bestseller amongst Caribbean groups in Britain and overseas, particularly in the US. It achieved its aim of disseminating information about the immediate post-colonial society in Jamaica, and extended Rodney's international reputation as a serious, well-informed and educated radical, unlike most of the African Americans who had emerged as major spokespersons in the late 1960s. He was not just seeking to acquire knowledge about Africa: he had direct experience of the most exciting and radical state on the continent – Julius Nyerere's post-Arusha Tanzania; he spoke and wrote about West Africa at a crucial point in that region's links with Europe which resulted in part in the African diaspora. *The Groundings* had a strong urgency and relevance for young Caribbeans in England eager to know something about the African past and to have that past linked to the Caribbean of which they knew comparatively little. It was not surprising therefore that *The Groundings* was reprinted in 1970, 1971, 1975, 1983 and 1990; the publisher's notes, introductions and editor's preface have become important additions to a valuable original document of protest in the struggles of Caribbean people both in the region and outside.

The text itself is a mere 56 pages. But within this space the reader hears the voice not merely of an angry young man, but a scholar who is master of a subject that had been conspicuous by its absence in Caribbean education circles – Africa as reality as distinct from Africa only as myth. Rodney linked African and the contemporary differential situations of Africans in the Americas, Europe and Jamaican society. He modified the radical language of Black Power leaders in the US to show how all shades of black people occupied subordinate positions in a world dominated by imperialism. Where many radical black Americans drew a simple line between black and white, Rodney's work hinted at a more complex situation in which racial and ethnic identities were wrapped up with the interlacing histories of a wide Atlantic world. In Jamaica and elsewhere imperialism had its supporters and such class interests cut against racial lines. This explained the Jamaican government's banning of the late Kwame Toure (then Stokeley Carmichael), H. Rap Brown, and James Forman, as well as books by Malcolm X, Elijah Mohammed and Hamilton and Carmichael's powerful and highly influential *Black Power: the Politics of Liberation*. Just as Rodney's lectures had had a marked impact on his audiences in Kingston, so in London *The Groundings* became an immediate success. It not only established Rodney as a leading Third World radical with an international status, it also launched the Bogle L'Ouverture Publications as a major independent publishing house operating within the black communities in Britain and through its subsequent publications served as a link with a wider diasporic world.

This point could be illustrated with reference to BLP's other publications, but it may be more relevant to do so through their continued links with Rodney, particularly given a growing interest in his work and his all too short career. For example, although BLP was not the first to publish Linton Kwesi Johnson's poetry, it was their publication of his *Dread Beat and Blood* (1976) which substantially introduced him to the British reading public and gave voice to a new generation of black British literature as distinct from Caribbean writers living in England. The Huntleys see Johnson's poetry as the voice of alienated black youths in the late 1970s and early 1980s which resulted in the explosions on the streets of British cities in 1979 and 1981. The simplified biographies of Marcus Garvey and of Cheddi Jagan by Eric Huntley for children, the poetry collections of Valerie Bloom, and the posters and cards produced over the years have been important. In 1990 BLP was declared bankrupt as a consequence of the combination of a number of factors: increased rent for premises, cutbacks in educational and library expenditures, pressing demands from the banks, the Huntleys not receiving payments for books ordered and sent to Nigeria as well as a bitter and unfortunate case with Patricia Rodney (Walter's widow) over royalties of her late husband's works. The last of these tribulations has left a deep and ugly scar in the legacy of Walter Rodney and has cast a shadow over the remarkable partnership the Huntleys and Rodney established to give voice to Caribbeans in the wider African diaspora.

The emerging historiography (see Lewis, 1998) around Rodney threatens to continue this unfortunate rift, but the hope must be that with time the scar will heal, and indeed there are signs that some of the protagonists are reaching out to each other across the barriers.

More immediately, having survived the tribulations of bankruptcy, by the mid-1990s Jessica and Eric were able to recommence publishing, but in a significantly changed publishing world. It would now appear that there are several mainstream publishers who are willing to publish young or relatively unknown Caribbean writers, or at any rate, there is now a recognisable British Caribbean writing tradition and young writers appear not to have insoluble problems with commercial publishers. Indeed, community-based publishers such as the Huntleys and LaRose forged a path and created a market, but it is the mainstream commercial publishers who are in a position to take financial advantage of that market.

BLP, Rodney and Africa

In these new circumstances, BLP may need to discover a new niche in a crowded publishing world, but there can be no denial that they have made a considerable contribution in the shaping of a wider Caribbean diasporic order. In recent years, however, BLP has shown a willingness to publish writers such as Hylton (1997b) and Walker (2000) who show keen interest in what they call an Africentric approach to scholarship, no doubt drawing on Asante (1998). This notion of Africentric scholarship is unlikely to provide the kind of niche in the market they could develop to make the contribution they made earlier. Indeed, much of the work produced in this genre is often poor derivative scholarship at the opposite end of the academic scale from the work the late Walter Rodney produced and encouraged as a scholar of Africa. The risk BLP takes with such work, however, may be just the kind of risk that is necessary for small niche publishers to take, because to paraphrase Durkheim's aphorism, today's oddity may be tomorrow's orthodoxy.

But to continue the story of BLP and Walter Rodney, it is important to narrate how the Huntleys played a central role in the production of Rodney's most well-known work, his polemic *How Europe Underdeveloped Africa*. This was simultaneously published by BLP in London and in Dar es Salaam in Tanzania by Tanzania Publishing House (TPH), under the leadership of Walter Bygoya, in 1972; it was a joint effort, with TPH having the rights for Africa and BLP the rights for the rest of the world. Far more than *The Groundings*, *How Europe Underdeveloped Africa* has come to occupy a central position in radical popular literature in the African diaspora and will probably be remembered as the central text produced by the first generation of post-colonial Caribbean scholars who benefited from higher education within the region but who more than any other generation before or since earnestly sought to link the various parts of the Caribbean Atlantic heritage. For Rodney, the aim of this work was 'to try and reach Africans who wish to explore further the nature of their exploitation, rather than to satisfy the "standards" set by our oppressors and their spokesmen in the academic world' (Rodney, 1972, p. 8).

Following a regular theme to be found in radical pan-Africanism going back to Edward Blyden in the nineteenth century and George Padmore, W.E.B. DuBois and Kwame Nkrumah in the twentieth century, Rodney wanted to understand and explain the relationship between Africa's underdevelopment and Europe's development subsequent to their contacts in the fifteenth but particularly the sixteenth and seventeenth centuries. Developing his argument in terms of the fashionable neo-Marxist underdevelopment or dependency school of the 1960s and 1970s, Rodney argued that Africa's underdevelopment was a consequence of Europe's development; the two futures of these closely linked continents were but sides of a coin. The argument had all the robustness of this genre of discourse as well as its drawbacks – neither of which are the subject of the present discussion; nor is the kind of prescription that flowed from the dependency position that Rodney and his associates sought to bring to bear on Guyanese politics between his return to Guyana in 1974 and his tragic death in 1980. The important point here is that the book caught the imagination of Caribbean and African intellectuals in the Atlantic world. The book's influence was felt even farther afield, however, as it was translated into Japanese, French, Spanish and German (the Huntleys insist that they never received any payment for the French publication).

However, from the perspective of this discussion of BLP, the more relevant point of interest is the story behind the production of *How Europe Underdeveloped Africa* which needs to become part of the growing narrative of the Rodney saga. With the quick success of *The Groundings* Jessica Huntley recalled that

> ... when we were to do the third reprint, I wrote to Walter and I said, 'look, is there anything new you want to add to this book? Do you want to change anything, and could you do an update?' And then he said that he would do something better for us. And then he sent us a proposal. And the proposal was that this book

was going to be chapters written by himself, Babu and Bhagat. [Interview with Eric and Jessica Huntley, 22 October 1992]

Muhammad Babu and Harko Bhagat were Tanzanian comrades of Rodney's, and both were later believed to be involved in the death of Sheikh Karoume in Zanzibar in 1971. Babu, a Zanzibari economist and minister in Nyerere's government in the United Republic of Tanzania (combining from 1964 the island of Zanzibar and mainland Tanganyika), was promptly detained by the government, while Bhagat escaped and applied for refugee status in Britain.[6] Jessica Huntley discussed the proposal with her confidante, the late Andrew Salkey who was a well-established novelist, poet and broadcaster with the BBC World Service, and

> ... Andrew said ... it would be really good if Walter could come up with another nice book all on his own to just put him right in the eyes of the publishing house and in the eyes of the world outside. ... Andrew wanted for Walter to do that, to back up, as Andrew would say, to back up the *The Groundings*. And when I wrote to Walter, then, he was livid. He was so angry at the suggestion, because he [Walter] said that Bhagat and Babu were good brothers and they had gone through the struggle ... [ibid.]

But with the imprisonment of Babu, and Bhagat in exile, the possibility of a collaborative work passed, and Rodney went on to produce the manuscript on his own. None the less, Babu did manage to do a brief postscript for the book. This account should help us better to understand the unconventional acknowledgement Rodney made when he stressed that

> Many colleagues and comrades shared in the preparation of this work ... But contrary to the fashion in most prefaces, I will not add that 'all mistakes and shortcomings are entirely my responsibility'. That is sheer bourgeois subjectivism. Responsibility in matters of these sorts is always collective, especially with regard to the remedying of shortcomings. [Rodney, 1972, pp. 7–8]

The different parts of the Atlantic-African diaspora are connected by complex relationships, and within this world two major Caribbean figures stand out above others during the second half of the twentieth century – Bob Marley, singer, poet, visionary, and

Walter Rodney, scholar and political activist. Marley achieved linking popular myths of Africa with the lived experiences of people across the wide Atlantic divide, and the invitation to be the guest performer at Zimbabwe's independence celebrations in 1980 was in many ways a telling and fitting recognition of that fact. One of Rodney's great achievements was to have produced a work that spoke not only to Africans on the continent, but to the whole African diaspora. His work has been variously celebrated throughout the diaspora. One instance of this was the Zimbabwean parliament's recognition of the Huntleys when, in late 1998, they attended the legislative body, immediately after morning prayer, the speaker said: 'I announce the presence in the Speaker's Gallery of Mrs Jessica Huntley and Mr Eric Huntley, the publishers of that truly ground breaking publication on [sic] *How Europe Underdeveloped Africa*' (Zimbabwe Parliamentary Proceedings, 1998). This statement was received by shouts of 'hear, hear' from members, reflecting the high regard with which Rodney and his publishers are held in Africa, particularly in those parts such as Zimbabwe which gained independence as a result of ardent and sometimes violent struggles against European encroachment and settlement.

JOHN LAROSE AND NEW BEACON BOOKS

Like BLP, New Beacon Books (NBB) had its inspiration in developments which occurred in the Caribbean. John LaRose had been an activist from his late teens in Trinidad, worked in Venezuela and had been in close contact with radical movements and individuals in the French, Spanish and English-speaking Caribbean and South and Central America. With this background, John was poised to become the quintessential Caribbean person who was best placed to perform the role he was to create for himself and members of his family in the heart of the Caribbean communities in England: a knowledgeable and well-connected, considerate and always helpful person through whom the interwoven experiences of Caribbean transnationality is individually and collectively lived.

While maintaining his close links with the Caribbean and developing new ones with Africa, LaRose entered a new phase of his rich transnational life around 1965, when he shifted from 'concentrating upon building up the relations with West Indians here [UK], especially those who had been involved in the revolution in the Caribbean, for further development of the struggle for revolutionary social and economic changes in the Caribbean itself' (interview with J. LaRose, 3 October 1991) to concentrating on Britain. But the new phase was also itself born of Caribbean concerns, namely, to 'go into publishing as a serious aspect of the thing' (ibid.). This 'thing' for him was earlier made clear in our conversations when he stated:

> I never thought that, considering what I had in mind for New Beacon ... it was never our intention to become beyond anything but a small to medium publisher and bookseller, and publishing institution. We knew the other political and cultural commitments that we had, and we continued to want to make, and that therefore we couldn't really think of ourselves as being a full-time, actually full-time publishers and booksellers, in the way that if you were going into this business as a commercial operation. [Interview with J. LaRose, 3 June 1991]

NBB was therefore born of Caribbean dreams. It took on tangible form when in August 1966 NBB published LaRose's own collection of poetry entitled *Foundations* under the name of Anthony LaRose. This was quickly followed by the re-publication of a major book in Caribbean and British historiography, John Jacob Thomas' *Froudacity* (1888). This had been first published as a well-argued and spirited reply to the English imperialist and racist historian Anthony Froude's negrophobic account of the post-emancipation West Indies. Eric Williams noted, in his survey of how English historians perceived the post-Emancipation West Indies, that Froude was the only professional English historian of the Victorian age who took the region seriously, and after his visit in 1887 recorded his support for the past slavery society in the region, his belief in black inferiority and English superiority (consistent with his disdain for the Irish and for Catholics) in his *The English in the West Indies, or the Bow of Ulysses* (see Williams, 1964, ch. 10). Thomas, who was born before Emancipation in 1838, was one of the first major Caribbean intellectuals and in 1869 had published *The Theory and Practice of Creole Grammar* (reprinted 1969). Thomas's two books had long been out of print, but they were known to LaRose and many of his contemporaries in Port-of-Spain in the 1940s and had inspired them in their intellectual struggles against imperialism. Thomas' riposte of Froude had been important in establishing what became a strong Caribbean pride in intellectual prowess that would match that of anything that the imperial intellectuals could marshal. An essential aspect of this tradition was that competition should be fair and the rules of competition should be transparent. In this way fair-minded people would be able to assess and judge fairly.

In re-publishing the text, LaRose first sought to get the distinguished Guyanese historian, the late Elsa Goveia, to write an introduction, and held discussions with Eddie Brathwaite (historian and poet) from Barbados as well as Wilson Harris (novelist and essayist) from Guyana about the text. Goveia was engrossed in research at the time and eventually Ken Ramchand wrote the Introduction, and Thomas's work became available again, particularly to a new generation seeking to repair the breach in an intellectual tradition the contours of which were little known. In the same year LaRose's premises became the meeting place for the newly formed Caribbean Artists Movement (CAM), to which we return below.

In a broader sense, it was the intellectual fervour of the late 1920s and early 1930s in Trinidad which had a lasting impression on LaRose and led to the founding of New Beacon Books in London over thirty years later. Born in 1927, LaRose was not himself part of the generation of national awakening which boasted C.L.R. James, Albert Gomes and Alfred Mendes. But LaRose had been deeply influenced by James and profoundly impressed by the efforts to found an authentic, indigenous but critical literary movement in Trinidad, at the centre of which had been Mendes and James. Gomes, who was to become one of Trinidad's first nationalist leaders, founded and ran the *Beacon* for two years (1931–33). Both Gomes and Mendes were of Portuguese backgrounds, their forebears having migrated to Trinidad after 1838 when the planters' response to Emancipation led eventually to the importation of cheap labour from as far afield as China and India, but initially from Madeira, where the failure of grape production encouraged a short period of indenture labour to the region (see Tinker, 1974; Wood, 1968). This new age of indenture labour was particularly important for Guyana and Trinidad, which had come into British possession relatively late in the eighteenth and early nineteenth centuries, respectively, and in which there was plenty of land to be settled by the new British masters.

The *Beacon* was a general magazine which published pieces on general culture and politics; it also carried short stories and reviews. It attracted contributors and readers from the different racial and cultural communities who made up Trinidadian society, and who were concerned about the life of the colony. With people from Britain, France, Spain, China, India, Africa and elsewhere, Trinidad for LaRose was a cosmopolitan society existing within a colonial order. But it was not until he came to live in England that he fully realised that he was the inheritor of this sophisticated, complex world in which the individual is invited to negotiate a way through and amongst people of initially different cultures, religions, customs, and so on. Out of this cultural kaleidoscopic world came a cultural explosion evidenced by a number of publications by the Beacon members. Chief amongst these were C.L.R. James's novel *Minty Alley*, published in 1936, the same year as the appearance of his seminal work on Toussaint L'Ouverture and the Haitian Revolution, *The Black Jacobins* (see also James, 1938).[7] Earlier in 1934 Mendes' first novel, *Pitch Lake*, was published. As Kenneth Ramchand reminds us in his Introduction to New Beacon's re-publication of *Minty Alley* (1971), the literary explosion which was taking place in Trinidad was part of a wider experience throughout the English-speaking Caribbean. It was a literary revolution which was to have its impact on new Caribbean communities in London several decades later, just as Rodney's lectures in Kingston were to have their impact in the 1970s.

LaRose's New Beacon Books was the realisation of a vision to revive and keep alive the work of the Port-of-Spain's Beacon group. Like its predecessor, New Beacon intended to spread its net wide, and publish books on every aspect of Caribbean life, including politics and the arts. This was because for LaRose and the Trinidad Beacon group, these aspects of human life are to be seen as closely interconnected and cannot be neatly separated or compartmentalised. Decades later and in what had been the centre of the imperial order, LaRose was to stress that 'everything begins and ends with culture' (interview with LaRose, 25 September 1991). The work of publishing and the meetings organised by CAM taught him that 'although we were talking about cultural things, we were talking about its history ... all kinds of relations: historical relations, political relations, economic relations, both inside the Caribbean and the rest of the world, and what it meant' (ibid.).

As noted, the new venture was concerned to provide a vehicle for poetry and re-publications of long neglected works such as those of J.J. Thomas. As noted, New Beacon went on to re-publish James's *Minty Alley*, Mendes' *Pitch Lake*, and Sir Arthur Lewis's *Labour in the West Indies*, which was first published in London in 1939 by the Fabian Society in an effort to bring to the attention of the British left the conditions and demands of West Indian labour during the period of sustained revolt in the region in the second half of the 1930s, culminating in the dramatic events in Jamaica in 1938 and the subsequent Moyne Commission (see, for example, Post, 1978; Munroe, 1972; Goulbourne, 1988a).

But New Beacon Books also sought, from its early days, to publish contemporary writers. Apart from LaRose's own *Foundations* (under the name of Anthony LaRose), NBB also soon published Adolphe Edwards' *Marcus Garvey* (1967), some critical essays by Ivan Van Sertima entitled *Caribbean Writers* (1968), and Wilson Harris's now famous critical essays *Tradition, the Writer & Society* (1967), which is a significant precursor of many postmodern literary debates about narrative, character and historical events. Like BLP, New Beacon Books' list has extended over time to include not only the Caribbean, but importantly the Caribbean in Britain, developments in Africa, the US, Central and South America, and elsewhere.

The New Beacon bookshop on Stroud Green Road in North London is an important aspect of this enterprise. Here LaRose's group has been able to offer what is widely regarded to be the best stock of books in Britain on the worlds straddled by Caribbeans in Britain – the Caribbean, Africa and parts of Latin America. Their stock include the full range of academic and more polemic texts, and the group's George Padmore Institute provides an added feature for researchers into the making of Caribbean communities in Britain.

SELF-HELP AND COMMUNITY ACTION

It is obvious that New Beacon and Bogle L'Ouverture have had a number of things in common in terms of the personalities involved, their beginnings, aims, size, scale of community commitments and activities engaged in as well as global outreach beyond race and ethnic boundaries. It is worth briefly commenting on aspects of these in order to convey similarities as well as a deep-rooted commitment to the larger African diaspora, and more specifically their commitment to the emergent Caribbean diaspora.

First, both publishing concerns have been comparatively small affairs, depending on family and friends for support rather than on banks and/or local public assistance, and refusing to be taken over by bigger companies in the marketplace. To a degree, many of the various radical publishing concerns that emerged during the same years in the 1970s have faced this kind of problem and have acted in ways that they thought best suited to their circumstances, such as being absorbed by larger groups. Whilst taken together the impact of NBB and BLP has been immense, it must be borne in mind that both publishers have been run more on the basis of domestic labour than on the basis of large-scale business enterprises. BLP, as noted, operated from the home of its owners; so too did NBB, until more generous space was found not far away on Stroud Green Road, where the bookshop as well as the group's Padmore Institute[8] are located. In the case of the Huntleys, some neighbours complained about the numbers and frequency of visitors. Premises were later rented at 5a Chigwell Place in Ealing where a bookshop was opened. After the murder of Walter Rodney in Georgetown, Guyana in 1980, the bookshop was renamed in his honour, but became the object of attacks by right-wing groups, which were particularly active in British cities in the wake of Margaret Thatcher's victory at the polls in 1979. One response by radical bookshops which were under such attacks was to form the Bookshops Joint Action group to campaign against right-wing activities. Taken together, the Huntleys' home and bookshop in Ealing became for well over two decades a central location in West London for visitors from abroad, for book launches, workshops for schools, and for the dissemination of news of developments in various parts of the African diaspora. For example, during those years such well-known figures as Selvon, Louise Bennett, Salkey, Johnson and Faustin Charles gave poetry and prose readings, and campaigns such as the anti-SUS laws in the 1980s were launched by BLP.

Second, whilst both publishing concerns were closely linked with international networks of writers and intellectuals, they also served as independent community advice and organising centres. As noted above, they doubled as bookshops – with NBB's presence as a bookshop being more pronounced than its publishing activities. In a sense, they became rather like the Caribbean barbershops of earlier decades, that is, sites for dropping in for news, discussions and renewal or maintenance of friendships and acquaintance. Although LaRose's home in Stroud Green was always open to anyone who cared to stop by for a discussion, his bookshop situated on Stroud Green Road availed the public of a place stocked with books, leaflets, pamphlets, information about groups in London, the Caribbean, Africa, the US and so on, as well as LaRose, Sarah White or one of their sons or helpers to discuss current or historical matters. Stroud Green Road is the main thoroughfare between Finsbury Park tube station and Crouch End, and the bookshop forms part of what has become a lively shopping area. This has been the result of settlement in the vicinity by groups of post-colonial immigrants from the Caribbean, East Africa, Southern Europe and the Indian subcontinent. The groups have given new life to the area, and the New Beacon bookshop enhances the locality's cosmopolitan flavour. Thus, to be with LaRose for a morning or an afternoon, any day of the week, is to experience a gentle but vigorous ebb and flow of intellectuals from Africa, the US, the Caribbean and elsewhere passing through and 'touching base'. Sometimes people drop in from the fringes of Britain or are visiting from continental Europe. There is always a steady flow of individuals off the street and from the immediate vicinity.

At Chigwell Place where the BLP bookshop was located the situation appeared less busy but was nearly always much the same as at Stroud Green Road. But, being farther from the dynamic main thoroughfare of cosmopolitan London, it is perhaps true to say that BLP was not as central as Stroud Green Road, situated close to Finsbury Park underground and frequent bus services to central London. While participation in conferences at universities may have been more actively pursued by BLP, the closer links between the New Beacon group and the wider British academic, social and left-wing communities meant that they tended over the years to enjoy the greater exposure. This has left the impression that New Beacon was the more varied in the coverage of cultural and political activities, as well as interviews with relevant topical publications and other media. In particular, LaRose was close to figures such as A. Sivanandan and his Institute of Race Relations, which publishes the journal *Race and Class* (with their headquarters on Pentonville Road in King's Cross) and the Brixton-based Race Today Collective, which published the now-defunct *Race Today*, and was led by Darcus Howe (a nephew of C.L.R. James and, later, a television personality, particularly as the notorious 'Devil's Advocate'). New Beacon was also more accessible to the national media than Bogle L'Ouverture as well as being closer to the English radical intelligentsia through Sarah White. Sarah's relationship to the local Caribbean and the wider communities is instructive with regard to what Americans in the late 1990s and at the beginning of the present century clumsily call 'cross-over' between different racial and ethnic groups: a scientist with an interest in Soviet science, Sarah came from the centre of the British intellectual establishment, her father having been a founding figure of the Arts Council with progressive views about cultures and peoples. Sarah's technical and intellectual contribution to the success of New Beacon has been immense, and all the more so in that she has set about her work almost silently and in an unassuming manner. Her contribution to this shared enterprise is therefore sometimes shielded or muted by the dynamics of the politics of racial or ethnic curtailment, that is, where it is perceived to be important to conceal the role played by individuals of different communities. This may be particularly strong in the Caribbean community in Britain, where there is a significant degree of collaboration at the public level as well as within families.

CONCLUSION

Two general conclusions must be drawn about the NBB and the BLP from the accounts of their activities sketched here. First, they have been closely associated and collaborated over major projects. One of these has been the Third World and Radical Book Fair which was initiated in the early 1980s by both groups and lasted for ten years, with support from Howe's group in Brixton. The groups, particularly LaRose's, were at the centre of the call for public investigations into the deaths of 13 young black people at a birthday party in New Cross in the 1970s. Earlier, both groups were involved with campaigns in London over education, busing, and related issues. Second, it must be clear that both groups were distinguished from several other similar enterprises by being deeply grounded within specific communities in different parts of the city. As noted, they have grown up with the Caribbean communities that have sprung up in the last decades of the twentieth century. They continue to be central to radical Caribbean diasporic consciousness, linking England with the wider African diaspora. Both John LaRose and the Huntleys have been honoured for their contribution: John and Jessica have been awarded honorary doctorates by Sheffield Hallam University and South Bank University, London, respectively and there have been a number of specific events held by members of their communities to recognise their contributions and to register appreciation. These are individuals whose modesty can easily mislead so that the casual observer would miss their seminal importance to Britain's Caribbean communities and the wider African diaspora. Both LaRose and the Huntleys would be first to say that their contributions to the definition and tone of Caribbean communities in Britain and its links with the wider African diaspora form part of a more general articulation of Caribbeanness and that other contemporary contributors also call for recognition.

7 Transnational Family Connections

This chapter describes some aspects of Caribbean kinship in Britain which strongly illustrate the transnational or diasporic characteristics of Caribbeans in the Atlantic world. The discussion principally focuses upon two key features of the Caribbean transnational experience as articulated through family and kinship relations: first, the provision of care and support across national boundaries and, second, the sense of self and national identities that is expressed through kin membership and participation. While the next chapter further develops the first of these points by focusing on the situation of returnees to the Caribbean in the 1990s, this chapter explicates some themes discussed in different ways in earlier chapters but discussed here within the nexus of relationships established through family and kinship.

The argument here is that Caribbean family and communal life in Britain is not fully understood without an appreciation of the continuing kinship links across national boundaries which provide necessary support for members but also impose duty and responsibilities on them. But it is necessary first to enter a further brief note about theory and method, particularly relevant to this area of discussion about meaning and function of Caribbean transnational kinship connections.

CONTEXTUALISING CARIBBEAN TRANSATLANTIC KINSHIP NETWORKS

In general, kinship systems combine descent by blood or genealogy – comprising the primary or core nuclear unit of the family, as well as the wider network of social relations based on affinity through marriage, co-habitation, residence and/or fictive relations. Kinship involves the ascription of individual and collective rights alongside reciprocal obligations and responsibilities. It is through the kinship system that a society sanctions forms of acceptable social behaviour and prohibits others (for example, incest, marriage rules, age of sexual consent). Kinship also provides the social context for procreation both within and outside the framework sanctioned by law, and the kinship system is a powerful agency for the transmission of values, customs and culture. Crucially, it is within the networks established through kinship that most individuals receive primary care and socialisation, the necessities for life in the wider social order, and develop the sense of belonging to discrete bio-social, or consanguineal and affinal, units. It is not surprising, therefore, that in sociological and anthropological discussions these networks are generally referred to as a system because they are identifiable institutions with a number of functions that are considered (for example, by Malinowski, 1963 and Smith, 1962) to be primary to the larger social order.

Whilst all human societies have established family and kinship systems, these differ and each must be understood in its own terms rather than through any extraneous overarching structure, functional schema or value system. Awareness of such specificities need not be as relativistic as this statement may sound, because in practice social orders are more remarkably similar in their broad structures, functions and values than they are distinct from one another. It is, however, more usual to stress the differences than the similarities between kinship systems. Of course, it must also be now recognised that while the traditional family has been in decline, there have been new forms of familial and related structures which are becoming generally acceptable as ways of organising household life. Examples of these changes include the general increase in female-headed households, single-motherhood households, men and women living on their own, as well as what Weeks et al. (2001) and his colleagues call 'families of choice', including same-sex relationships of which some Caribbeans, particularly Jamaicans, have become notoriously intolerant.

These general remarks are as apposite for the autochthonous as they are for the new minority communities in contemporary Britain. With regard to Caribbean communities, however, work on the 1991 national census supports a general observation that there is a greater tendency for marriage or co-habitation to be exogenous (see Owen, 1996; Berrington, 1996; Modood and Berthoud, 1997) than is the case with other communities. Berrington sought to explain this in terms of the relative sizes of minority ethnic communities, their density and the preponderance of the white population (Berrington, 1996, pp. 198–9), but there are other more relevant correlative factors such as the already mixed lineages and linkages of Caribbean families and kinship.

Moreover, there is the tendency for Caribbean culture to be outward-looking in orientation. The important point here, however, is that the general willingness to form unions with individuals outside the ethnic or national community gave, and continues to give, rise to kinship patterns that transcend the boundaries of the nation-state. Expressed another way, it may be said that Caribbean families in Britain more than others exhibit and live within multi-ethnic, multicultural contexts. Migration and family reproduction in Britain have given a new dynamism to this process, but it was one which commenced within the Creole societies which developed out of the slave and plantation systems in the region (see Brathwaite, 1978, 1997; Patterson, 1967).

Whilst there is comparatively little attention, whether of an empirical or theoretical kind, paid to the transnational relations of Caribbeans in Britain, there is usually a general ideological and policy concern over the success or failure of Caribbean kinship systems to perform the universally expected functions mentioned above. In particular, some observers are wont to take the bare statistics that over 50 per cent of mothers of Caribbean backgrounds are lone parents and the fact that less than half of all Caribbean families are outside the nuclear unit to mean that the Caribbean family is dysfunctional, or at least members of the family and the kinship group are unable to provide the necessary support required by members and therefore reinforce welfare dependency (see Dench, 1992, 1996).

The research into the living arrangements, family structure and social change of Caribbeans in Britain that my colleagues and I conducted in the late 1990s therefore sought to test the hypothesis that contrary to this view of dysfunctionality, it has been their strength and resilience in unfavourable conditions which have provided the Caribbean family and kinship groups in Britain with the wherewithal to establish communities, and to sustain and reproduce themselves. The accounts of mutual support across distance, the closeness between members of the network, the ways in which knowledge and values are transmitted suggest that the kinship system does provide the emotional and material factors necessary for meaningful individual and collective life. These do not mean, however, that Caribbean families can, or have sought to, live in isolation from the wider British social system and survive through their kinship groups exclusively. Caribbean kinship networks do not account for the total social incorporation of individual members, because kinship groups operate within the wider context of the social systems of the national labour market, educational institutions and the judical-political units of the British state.

Thus, for example, we found relatively little in the histories of the families studied to suggest that their kinship networks could provide employment for members, or that kinship was used with respect to the political system. Whilst there was evidence of individuals taking limited advantage of the economic opportunities provided by the international kinship system, in general these opportunities have not been fully exploited by members of these networks. While in the 1990s and the beginning of the present century Caribbean governments and businesses have demonstrated an interest in exploiting the export and investment opportunities made available by the vitality of the Caribbean transatlantic community, this interest pales in significance when compared to the Chinese and the Indian diasporas.

The second hypothesis which guided our research asserted that, arising from their historical antecedents, Caribbean families and kinship networks exhibit modernist features to an unusually high degree. This is clearly seen in the tension between collective control and the freedom of individual members in each family discussed below. The overall value system which informs Caribbean societies is not discordant with the dictates of the impersonal, contractual rules which characterise and mark off modern societies from earlier social formations that the founding figures of sociology such as Marx (1974), Durkheim (1933) and Weber (1995) stressed. At another level within these social orders, a variety of modifications have occurred, combining patterns of resistance and innovations which draw on pre-Columbian and African roots, but in ways not clearly recognisable as African, European, or otherwise. In short, the tension between the desire to control or restrain individual behaviour through kinship ties and obligations and at the same time strongly assert individual freedom reflects an absence of traditionalism or autochthony (see Mintz, 1993; Mintz and Price, 1992; Goulbourne, 1998, chs 1 and 2).

The tension involved here is not bred of postmodern conditions, as theorists such as Anthony Giddens might suggest. Rather, the tension has long been part of the Caribbean reality in the post-Columbian era, that is, as part of the region's experience of modernisation. In other words, it is non-Caribbean Western societies which had a variety of traditional pasts for whom these features are 'postmodern', not the Caribbean nor Caribbeans across the wider Atlantic world.

It is difficult for scholars in the North Atlantic to grasp this point, because they are generally heirs to academic and intellectual traditions which ideologically takes the white West as central, as the sole core, of human development over the past half-millennium. Any interpretation that disturbs this ideological understanding of the world order, particularly from within its own orbit, is unacceptable and is therefore difficult to grasp as part and parcel of the lived experience of what they like to call 'the West'.

Although not significantly explored here, our data provide ample evidence of the tension between individual autonomy and the burden of collective obligation which Durkheim (1933) saw as a fundamental problem at the root of modern societies and which continues to be problematic (see Finch, 1989). For example, nearly all our respondents who were brought up in the Caribbean spoke about the severity of the physical punishments they received, usually from their fathers; respondents tended to speak about father's 'strictness' and mother's sternness, reflecting moral codes to which they came to adhere. Whilst parental authority was exercised through the threat or use of physical force, respondents felt that such punishments were administered not out of hate, malice or cruelty but out of deep concern for the long-term well-being of children in the hostile world of the wider social system which had the hallmark of social inequalities based on dominant majoritarian perceptions of racial differentiation. Sometimes punishment was justified by reference to more moderate rules such as learning 'good manners' and the need to be 'presentable' (that is, dress and behave in acceptable ways) in the perception of the wider world. There was always a concern over whether the behaviour of the individual would bring shame onto the family or the larger network of kin, or make them collectively to feel proud.

At the same time there has been and continues to be a profound respect for the individual's freedom to act, even where the rules and boundaries of good behaviour are breached. This is perhaps most clearly expressed over the deep fear about girls becoming pregnant prior to marriage, co-habitation or a clear signal of commitment by a male partner. Consequently, girls are kept on a short leash, particularly by mothers. Once children arrive, however, they are warmly welcomed as members of the family and kinship group, with the girl's mother exuding pride at becoming a grandmother; the grandfather radiates confidence and warmth even when the sense of failure lingers. This is consistent with several points made in what must now be regarded as the classic studies of family and kinship as regards the African and mixed populations in the Caribbean (see Blake, 1961; Clarke, 1957; Henriques, 1953; M.G. Smith, 1962; R.T. Smith, 1988; see also Mohammed, 1988; Barrow, 1996). Even where the nuclear family continues to exhibit hostility or reserve about the new child, often members of the wider kinship network will assume responsibility, and with time the child is likely to be endowed with the same rights as children born within wedlock.

Although only a limited number of interviews are drawn upon in this discussion, our data set includes 180 interviews with 60 families with backgrounds in Barbados, Jamaica and Trinidad & Tobago. Our starting-point, however, was the UK, and our respondents presented us with material covering the memory and perceptions of experiences of four and sometimes five generations of their families. Whilst we collected statistical data in Britain and the Caribbean, our main methodological tool was the life-story approach (see Vansina, 1965; Thompson, 1978) which, unlike more conventional in-depth interviews seeks to capture the longer perspective of a person's life, including its rhythm, cycle and changes. Where the conventional in-depth interview technique generally focuses upon specific instances and events, and is particularly useful for conducting research amongst organisational, corporate or political leaders, the life-story approach seeks to capture the lives of individuals and communities who are not necessarily the shakers and movers of major events, but whose lives are parts of the day-to-day fabric of social structure and action. The life-story approach is therefore particularly apposite to the study of family and kinship systems because the social investigator places the emphasis on the micro and subjective dimensions of life as distinct from the macro and aggregate aspects of social and political life. This approach helped us to avoid the danger of committing what Gundar Myrdal (1969, 1944) and Frantz Fanon (1968) saw in their different ways as objectivity being used against the interests of the excluded and the colonised. The extensive questionnaire guideline we constructed to capture the intricacies of the subject's life covered such matters as childhood, education, work, aspiration, ageing, and the home from the subjective perspectives of actors. There was little or no input of a behaviouralist kind. Whilst this may be seen as a limitation because the merits of sociological observation and the partial participation in community life by the social anthropologist are missing, it should be borne in mind that our questionnaire guideline also enabled us to come closer to the individual's understanding of the relationships between parents, grandparents, siblings, lineal and affinal aunts and uncles, cousins and other members of the kinship network across generations and distance.

Expectedly, members of the families interviewed tended to utilise the kinship network as primary institutions for equipping individual members for fulfilled lives in a competitive and generally hostile world. Where what M.G. Smith (1974, 1988) called differential incor-poration into the social fabric is involved, as with Caribbeans in Britain, family and kinship links and obligations may be of particular importance. Education, the building of confidence, the acquisition of collective self and community awareness (which do not find support in the public domain), a sense of individual well-being and happiness, and the devising of survival strategies are all vitally important functions of kinship networks. Our data suggest that maintenance of transnational kinship in the Atlantic world is central to these functions in Caribbean communities in Britain in the 1990s.

The theme of transnationality that is explored in the remainder of this chapter is not new but has not hitherto been properly focused upon. The work of Thomas-Hope (1980, 1992), Goulbourne (1980), Western (1992), Olwig (1996), and Chamberlain (1997) are of particular importance in providing invaluable doumentation of the Caribbean transatlantic experience, but British and European schol-arship may not be as developed as appears to be the case in the US (see Sutton and Chaney, 1987; Foner, 1987; Basch, 1987). For example, Patterson in her work on migrant Caribbean settlers in Brixton at the beginning of the 1960s spoke about 'the close trans-Atlantic consanguineous links between migrants and their kin at home' (Patterson, 1965, p. 261), and she noted that 'the single-room society' of these settlers distanced from families in the Caribbean was inadequate 'to satisfy the individual's basic social and economic needs' (ibid., pp. 260–1). By the end of that decade and into the 1970s, marriage amongst Caribbean migrants was increasing (see Rex and Tomlinson, 1979, ch. 3; also Driver, 1982), but the figures referred to above from the 1991 national census suggest that Caribbean marriage patterns are reappearing amongst British-born offspring. The much commented upon national trends toward divorce and delayed first marriage (see Newman and Smith, 1997, pp. 16–17) would appear to both reflect and reinforce this Caribbean practice. Despite these changes over time, one factor has remained constant, namely, the close transatlantic consanguineous links referred to by Patterson. Whilst she measured this by reference to the high volume of remittances, it is significant that our respondents in the mid-1990s hardly mentioned remittances, but rather stressed other, perhaps less immediately material, links between themselves and their families 'back home'. To be sure, there are several practical links across the Atlantic as outlined in Chapter 2, which need not be reiterated here.

Two features of transnationality across the Atlantic are described in the remainder of this chapter. These are the care and affection which members provide for each other and their sense of self and national identities which are expressed through their kinship network across the Atlantic. The discussion focuses upon the lived experiences of three families, the Forbishers who are in the main Barbadians, the Whaites with backgrounds in Jamaica, and the Smiths who are predominantly Trinidadian. Each family exhibits several of the features discussed here but in their own unique ways that cannot be compressed into a general story without losing the nuances which make their narratives distinctive and meaningful. The following diagrammatic expressions of the three families focused upon in this discussion illustrate formal structures and suggest relationships. The discussion does not directly address questions of family size, composition, residence, occupation and class, gender and generation, but it is hoped that the outlines of the experiences of selected members of each family will convey the powerful meaning that they give to the transnational dimension of their individual lives and particularly their respective kinship groups.

CARE AND AFFECTION ACROSS NATIONAL BOUNDARIES

First, family and kinship networks are maintained through the regularity and frequency of visits, or what the Forbishers variously describe as the 'back and forth' movement of kin members (see Figure 7.1). Thus, Annie's seafaring maternal uncle, James, who had traversed the seas before settling in Nigeria in the 1960s as a businessman in the construction industry, decided to resettle in London with his wife whose first husband was an Indian who died young after they had produced a daughter. A number of Annie's siblings received their training in England,[1] and her family of creation has had frequent visits from members in Barbados and North America.

When Annie fell and damaged her ankle, her father, the Revd Theophilus Thompson said, 'Well, Carmen is in school, the husband has to be at work, so she'll need somebody. So, I pack my things and went to her' in London for the second time (BG120/1, Tape 2 Side A/p. 9). His great pleasure was that he could be of some help to his eldest child's family by being around, carrying Carmen on his shoulders. He also visited another daughter, Jane, and her family in Ottawa, where after praying for her neighbour's diabetic child, the Revd experienced how a kind human act can transcend apparent barriers of race.

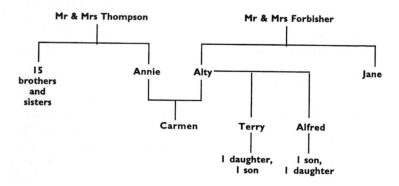

Figure 7.1   Kinship networks: the Thompsons and the Forbishers

The importance of visits is most forcefully expressed by Carmen, Annie's daughter, who started visiting her grandparents and other relatives in Barbados from as early as when she was four years old.[2] Until her fourteenth birthday Carmen visited her kinfolk in Barbados every summer. As a result her childhood memories became as filled with moments when she played with children on her street in London as when she romped in the sand in Barbados. Consequently, she could say 'I mean, by now, I know Barbados off the back of my hand. And it's almost as if, in a way, I feel as if I'm very nearly a Bajan, so to speak, but I know that I'm not' (BG091/3 Tape 1, Side A/p. 8).

There was also much practical assistance involved here. The family suffered from diabetes, and the greatest sufferer was Carmen's grandmother, who lost a leg and two children as a result. Carmen says of her grandmother:

I used to help her on with her false leg, and, basically, help her out, get a magnifying glass, and all those little things. And there's one thing I always used to remember about her, was her mole, on her, on her face. I always used to sit on her lap and play with her mole, and she used to tell me stories, and things like that. And she was, I mean, she was almost like my mother, you know, a very close bond with her. So when she did die, and I was not there, which really hurt ... it was ... oh, it was a very strange feeling, because I felt, 'Why couldn't my mum have taken me with her, so that I could see my gran for the last time?' But luckily in a way, because unlike my other cousins who live here, I, I was there every year, up to her death, in the summer, whereas they only saw her about four times. [BG091/3 Tape 1, Side A/p. 7]

These visits also helped to maintain continuity of family traditions and customs such as the laying of the table for meals, saying grace, eating together at points in a busy day, retaining religious beliefs and practices and seeking the views of family members and kinfolk. 'Talking to back home' over the telephone, writing and the sending of photographs of family members reinforced continuity and bonding across distance and came close to influencing day-to-day activities, thereby giving meaning to what Castells (1996) calls 'the network society' brought about by the informational revolution, not the existence of a global village.

The same concern about the welfare and well-being for their kin in England, the Caribbean and North America is shown by the Whaites (see Figure 7.2). But their kinship network went beyond the Atlantic world. For example, Jerry, the family historian, found that some cousins from Jamaica were living in Japan. He explained that a cousin worked in the tourist industry in Jamaica, and on one occasion she was involved in 'ushering' a group of Japanese tourists:

... and one of the guys took a liking to her, and it developed from there. Took her back to Japan, married her. And one of her brothers followed her up, well, two of her brothers followed her up, to visit, as members of the family. One of them stayed and married a Japanese girl, and he is still living there. [JF022/Tape 1, Side A/p. 9]

This young man, Kris, appears to have started a business in Osaka, marketing Jamaican health foods. Jerry also had a keen interest in

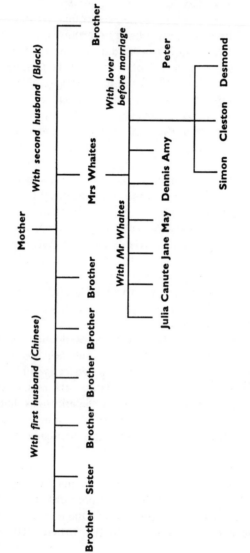

Figure 7.2   Kinship networks: the Whaites

travelling, and was planning to visit his cousins and their families in Kyoto and Osaka. The family depended on Jerry to keep members of the network in touch with each other, and he has actively encouraged them to visit each other in different countries. He himself had a strong urge to visit Jamaica which he had reluctantly left in 1966 to join his parents in London. Although Jerry went on to become the first black head boy of his school and had the opportunity of having a career as a sprinter, the coming to England was 'traumatic' for the 12-year-old boy and he longed for home. He expressed the point thoughtfully when he said:

> I decided ... if ever I'm going to go home, I'll have to do it myself, because initially, I was sent for, and it's as if, subconsciously, I was waiting to be sent back, you know. And I thought, 'No', well, obviously my parents are not going to send me back, so if I want to go, I'm going to have to do it. [JF022/Tape 1, Side A/p. 3]

Jerry first visited Jamaica in 1979 when he was 25 years old, paying for his ticket in instalments to a local travel agency. Although we do not know what impressions this first visit had on Jerry, we may surmise that the visit was important, particularly because when later he is confused and bewildered by life in England it is to Jamaica that he turned as a way out of his problems. At the age of 19, he made 14–15-year-old Yvette pregnant with their first son Simon. A white, ex-colonial family was to take care of baby Simon, because Jerry and Yvette and their families could not cope with the situation. After a year, baby Simon joined his parents and paternal grandparents in the family home. Some years later Jerry set up house with a second woman, Thelma. But his conscience got the better of him, and he returned to live with Yvette and Simon at his parents' home. Six months later he learnt through a friend that Thelma was in hospital, and rushed there to discover that he had fathered another son, Desmond. Thelma had learnt from friends that Jerry had a son with Yvette, and Jerry now wished to avoid this embarrassment being repeated and therefore informed Yvette about his son with Thelma before Yvette could hear of him from others. Both Jerry and Simon told us that Yvette was deeply upset by this news. Simon did not know this, but so too was his father, Jerry; he was caught between the mothers of his two sons, and could see no clear way forward. In 1983–84 Jerry decided that he 'had to go and chill out and sort out what I was going to do, you know' (JF022/Tape 2, Side B/p. 5). Earlier he had stated 'that's one of the reasons why I went to Jamaica for the year, because I was being pulled like here, and pulled out there, and everybody's hurt, apart from me. And I'm thinking, "No, this can't work. I've got to go away and clear my head and sort myself out"' (ibid.).

Jamaica is not only the home longed for; the island becomes a refuge, a resource to be depended upon in time of deep psychological or spiritual need. Jerry spent a whole year there, working for a maternal uncle who had a number of small businesses, but, failing to secure long-term work in Jamaica, Jerry returned to England, after sorting himself out and deciding to settle down with Yvette and his first son, Simon. Jerry and Yvette co-habited for some years before their spontaneous marriage during Yvette's first visit to Jamaica with the family for the wedding of one of Jerry's cousins.

Apart from visiting his maternal grandfather and meeting a number of cousins in Canada, Simon was keenly aware of his father's feelings about the need to maintain family contact across generations and across countries and was 'very proud of his Jamaican heritage, and that' (JF021/Tape 1, Side A/p. 2). In 1979 Jerry had planned to take Simon to Jamaica, but this did not happen, so that 'when he [Jerry] actually left, I remember crying at the airport, because I wasn't going with him' (ibid.). But this was part of the family's recent history. Jerry said that when 'my father left, it is sad, everybody was sad, you know' (JF002/Tape 1, Side B/p. 1). This was repeated when later their mother departed to join their father in London, particularly for their mother who was leaving her young children behind and entering an uncertain future. This theme of sadness was accepted as part of the experience of migration, but for Jerry and other members of his family and kinship group the opportunities appeared to balance their experience of dejection as a result of temporary separation. Jerry told us:

I remember once, one of my uncles went to the States for a while, and he came back. And the thing that struck me was the type of clothes he wore, the belts he wore, the watch he wore, the shoes he had, you know, the trousers he had. I mean, it's a visual thing, because, I don't know, maybe because the Caribbean is lots of bright colours and stuff, you pick up on these things that are different, you know. And some of the stuff was new and smelt good, and, you know ... those are the things that, you know, stuck in your mind, or stuck in my mind, anyway, you know. So I wanted to experience some of these things, cos, although they were telling you stories about it, you wanted your own experience. I mean, as young as that, I was thinking those sort of things. [JF002/Tape 1, Side B/p. 1]

This was the magic of travelling, experiencing difference and seeing the allure of new opportunities that has never left Jerry. Indeed, the lure of travel has become intertwined with family responsibilities and the need to keep members of his transnational kinship network in touch with each other.

But in addition to the sadness of family separation, the demands of family and kin spread over vast distances can take their toll on the nuclear family unit. Having experienced separation from their parents, when Jerry and his siblings arrived in London not only did they find their youngest brother, Denis, demanding the attention of their mother, but also that when 'evening comes, he said, "Mummy, you're not going to let these, these children stay here. They're not ... you have to send them back to their mummy. They can't sleep here!"' (JF020/Tape 1, Side A/p. 12). But mutual readjustments came with the family being together again. Unfortunately, this was to be fractured, because of the dual pull of kinship responsibility and possible opportunity. Having secured a job as an assistant at a medical research laboratory, Mrs Whaites had to rush to New York to help her sister-in-law take care of her mother, who was suffering from diabetes and high blood pressure. On arrival Mrs Whaites discovered that her sister-in-law herself was ill and in desperate need of help; additionally, she was keeping the three children of her sister who was ill in Jamaica and had sent them in desperation to New York. Mrs Whaites postponed her return to London and turned to cooking, washing and taking care of her in-laws and their children.

As could be expected, Mrs Whaites lost her job in London, but secured employment, illegally, as a home nurse with an elderly Jewish family. The stay in New York lasted three years, by which time (we learn not from her but from her son Jerry) she was hoping to get her green card and stay in the US and later send for her family. During her absence her husband had to manage as best he could with the family, and felt that it was his failure that one of the girls became pregnant in her early teens and then Jerry having a baby with Yvette, at the time an under-age schoolgirl. From all accounts, the family suffered as a result of Mrs Whaites' long absence, and her return provided the family with the vital missing element.

Unlike the Forbishers, the Smiths wished to avoid their kin, but they were none the less pulled into the sharing of responsibilities and the use of the network as a resource from time to time (see Figure 7.3). Thus, although his mother does not tell us, Jon recalled, and his grandmother confirmed, that there was a time when Jill and Jeremy were in such need of help that they sent Jon to Trinidad to stay with relatives for the better part of a year. Jon's memory of that period was understandably vague, but it was a time with the wider family network that he looked back on with some nostalgia. Second, when Jill's eldest sister died in 1991, Jill and Jeremy decided to take care of Ruby, the sister's ten-year-old daughter. Ruby was taken to London and brought up as a regular member of the family alongside Jon and Don, and in 1996 was preparing for her GCSE examinations at a reputable school in North London. Third, the Smiths, like the other families, made frequent visits 'back home', so that the children could meet their kin and feel that they were part of the kinship network. Again, like the other families, members of this network live in North America, particularly the US.

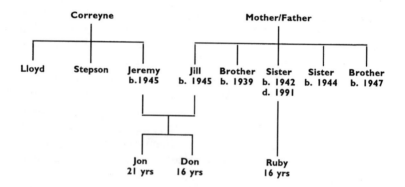

Figure 7.3   Kinship networks: the Smiths

Not surprisingly, like the other families the Smiths are also a multi-ethnic and pan-Caribbean family, with a long history of migration between islands in the Eastern Caribbean. Jon's grandfather and grandmother met in Trinidad, but they are both Grenadians whose parents migrated with them to that island. When Jeremy's mother was pregnant with him, and her lover left Trinidad to train as a dentist, family circumstances obliged her to return to Grenada so that the boy was born there. His father returned to Grenada, and according to Jon who visited and established his own independent link with his grandfather, he rose to some public prominence and wealth with his wife who was described to be from a half-white, Creole, family. Jill said of her mother, 'She's mixed with Portuguese and African Negro, that's not really politically correct! I don't know what to say. Negroid. And then my father, he was mixed with Chinese and Negroid, so there's three different mixtures. Three different races, rather' (TO 01/Tape 1, Side A/p. 1). This, as noted in an earlier chapter, is not unusual for Caribbean families in Britain. The implications of this diversity of the inner lives of Caribbean families are not, however, fully appreciated.

TRANSNATIONALITY OF SELF AND NATIONAL IDENTITIES

The second example of kinship maintenance across national boundaries is expressed through a strong sense of self and national identity through time and across distance. Figures 7.1, 7.2 and 7.3 illustrate the complexity or plurality of the transnational identities of each of our three families through their dispersed kinship network across the Atlantic. A detailed description of the structure of these relationships need not detain us from describing the meaning of this transnationality for the actors themselves.

Overt, expressive nationalism is relatively muted in the Commonwealth Caribbean, and this is perhaps more evident in Barbados than in some of the other islands. There is, however, a strong and confident and, therefore, relatively calm feeling of national identity and commitment to the country. Our Barbadian respondents, representing different generations, expressed this deep sense of national identity which posits that it does not matter where a person is born nor where they live, if there is a Barbadian connection this is what matters. National identity is least strong in Annie Forbisher, but she too expressed a view about such matters. After having enjoyed a relationship with a Kenyan Asian for seven years, his family arranged, unbeknownst to Annie, his marriage in Nairobi, bringing the relationship to an abrupt and 'very heart-breaking' end (BG 070/2, Tape 3, Side A/p. 4). It is not mere rationalisation *post factum* that led her to say, 'Well, I don't regret it, looking back now, because I'm glad I stuck more to my culture, you know' (ibid.), which was the point expressed by her father in Barbados, who was aware of the pain the breakup caused his eldest daughter. In his view it was not so much a matter of where a person lived or was born; of greater significance was the person's culture. Love for the place of birth or parents' place of birth came first in the individual's sense of identity; to disregard this is to jeopardise the well-being and happiness of the individual and the children who would result from the union.

The objection was one to do with culture and religion, not race. The arranged marriage was something they could no doubt understand, because the Thompsons, although predominantly black, had both European and South Asian predecessors, and indeed, Mr Thompson's marriage was an arranged one in the Hindu tradition. He was also of the view that a wife should follow her husband's lead, and, he believed, this would have resulted in a great deal of pain for his daughter had she married into an Indian family. Indeed, Mr Thompson expressed most clearly the sense of being Barbadian and in terms that would be understood readily by nineteenth-century European Romantics who reacted against the cosmopolitanism of the Enlightenment. He opined in terms that the German Romantic and humanist poet Herder would approve:

> Now, see the point now. If you went now, and went to the utmost, let me say you go to Germany, you might see a girl, and everything as of her appeals to you, everything. But for me, now, I'm saying it's not wisdom to make her a wife. And this is the thing now, that I showed her [Annie]. Every person that comes up at a certain level, he thinks his land to be the land. And he so yearns for it, the more he goes into old age. I can't speak with authority, but this is feeling, that the majority of people always wish they could return home, see. Now, if you marry a German woman, she has that same thing for Germany. And then you make children, see? You raise them in Germany or you raise them in Trinidad. If you raised them in Trinidad, the tendency will be Trinidad. But the mother's journey is Germany, and then you're tearing her apart when she would love to go to Germany. But then you love Trinidad. And the children now, is torn. They love you, they love her. Who must we cater to? So those are things that I show her. I said, 'the Indian, whenever he's coming up to old age, he is going to desire India'. I says, 'and not only that, as the man, you've got to give reverence to him. And he, not knowing the true God, but has a love for what is not God, but is God for him', I says, 'he's going to want his children to be trained that way. And if you are not going to have quarrels and fight and things, you gonna have to give way to him, sending your children to what is no God, and selling him. Because if you resist him ... without his

permission, then you're breeding thing'. And she saw it. [BG
120/1, Tape 2, Side A/pp. 8–9]

Several emotions or feelings about identity, conservation and per-
petuation of self, a sense of care for the future and well-being of
family and kin are involved in this expressive Romantic statement
which dismisses the challenges and opportunities of social participation that transcends mono-culturalism or the assumed cultural
singularity which is perceived to be the basis for the nation-state (see
Goulbourne, 1991a). But the location of the statement within the
contention between Enlightenment and Romanticism is not the
point here. It is sufficient to note the passion expressed about
belonging to a community through family and kin that even
unassuming nationalists within an outwardly oriented culture can
articulate in order to preserve the kin.

For Carmen, Annie's daughter and Mr Thompson's granddaugh-
ter, the tension involved in maintaining an identity across national
boundaries is obvious. Brought up in an ostensibly multicultural
Britain, she is far better equipped than either her grandfather or her
mother to understand the world of ethnic and racial pluralism, and
is at relative ease within this world of diversity. Complex questions
about mixed unions can be answered by reference to her kinship
network across the Atlantic. As she stressed:

Well, I mean, okay, you can't choose who you fall in love with,
put it that way. I mean, if it happens, it happens, whoever it's
with, whether it's with a white guy, or an Indian guy, or a Chinese
guy or an actual black guy. But there is, you've got to, people who
are in mixed relationships, you've got to have a very strong personality to put up with what people say, because one of my
friends, she had a white boyfriend, and she said that people used
to ring her house and just abuse her, saying, 'what are you
deserting your race for?' And all this.

Black friends?

Yeh. But she really liked him, and he liked her too, but ... she
couldn't take the pressure no more, so she just ended it. So, I don't
know, you've got to be able to, you've got to know that you're
going to get that sort of thing, just on the street when you're
walking, I mean.

Right. How do you feel, for instance, if one of your family relations gets involved with somebody from another race? You know, relations being cousins, that kind of thing. Does that bother you?

I don't think it does, because my Auntie Jane, she, she was married and she divorced, and she was bringing up her four kids by herself, and she was, she married, I think it was two years ago, to a white guy, a white Canadian, and, I mean, I don't ... well, he's Uncle Tim, and I don't see him any different. I mean, he fits in so well, because he has such a strong personality, and everyone warms to him. And she is happy, which is the main thing. And the bonus is that we all get along with him. So it doesn't really bother me. I mean, it would only bother me with it, any of my cousins, if it wasn't a person who could, you know, fit in with us. I mean, the point is, our family in Barbados, we're very strong, very close knit, and if someone ... you've got to be able to get on with everyone, you've got to have ... not a musical interest, but you've got to be able to adapt to surroundings. I mean, we're a very close lot. So you've got to be someone who will fit in, otherwise you'll be left on the side. [BG 091/3, Tape 2, Side A/pp. 4–5]

Carmen, not unlike other young persons of Caribbean backgrounds in Britain felt that she was 'black Caribbean', because of her parents. Not being white, Carmen did not feel that she was English or British, even though she was born and brought up in London and is a British citizen. Parentage and colour marked her off from her white mates; she was also conscious that she was somewhat different from other young people of Caribbean backgrounds whose parents came from the same island, and suggested that the mixtures were 'going to be pretty hard. People are going to have an identity crisis' (ibid., p. 5). If it had not been for her kinfolk in Barbados 'I wouldn't have much of a family really, if I think about it' (ibid., p. 6), and although, as noted earlier, she knew she was not Barbadian, she none the less looked forward to migrating to the island that her mother had left for England – the country that her grandfather saw as a great opportunity for his eldest child in the struggle for self and social improvement.

Jerry Whaites, family historian, is also a Jamaican patriot, but his patriotism is not an exclusive kind. It led him to insist that Yvette visited St Vincent where she was born before she visited Jamaica, and with Yvette's mother they went on a two-month tour to meet her kin and acquaint themselves with St Vincent. Indeed, Jerry had set it out as a condition of their being together that Yvette would visit St Vincent to renew links with her roots. He insisted that

> ... if she was going to be my partner, she would have to travel also. And one of the things that I insisted upon was that she went home, wherever it was she came from, she had to go back there to be at peace with herself, settle some of the memories she had from home, instead of just thinking about it, the way I found whatever it was I was looking for at home. So I didn't want her to come to Jamaica, initially, until she'd actually gone home first. [JF 022, Tape 2, Side B/p. 7]

These are sentiments with which the Barbadian Revd Thompson would agree: the migration process appears to require a return, a journey back to the point of departure. Travelling and meeting relatives in the islands clarified and gave coherence to the relationship between Jerry and Yvette. The journey back to roots seemed to have acted as an agglutinating factor in their lives and allowed them to move from an informal living arrangement to the formal marriage status. It was as if there were a deep unspoken matter regarding kinship affinity, self-identity and wider national or communal solidarity to be settled. A Durkheimian solidarity is achieved not through a guild or occupational group, but through the repeated theme of return (as well as the actual ability to return in both directions more than once), and the renewal of affinity. Like Carmen and her parents, Jerry felt:

> It's all well and good asking me how I see myself, especially in this society, it's how people see you. They see me as a black person, you can't hide, right? I see myself as a human being first, and as a black person of Afro-Caribbean descent. I've become a British person through rules and regulations, but I can never ever be English. Not even my sons who were born here, they might be English on paper, but they will not, they will not be regarded as such. They will always be Afro-Caribbean, or West Indian .... or black, yes. And this is why I'm, I'm insistent about them learning about where their parents are from, right? Taking Cleston and Simon, and even Desmond's been back to the Caribbean, so at least they've got an idea of where their parents are from, which I think is very important, you know. I mean, I always thought that

we've got this escape hatch in the back of our minds, those of us who are not born here, where we can always go back to. But those who are born here haven't got that, it's just stories to them, you know. [ibid., p. 13]

For Jerry the Caribbean background, like the more distant African past, is a resource for Caribbean families in Britain, but there is a responsibility on the part of parents to ensure that their children experience this heritage through deliberate and direct exposure, and not to leave it as 'just stories'.

The crucial set of questions that released Jon Smith from an English reserve to express his frustrations with being British of Trinidadian background is this:

What about other young black people in England ... do you think that it's difficult for them to get on in Britain?

Yeh. It is difficult to get on in England. It kind of creates a ... well, my theory is that the reason there are a lot of black people in mental institutions, a higher proportion than in the normal population, 'normal', well, indigenous population, is that you have to, you don't have to, but you find yourself having to divide your mind. And you're working in a white environment, living in a white environment, and then you find yourself in a black environment with your family and your friends, so that creates, that creates a lot of pressure for people, and they find, like, they're not accepted in the white community fully. I mean, they're accepted. But there's always the odd slight, or the odd patronising remark, or outright discrimination. And in the black community, there's people who still, who, like, retreat into the bunker to cope with the problems in Britain, and they see a white person and they just cut them dead. So a person who has been in a white environment with white people, if they see you're like that, then they'll cut you dead, and that creates a stress in people's minds, so that sends them over the edge. So, I think that's why it's difficult for black people, because they have to try and assimilate, not assimilate, kind of get on in the white environment, because those are the people who control everything in Britain. But at the same time they want to stay, you know, you have to stay true to your roots, so that creates a big pressure. [TA 015, Tape 1, Side A/p. 14]

It was never explicit but nearly always implicit in the discussion with the Smiths that in order to succeed, a distance between extended family, kin and the nuclear family had to be maintained. Consequently, the transnational kinship network was not seen as a resource, but more as a drain on the nuclear unit or as a constraint on the accumulation possible within that narrow frame. For example, in multicultural Britain Jon interpreted the pluralism to which he is heir as a drawback: 'when I go home it's always reinforced that you're black and Trinidadian, West Indian, and you know, it's just, it's embedded into your head that, you know, you're different. I can't really explain it (TA 015, Tape 1, Side B/p. 8).

Like his parents, Jon felt that he had always been committed to the ideal of the nuclear family. He could not, therefore, understand his paternal grandfather who did not see his son, Jeremy, until he was an adult and sought out his father. But, then, Jon admitted that he had 'always been fed ... my grandmother's line, you know, that he [his paternal grandfather] ran off or whatever, he treated her badly' (ibid., p. 4). Jon was always concerned about meeting this prominent Grenadian public figure who had made his name as a professional man, but whom he found to be 'quite fierce, he's quite an intimidating person' (ibid.) with whom he managed to get on well. Would-be monogamous Jon learnt that this grandfather had 'other children sort of dotted around, you know ... and plus he married somebody else, and had children. He's got grandchildren from that wife, yes' (ibid., p. 5).

Additionally, and more confusingly, Jon had a steady white girlfriend, but he felt that her family was less than comfortable with him. Jon described them in the following terms:

> Her parents, I think, although they're polite, I still think they're a bit, I don't know whether they're used to it now, but at first they were a bit uncomfortable with it. Not disapproving, just worried about what I'd be like, you know, they're very ... I still find them quite formal when they're with me, sort of desperate not to put their foot in the wrong place, offend. [ibid., p. 6]

Jon had a close understanding of the British youth scene, but was keenly aware that he was not English, 'because England isn't home' (ibid., p. 7). He always thought of himself as being Trinidadian, although he was born and brought up in London and his parents were of the view that Jon saw himself as English, and his mother wanted her children to adapt to British society. Jon himself, however, said that he

> ... always felt blood is, blood is what you are, not really the type of ... not really the place where you are born, it's more blood, blood-related, I think is what you are. And I've always seen Trindadian, Trinidadian especially, as opposed to West Indian, because in Britain, everyone's a Jamaican it seems! [Laughs] So I've always been quite strong on this, like, people say, 'Are you Jamaican?' I say, 'No, no, I'm not. I'm Trinidadian' I've always been quite proud of that, yeh. So I'd say half, half British, half Trinidadian, yes. Yes. [TA 015, Tape 1, Side B/p. 8]

Many of the sentiments expressed reveal tensions caused by the wider social order for families and kinship groups and these straddle the public and private spheres of life in several ways. What is clear, however, is that these tensions raise questions about what is seen, not uncontentiously, as a multicultural Britain, as discussed in earlier chapters. For example, what might come readily to the mind of many is Lord Tebbitt's attack on the multicultural society at the Conservative Party's annual conference at Blackpool in the autumn of 1997 as inappropriate for modern Britain. However, his antipathy to what many liberals understand as a multicultural society (tolerance of diversity) has been frequently expressed by him since at least the late 1980s (see, for example, Tebbitt, 1990; Mishan, 1988; cf. Goulbourne, 1991a).

CONCLUSION

The discussion in this chapter has emphasised one dominant theme in the living arrangements of Caribbean communities in Britain, namely, the transnational dimension of family and kinship across the Atlantic as an example of the Caribbean diasporic experience. The discussion has focused on the care provided to members as well as the maintenance of self and communal identities, and although these features are not unique to these segments of the national British community, the characteristics described may be more pronounced where Caribbeans are concerned. It is therefore necessary to take this powerful feature into account when assessing development and continuity in Caribbean communities in Britain. The variety and complexity of these kinship networks should serve as a caution against hasty conclusions about the capacity of these communities to provide the wherewithal for their survival. Racially and ethnically diverse, the transnational character of Caribbean kinship is a significant aspect of a deep-rooted strategy for survival, in terms of well-being and identity, within the wider social system in which Caribbeans are differentially, and therefore inequitably, incorporated. These features, however, raise pressing questions of policy for the immediate future, as the next chapter suggests.

8 Returning 'Home' from the 'Mother Country' in the 1990s

A major feature of the summer of 1998 was the media and community celebrations of the fiftieth anniversary of the docking of the SS *Empire Windrush* at Tilbury with nearly five hundred Jamaican migrants. This event has been long regarded as marking the beginning of sizeable migration to post-war Britain, or what Jamaica's celebrated poet, Louise Bennett,[1] humorously described as 'colonisation in reverse'. While the celebrations properly highlighted the significance of black entry to and settlement in Britain, the return process has also been a dynamic aspect of the Caribbean diasporic experience.

This has been reinforced by several factors, including the long-cherished motivation of the immigrant generation to return, their ageing in the 1980–90s, the problems they and their offspring faced in Britain, and the relative ease with which the desire to live in the Caribbean could be realised by the more fortunate in the 1990s. Whilst the phenomenon of return is far from being new, it is suggested here that the volume and patterns of return in the 1990s created new opportunities as well as raised problems for families and fresh social and policy issues for relevant authorities in Britain and those Commonwealth Caribbean countries, such as Barbados and Jamaica, which are immediately affected.

THE VOLUME AND NATURE OF 'RETURN'

As noted in the first chapters of this book, the period of significant migration to Britain from the countries which now comprise the Commonwealth Caribbean occurred between 1948 and 1962 but, following the Commonwealth Immigration Act 1962 which established a quota system to restrict drastically the entry of black and brown immigration into Britain, the Caribbean-born population has consistently utilised the option of returning to their homelands. Several observers have variously commented on this tendency-to-return phenomenon from the 1960s (see, for example, Thomas-Hope, 1980; Patterson, 1968). In the 1990s studies by Byron and Condon (1996) and Peach (1991) have concentrated on the ageing Caribbean-born population and their return to the region and, to a lesser extent, their possible re-migration (most likely to North America). Peach showed that from a high of over 330,000 in 1966 the Caribbean-born population declined to 233,000 in 1986–88 (Peach, 1991, p. 2). After taking into account 1,457 deaths over the period, he concluded that re-migration to North America and return migration to the Caribbean must have accounted for the majority of the 97,000 decline in this element of the UK population. Drawing on the 1991 British national census and the regional census by CARICOM (the Commonwealth Caribbean economic community) of the same year, Byron and Condon (1996, p. 96) suggested that between 1981 and 1991 the Caribbean-born population in the UK declined by 26,988 persons or approximately 9 per cent, after taking into account the deaths of 3,600 persons.

With respect to destination, Peach (1991, pp. 12–14) speculated that during the two decades from 1966 over 50 per cent of returnees, or about 48,000, would be destined for Jamaica, with Barbados receiving the next highest number of returnees at about 7,000. This was because over 50 per cent of Commonwealth Caribbean migrants to Britain came from Jamaica, with Barbados being the next largest sending country (see Peach, 1968; also, Deakin, 1970, chs 3 and 4) and the 1991 census returns confirmed a continuing predominance by people of Jamaican background in the Caribbean community in Britain (see Owen, 1994). It is not surprising, therefore, that Jamaica is the destination of the vast majority of people returning to the region.

Table 8.1   Number of returning residents to Jamaica, 1993–97

Year	UK	US	Canada	Other	Total
1993	919	988	278	174	2,359
1994	1,145	999	333	110	2,587
1995	1,007	905	288	153	2,353
1996	995	863	296	114	2,268
1997	995	762	244	91	2,092
Total	5,061	4,517	1,439	642	11,659

Source: Returning Residents Facilitation Unit, Ministry of Foreign Affairs & Foreign Trade/Jamaica Customs & Excise, 1997

A strong indication of this was the fact that the government of Jamaica was the first to provide a structure for the management of

Table 8.2   Number of returning residents to Jamaica by month, 1993–94

Month	UK 1993	UK 1994	US 1993	US 1994	Canada 1993	Canada 1994	Cayman 1993	Cayman 1994	Other 1993	Other 1994	Total 1993	Total 1994
Jan	44	99	58	75	10	25	00	00	9	11	121	210
Feb	36	70	45	47	03	18	00	00	6	11	90	146
Mar	38	96	53	69	17	29	00	00	14	9	122	203
Apr	67	86	62	72	07	18	00	00	14	8	150	184
May	78	100	67	85	23	25	00	00	21	7	189	217
Jun	74	78	75	98	19	29	00	00	14	6	182	211
Jul	85	83	91	114	32	37	00	00	15	7	223	241
Aug	74	78	113	105	34	28	00	00	23	9	244	220
Sept	78	73	105	86	28	25	00	00	21	7	232	191
Oct	92	118	84	76	19	32	00	00	8	10	203	136
Nov	150	124	105	70	43	33	00	00	19	11	317	238
Dec	103	140	130	102	43	34	00	00	10	14	286	290
Total	919	1,145	988	999	278	333	00	00	174	110	2,359	2,487

Source: Returning Residents Facilitation Unit, Ministry of Foreign Affairs & Foreign Trade/Jamaica Customs & Excise, 1995

the process of returning citizens and residents through the establishment of the Returning Residents Facilitation Unit (RRFU). Before, however, considering the arrangements in place in Jamaica and Barbados for returnees in the last decade, it is first relevant to indicate further the volume of return to Jamaica, the country with the largest migrant population and for which data were available by the end of the 1990s.

In the first instance, Table 8.1 shows the obvious fact that the vast majority of people who returned to Jamaica were from North America and Britain. The table does not show the figure for 1992, but according to the RRFU in that year 1,552 persons returned to Jamaica 'who would have met the criteria of the Returning Residents Programme' (RRFU, 1997) had it been in operation at the time. The numbers increased and remained at over 2,000 in the four years from 1993 to 1996, as Table 8.1 shows. The RFFU identified the British dependency of the Caymans as a specific departure point, but since 1996 the Caymans is subsumed under the 'other' category, no doubt because whilst there was a steady flow of returnees there were never many Jamaicans returning from this prosperous and nearby dependency.

The second characteristic to note from Table 8.1 and subsequent tables is that whilst the returnees from North America constituted a simple majority, the single largest contingent of Jamaicans returning to the island was from the UK. This difference may have been due to two important factors. First, sizeable post-Second World War migration from Jamaica and the rest of the then British West Indies to North America occurred later than migration to Britain, due largely to the restrictions placed on Caribbean migrants by the American Congress's McCarran-Walter Act of 1952 (see Roberts and Mills, 1958; also cf. Fryer, 1984, ch. 11; Peach, 1968). Consequently, there may be proportionally more of this cohort of elderly Jamaican-born people in Britain than in North America. It was not unreasonably generally assumed that the elderly are the larger proportion of those returning, suggesting that the 'myth of return' that Anwar (1979) spoke about almost two decades ago has less relevance for Caribbean communities in Britain than for Pakistanis with whom he was concerned. As returns from the 1991 census showed, the elderly in the Caribbean population in the UK came closest to the broad apex in the age pyramid of the indigenous white population (Owen, 1996; see also Warnes, 1996). Second, the proximity of Caribbean points of departure and North American destinations facilitated greater frequency of visits and may have also meant that there was less of a felt need to return on a long-term or permanent basis. Two examples may be in order here. Statistical returns from the Jamaica Ministry of Tourism showed that 64.5 per cent of 'stop-over visitors' in Jamaica in 1995 were from the US, with another 9.5 per cent from Canada; in contrast, the percentage for the UK was 9.9 per cent. The figures for the preceding years from 1991 were similar for these three countries (Planning Institute of Jamaica, 1996, Table 14.3). Permanent visas issued in Kingston by the US and Canadian embassies and the UK High Commission told a similar story: 14,239 permanent visas to the US; 3,577 to Canada; and a mere 242[2] to the UK (ibid., ch. 17). In other words, regular and frequent contacts between North America and Jamaica far out-distanced those between the island and the UK, and these contacts along with the relative proximity may partly explain the motivation to return on a long-term basis by UK residents.

Table 8.3   Number of returning residents to Jamaica by month, 1996

Month	UK	US	Canada	Other	Total
January	84	62	25	07	178
February	57	52	14	08	131
March	58	43	13	09	123
April	65	59	16	05	145
May	78	63	17	11	169
June	66	73	20	05	164
July	75	85	33	13	206
August	62	85	27	17	191
September	68	70	27	13	178
October	138	98	32	13	281
November	125	80	32	06	243
December	119	93	40	07	259
Total	995	863	296	114	2,268

Source: Returning Residents Facilitation Unit, Ministry of Foreign Affairs & Foreign Trade/Jamaica Customs & Excise, 1997

The overall picture conveyed by Tables 8.1 to 8.4 is of a 1990s Jamaica experiencing considerable levels of re-migrations from across the Atlantic or North America. Table 8.2 shows the number of returnees to Jamaica on a monthly basis throughout 1993 and 1994 from the UK, the US, Canada and other places. Apart from July, September and November there were increases of returnees from the

UK throughout 1994, and there was only a marginal difference between the numbers returning from the US and the UK, although the Jamaican community in the US is larger than that in the UK. However, Table 8.3 shows that whilst the volume of UK returnees remained larger than that from the US, the North American volume continued to be slightly larger throughout 1996 and 1997.

(There are, of course, important aspects of the return phenomenon which these figures did not tell. For example, it should be stressed that the return migration phenomenon was not simply a matter of migrants returning to the region after their sojourn in Britain. Many of those described as returnees were in fact migrants to the region, because they were born and brought up in the UK or they were spouses of individuals from, or with close links in, the region. These characteristics of the Caribbean communities in the UK were reflected in the difficulty officials in the Caribbean have in describing the status of returnees who are variously referred to as 'returning residents', 'returning citizens' and 'returning nationals'. However, none of these is an adequate description of all the people involved in the process, confirming King's (1986) observation that there are several models of return migration. /

Three factors help to explain this situation. First, from at least the 1970s the majority of people of Caribbean background in Britain were born in the UK but due to their well-documented unfavourable differential incorporation many share the long-term aspiration of their parents to live in the Caribbean and a small minority take the step to fulfil this dream. Second, as noted in an earlier chapter, people of Caribbean backgrounds in Britain exhibit a strong tendency towards exogenous marriages and living companionships, with a significant percentage of children (over 20 per cent) in this segment of the community having both Caribbean and indigenous white parents (see Owen, 1996). It is not surprising, therefore, that some individuals from Caribbean communities in Britain who are treated as returnees are in fact migrants, but who go to the Caribbean, not unlike Caribbean migrants to Britain between 1948 and 1962, with an initial sense of belongingness (see, for example, Carter, 1986; Cross and Entzinger, 1986). After all, many would have visited the Caribbean to see members of their kin networks or visited as tourists, as suggested in the last chapter. Third, as earlier noted, there is no legal obstacle to the fulfilment of the desire to live in the region.

Table 8.4   Number of returning residents to Jamaica by month, 1997

Month	UK	US	Canada	Other	Total
January	97	61	20	11	189
February	74	50	16	11	151
March	66	55	14	10	145
April	72	46	13	07	138
May	75	57	18	04	154
June	84	64	20	10	178
July	83	77	25	04	189
August	52	75	20	11	158
September	90	78	21	10	189
October	113	65	25	03	206
November	93	54	23	07	177
December	96	80	29	03	208
Total	995	762	244	91	2,082

Source: Returning Residents Facilitation Unit, Ministry of Foreign Affairs & Foreign Trade/Jamaica Customs & Excise, 1998

Another aspect of the return migration experience that is extraneous to the figures the tables suggest is that the return is not a permanent or static feature but is rather a recurring and dynamic process. This is also no doubt an important difference from earlier experiences of migration and return (to Panama, Cuba) in the region (see, for example, Richardson, 1985). In other words, the experiences of families reveal a fairly regular pattern of return to the Caribbean often followed by 'return' to the UK. This is true both for the elderly Caribbean-born returnees as well as young people who were born and brought up in the UK and who, on 'returning' to the region with some members of their families, do not necessarily close off their options to find their way back to the UK. As Byron and Condon (1996, p. 91) noted, the act of return to the point of departure is not necessarily a 'completion step in the process' of the migration experience. Members of the Caribbean community in the wider Atlantic world constitute a fairly well-integrated world which transcends the boundaries of the nation-states to which individuals are obliged to belong.

THE STRUCTURE AND CONTENTS OF SUPPORT

The return phenomenon raises questions about the nature and structure of support for returning residents or citizens and their families. These include informal supports such as are provided by families themselves as well as the more formal public structures through which support is channelled. The latter includes the facilitation units mentioned earlier, established by the Jamaican and Barbadian governments, island associations and a variety of welfare bodies that Caribbean communities have established over the years in Britain and increasingly in Jamaica and Barbados; and the formal structure of relations between Britain and Commonwealth Caribbean states, as outlined in Chapter 2. The nature of family support across the Atlantic was discussed in the last chapter, but a brief comment on aspects of the formal mechanisms of public support in the UK and particularly in the Caribbean may be useful here.

((Whatever the actual size of return migration during the years since the 1960s, it was not until the 1990s that governments in the Caribbean have been forced to take account of the volume and patterns of return of citizens and their families. As stated earlier, Jamaica was the first to do so, followed by Barbados. St Lucia, which is also experiencing a significant volume of returning citizens and their families (Abenaty, 2000, 2001), by 2000 was also set to follow the Jamaican and Barbadian lead. In contrast to Barbados and Jamaica, officials in Trinidad & Tobago in the late 1990s had not felt a need to establish any special unit to facilitate returnees, because the volume had not been significant (interview with Arthur Harper, 29 July 1996; interview with Jennifer Sampson, 29 July 1996). The work of Jamaica's RRFU and Barbados' Facilitation Unit for Returning Nationals (FURN) may none the less be the direction for the future as more of these small and vulnerable states are forced to take seriously the flow of returnees in their various guises.

In Jamaica, the RRFU was established under former Ambassador Don Brice in 1993 within the Ministry of Foreign Affairs and Foreign Trade. Brice had served in Barbados and had led the Jamaican team in the negotiations to extend membership of CARICOM beyond the Commonwealth Caribbean (interview with Don Brice, 7 August 1996). The appointment of this senior diplomat would suggest that the Jamaican government was giving priority to this initiative. Following suit, in 1996 the Barbadian government established the FURN, also within the Ministry of Foreign Affairs under the coordination of Jeffrey Hunte, a senior foreign service official who had served in London and knew the Barbadian community in the UK well (interview with Jeffrey Hunte, 1 August 1996). Like the Jamaican RRFU, one of the first actions of the FURN was to publish a booklet setting out the government's generous concessions to intending returnees, and in the view of some Jamaicans in London the Barbadian Charter for Returning and Overseas Nationals is much more generous than its Jamaican model, the Charter for Long-Term Returning Residents. Consistent with the establishment of these bodies, the Jamaican and Barbadian governments took steps actively to provide relevant information to intending returnees, and their high commissions, embassies and consulates in Britain and North America have accessible facilities for families with such plans. In particular, coinciding with the promotion of JamaicaExpo exhibitions to the UK from the mid-1990s, Don Brice and Lloyd Wilkes at the High Commission organised seminars in London to inform and advise potential returnees about the facilities, opportunities and difficulties in Jamaica. These meetings were usually well attended, and lively and well-informed discussions took place about the issues returnees and intending returnees raised. In addition, the Jamaican *Gleaner* newspaper, which is widely circulated in the Jamaican and Caribbean communities in Britain, from time to time published a returning residents supplement and newspapers in Barbados sometimes carried important news about returnees. The unit also early established a website accessible to all who wished to consult it for information about the developing situation across the Atlantic.

The Barbadian and Jamaican facilitation units collected relevant data about returnees and their families from customs, embassies, high commissions, community associations and other relevant bodies. They provided information about the total process of return, including government concessions with respect to customs and excise duties, the expected pitfalls of return, the opportunities available to returnees, and a databank of the skills of returnees with the aim of facilitating their contribution to the Jamaican and Barbadian economies. During the course of our research, particularly in 1996–97, the skills databank in Jamaica was in the process of being developed, but in London the Barbadian National Resettlement and Development Council, coordinated by the High Commission, already was keeping details of intending returnees' skills. In discussions with the units' directors in Bridgetown and Kingston in 1996 it was suggested that it would be useful to researchers as well as policy makers for the data to be disaggregated according to gender, age and intended areas of re/settlement, and we have been assured that these suggestions will be taken into account in the development of these databanks. By the beginning of 1998, the unit in collaboration with a range of public and private bodies in Jamaica, the Jamaica/European Commission joint project for Return and Reintegration Programme of Jamaican Nationals for Development under the International Organisation for Migration (IOM), had been able successfully to assist individuals – several from the UK – to secure senior posts (Ministry of Foreign Affairs and Foreign Trade, 1998, appendix ii).

Returning nationals and their families as well as the governments of the respective countries benefited from the activities of island and welfare associations on both sides of the Atlantic. The island associations were generally established during the period of entry and settlement in British cities, particularly from the mid-1950s (see, for example, Goulbourne, 1990; Fitzgerald, 1988; also Heineman, 1972). But while it was generally thought that with time these organisations would atrophy through lack of support from migrants' children, many of these organisations have remained buoyant with the active support of retired migrants as well as younger people who wish to maintain and celebrate their parents' Caribbean heritage which is a living part of their present. For example, Hinds (1992) found that there were 15 such associations operating in London; the dozen amongst which he conducted research had a total of 2,854 members. Of course, memberships vary, but Hinds' figures suggested that each association had an average of 238 members. In other parts of the country researchers have reported similarly (see, for example, Hylton, 1997a; Goulbourne, 1990), suggesting that these bodies were very much alive and active in Caribbean communities. During the course of our own research we found these associations to be invaluable in gaining access to members of specific island communities in Britain as well as 'back home'.

In the main, these associations have been concerned with maintaining close links with their members' homelands, the preservation of island cultures, helping members with welfare problems, providing assistance to nationals in Britain and the Caribbean and on specific occasions mobilising around political or natural crises 'back home'. In the 1990s, the return migration process is another factor that gave new life to these bodies, because they were well placed to provide assistance to members planning to return or re-migrate. Along with their other functions, these associations served as forums for transmitting information about those who had taken the step to return and from time to time visit families and friends residing in what Rastafarians call 'Babylon'.

Just as Caribbean migrants to Britain formed associations to provide for their needs, so too when they returned to the region they were busy forming returning residents' or nationals' associations in the 1990s. There were associations in all 14 parishes, or administrative units, in Jamaica (interview with John Small, 7 August 1997; interview with Steve Batchelor, 5 August 1996), and they are also widespread in Barbados (interview with Melvin Drayton, 2 August 1996). These bodies may have been seen as Caribbean extensions of their British counterparts, because they were inspired by much the same concerns about integration in the local community, defending their interests and bringing their comparative experience to bear on particular situations. Immigrants to Britain needed to protect themselves, to provide companionship and help for each other in a less than friendly environment; on returning to the islands they soon found that the experiences during their sojourns had changed them, unaware, into English men and women. They were discovering that they speak differently, walk, dress, shop and go about their daily routines in ways that were not merely 'foreign', but peculiarly 'English' in the eyes of their erstwhile countrywomen and men and those who had not travelled, or whose sojourn had taken them to North America and elsewhere closer home. The returnee from Britain was often an incomprehensible oddity closer to Noel Coward's 'mad dog and English man out in the mid-day sun' syndrome, than to the relaxed stoical person who embarked on the migration route some decades ago.

Of course, the situation in the 1990s was not helped by the fact that the returnee frequently decided to re/settle in an area some distance from where they had close family connections, thereby realising another aspect of the Caribbean migrant's dream, that is, self-improvement defined in terms of physical relocation or residential upward social mobility (see Thomas-Hope, 1992). For example, in Jamaica the hill town of Mandeville has acquired the reputation of being a desirable destination for returnees who have created a prosperous ghetto characterised by some English pastimes: the cultivation and display of well-manicured lawns and gardens ordered more for aesthetic satisfaction than for practical use, which stand in sharp contrast with the utilitarian kitchen and fruit gardens of rural Jamaica; and the rounding off of the afternoon with English tea. Some would see an irony here because the town of Mandeville in the parish of Manchester, like Simla in the Himalayan foothills, used to be the retreat for British administrators during the hottest months in the colonial past. And while not new colonalists, by the end of the decade returnees have come to be seen as highly visible and easy targets by robbers and gunmen, as the British press reported from time to time from the late 1990s and into the present century.

But there is also a salutary display of the wish to help the less fortunate who did not travel, or who travelled but suffered at the hands of service providers and lawyers at the point of return, therefore consciously or unconsciously building on a long tradition of Anglo-Caribbean philanthropy (see, for example, Bryan, 1990). As the Foreign Minister, Seymour Mullings, acknowledged, returnees 'are quietly reintroducing to Jamaica by example the tenets of civil society – the spirit of community' (Ministry of Foreign Affairs and Foreign Trade, 1998, p. 25), and he highlighted their voluntary contributions in health, education and social care for children and the elderly. It is significant that in Jamaica, returnees from North America did not felt the need to organise to promote or defend interests particular to themselves whilst the less numerous British returnees have been compulsive organisers whose voices are now being heard, if only in a minor key, by policy makers. This suggests that the important differences in British and North American migrant experiences that some commentators have pointed to (see, for example, Thomas-Hope, 1992) remain and have significant implications in the return loop of the Caribbean diasporic experience.

There has, of course, been a well-established structure of relations between the British state and states in the Commonwealth Caribbean. This provided an overall context within which the process of return could be managed and made relatively easy, even if not as easy as movements between metropolitan France and her overseas territories in the region (see Byron and Condon, 1996; also, Hintjens, 1997, 1995). This includes the state-to-state relations between specific Caribbean and UK governments through membership of the Commonwealth but also independently of this body. For example, Commonwealth membership helps to ensure the enjoyment of dual citizenship status, residential and voting rights where local by-laws and regulations (such as residency or entry on the electoral roll) are met and the sharing of a number of judicial and political institutions, some of which are about to change (see, for example, *The Lawyer* 14 July 1998, p. 48; S. Goulbourne, 2001).

One arrangement which is independent of Commonwealth membership and is of paramount importance for the returnee or those migrating from the UK to the region concerns pensions and benefits. Whilst there have long been provisions for a person to exercise their pension rights abroad, there are restrictions regarding the receipt of benefits, inflation rise, and specific bilateral agreements which have had to be entered into with Britain. In the late 1980s the British Commission for Racial Equality investigated this matter after they were alerted by a Rastafarian group in London to the potential for unfair discrimination against members through the benefits rules. The CRE's report (1992) revealed that whilst some countries had entered into agreements with the UK, there were some such as Grenada, which had not and this worked against their (returning) citizens' interests. In the case of Barbados and Jamaica, fortunately there have been agreements from which returnees can now benefit. Jamaica was one of the first countries in the 1970s to take advantage of this regime and in 1992 Barbados did the same.

There are, however, several kinds of benefits and each bilateral agreement must specify which are covered. For example, in the case of Jamaica only six benefits were covered (whereas a similar agreement with Cyprus covered nine); however, whilst the Jamaican agreement did not cover invalidity benefits at the time of the report, it now does, as will be seen from the details on Table 8.5. The CRE report noted that there were three conditions which appeared to govern these agreements: reciprocity, that is countries entering into such agreements with Britain should have similar systems in operation to that in the UK; substantial population exchange; and third, there should not be a situation of Britain 'exporting benefits' to another country. These and related issues remain to be further researched and their implications for transnational families considered, but at this point it is pertinent to turn to some of the problems and opportunities involved in the return phenomenon.

PROBLEMS, OPPORTUNITIES AND POLICY ISSUES OF 'RETURN'

Several problems and opportunities are generated by the process of return and resettlement. These include both psychological and practical difficulties involved in the decision to move from one physical and social location to another, and these are often compounded by the returnees' memories and expectations. Problems associated with customs and excise rules, health services, house prices and residential choice and concentration as well as the less than professional behaviour of some lawyers have been at the root of the returnees' practical concerns and these have tended to influence not only the final decision to return but also the day-to-day struggles involved in the process of re/settlement.

As noted earlier, the Jamaican RFFU and the Barbadian FURN set out terms that were generous to returnees. In the first place, the returnee is generously defined with respect to nationality law and the number of years spent abroad in order to qualify for the concessions offered. The Jamaican charter described a national as a person who had attained the age of 18 and who had 'been resident overseas for not less than the past three consecutive years' (RRFU, 1995, p. 5); the Barbadian charter spoke of a 'citizen by birth, descent, registration or naturalisation' returning to the island after ten years abroad (FURN, 1996, p. 5). While Jamaica has been more lenient with the number of years spent abroad to qualify as a returning resident, Barbados was more generous about specific concessions regarding personal possessions and cars, but both charters were careful to set out in considerable detail the provisions for returning nationals about household and personal possessions, motor vehicles and tools of trade, each of which was carefully defined and described to avoid ambiguity and uncertainty.

None the less, and as might be expected, intending and actual returnees complained about the restrictions imposed on items such as the number of televisions, furniture and so forth that they could take without charge into Barbados or Jamaica. There were also complaints about the level of tax placed on more expensive items such as cars. In Jamaica returnees frequently complained about more day-to-day aspects of life such as the rough-and-ready or brusque manners of public functionaries such as customs officers, lawyers, secretaries and others with whom returnees come into close contact at the time of return and soon thereafter as they resettled.

In Barbados there have been signs of a degree of resentment against returnees receiving favourable differential treatment at excise and customs. Many of these issues were discussed by their associations in Britain and the Caribbean. Both in Britain and Jamaica a number of these associations published fairly regular newsletters for the benefit of members, and meetings were organised around actual or potential difficulties returning residents or nationals will face. Jamaicans were particularly vociferous about these issues, and they felt that having lived and worked hard for their possessions in a hostile British environment, they should be allowed to take them without too much let or hindrance back to a Jamaica which they had continued to regard as home during what many saw as their painful sojourn. A long-standing issue faced by some returnees has been that of dishonest estate dealers and lawyers (see, for example, Ministry of Foreign Affairs and Foreign Trade, 1998). There have been cases of individuals returning with their families to find that the properties they thought they had been paying for over several years from hard-earned savings either did not exist or were owned by others. In addition, whilst some elderly returnees tend to express the view that they had no desire to return to the UK, there was a general feeling that they might visit family members, especially their children and grandchildren who continued to live there. Any actual or perceived restriction on entry by those who did not register under the British nationality laws of 1981 and 1983 were generally seen as unreasonable and unnecessary. This folk-like simplicity about nationality rights (of movement, etc.) has been a powerful expression of a feeling of belongingness within a wider Atlantic world, however uncomfortable this may be as a result of differential incorporation within this world.

This question is closely tied to the most deleterious set of problems faced by returnees, namely the sensitive area of health. Many returnees were, as noted earlier, young people who may have been expected to be healthy and easily insurable by the many of the private companies active in the region. It may be supposed, however, that the vast majority of returnees were born in these countries and are now in their twilight years of retirement, the period of life in which these individuals look forward to reaping some of the small benefits of a life of hard work in a foreign land, even if that land was regarded by some as 'the mother country' in an imperial myth that was central to the colonial Caribbean they left four or five decades. The age profile of the majority of returnees sets the framework for the kinds of health problems they were likely to face: high blood pressure, diabetes and old-age infirmities. Returnees from Britain faced particular difficulties, and Jamaicans appeared to face greater problems than Barbadians. In Barbados the health and social security systems were more comprehensive than in Jamaica and the less fortunate returnees were more likely to receive help than in Jamaica where assistance appeared to have been less progressive (interview with Dr Beverley Miller, 1 August 1996; interview with Dr Peter Phillips, 25 July 1996). For example, in Barbados it was possible for persons with pensions which fell below the national average to be topped up, and by 1996 there had been at least one such instance of assistance to a returnee from the UK, as pointed out by officials (interview with Lloyd Bradshaw, 1 August 1996; interview with Charles Corbin, 1 August 1996).

In Jamaica, returnees appeared to be in need of state assistance in making adequate health arrangements for their later years. This problem may have stemmed from a widespread view in Britain that it is the state's responsibility to provide medical care for citizens who contributed their taxes to the public purse and therefore the individual need not enter into private arrangements with insurance companies or medical firms. The reliance on private providers of health care is still relatively new to the post-Beveridge British public as a whole and Caribbean returnees shared this ideology of cooperative or socialised medical provision which may be inappropriate to specific Caribbean countries such as Jamaica, whose health and public services suffered as a consequence of persistently worsening economic situations in the 1970s, 1980s and the first part of the 1990s. In contrast, people returning from the US appeared not to have this problem, because in that country the general assumption is that the individual will see to his or her family's health needs through private arrangements. Jamaican returnees from Britain were therefore in need of the assistance of the UK and the Jamaican governments to establish schemes with medical insurance companies, and in the late 1990s there were discussions taking place along such lines between some leaders of returnees, the Jamaican government and the American company Blue Cross. In the meanwhile, it appeared that for those who can afford it, one option was to visit the UK periodically for monitoring and treatment of health conditions and to purchase drugs less expensively. Obviously, it is in situations such as this that family members still in the UK may provide assistance to those who have returned to the Caribbean.

Apart from the frailties of old age (see, Blakemore and Boneham, 1994), it is becoming better known that members of the Caribbean community in Britain are more likely to suffer from some ailments than the majority ethnic community (see, for example, Ahmad, 1993; Ahmad and Atkin, 1996). The health problems frequently referred to include diabetes, high blood pressure and various heart conditions, and these are also some of the health problems that leaders of returnees associations (interview with Steve Batchelor, 5 August 1996; interview with Gloria Riley, 6 August 1996) and medics have pointed to as matters of immediate concern.[3]

There is no intention to leave the impression that returning to the Caribbean is nothing but a fraught business. It must now be obvious that whilst there were and are likely to be a number of problems facing many of those who decide to return and settle in Barbados and Jamaica, there have also been many opportunities for those seeking to make or re-establish their homes in these countries. In the first place, in both Barbados and Jamaica there appeared in the 1990s to have been little difficulty in securing employment by individuals who returned with skills varying from secretarial to legal work, small-scale farming, and employment in the manufacturing, tourist and other industries. As noted, both the RFFU and the FURN had structures in place for helping returnees and their families and the skills databanks they proposed were expected to prove helpful to employers and returnees alike. I have already suggested that there may be more young women than young men involved in the return experience and that these young women appear to be well educated and trained (often with university and professional qualifications) and to have little or no difficulty in securing gainful employment in Barbados and Jamaica. This gender difference also reflected the higher levels of education achieved by girls of Caribbean background in Britain than those attained by boys of the same background (see, for example, Goulbourne and Lewis-Meeks, 1993; Tomlinson, 1983; Rampton, 1981; Swann, 1985) as well as discrimination in the UK labour market for qualified black females. It is not unusual for employers in the region to express a preference for UK-trained female staff, because of their apparent greater sense of duty, self-discipline and attitude to work. This, of course, may be nothing more than the behaviour of the immigrant, because similarly employers on the other side of the Atlantic may prefer the work ethics displayed by immigrants from the Caribbean to that of workers in Britain.

One obvious and significant opportunity that arises from the return phenomenon is the considerable financial contribution made to the economies of Barbados and Jamaica. Such financial contributions include the transfer of savings and investments, and gifts and contributions from family members in the UK. It is not possible to quantify family contributions and gifts but it is relatively easy to quantify the transfer of pensions and benefits from the UK to the Caribbean. Since June 1994 the Pensions and Overseas Benefits Directorate in Newcastle upon Tyne has kept information on the number of beneficiaries abroad and the amount paid; they do not, however, keep statistics on beneficiaries' age or gender, nor do they have projections for future years. Another drawback with the data is that by the very nature of pensions and benefits the directorate is

Table 8.5 Pensions and benefits from the UK to selected Caribbean countries, 1995–97

	January–December 1995*			January–December 1996**			January–August 1997***		
	RP	WB	STB	RP	WB	STB	RP	WB	STB
Barbados	£4,261,576.78	52,950.45	39,893.49	5,474,839.54	68,321.25	5,360.31	3,567,776.08	30,503.81	9,620.47
No.	2,499	30	NA	2,805	35	NA	NA	NA	NA
Jamaica	£38,005,476.97	785,992.55	411,157.06	45,072,245.90	927,987.30	29,746.15	27,739,071.10	560,307.78	24,976.23
No.	20,044	370	NA	21,192	367	NA	NA	NA	NA
Trinidad	£768,601.63	13,169.82	3,158.42	851,636.49	15,749.67	00	568,544.61	8,739.44	00
No.	553	11	NA	644	12	NA	NA	NA	NA

Key: RP = retirement pensions WB = widows' benefits STB = short-term benefits NA = not available

Notes: *   February excluded; data not available
 **   March excluded; data not available
 ***   Data not available for the remainder of 1997

Source: Pensions & Overseas Benefits Directorate, Department of Social Security, 1997

not able to have exact figures about the numbers of beneficiaries and therefore concentrates on taking an annual 'snapshot' to determine the numbers of persons receiving pensions.

Even so, Table 8.5 is a relatively clear illustration of the considerable flow of retirement pensions, widows' benefit and short-term benefits (that is, sickness and invalidity benefits, and severe disablement allowance) into the Barbadian and Jamaican economies over a number of recent years. It should be noted that the returns for 1997 are incomplete because they were calculated in the autumn of 1997. By March 1998, however, the directorate was able to confirm that for 1997 as a whole the number of retirement pensioners was 3,083 and 37 widows' benefit holders in Barbados; the total for Jamaica was 22,051 retirement pensioners and 354 widows' benefit holders; the respective figures for Trinidad & Tobago were 742 and 14. The total amounts paid out as well as the number of people receiving short-term benefits were not available. Overall, these figures and those in Table 8.5 confirm that Jamaica is the major destination of returnees and consequently the major recipient of pensions and benefits accruing to families from the UK with regard to the Caribbean. In general, the differences between Jamaica and Barbados remained consistent over the years: for example, in 1995 over £38m was paid to 20,044 pensioners in Jamaica as compared to over £4m to 2,499 pensioners in Barbados; the respective figures for 1996 were nearly £46m to 21,192 pensioners and nearly £5.5m to 2,805 pensioners. Widows' benefits and short-term benefits realised in these countries also reflected the relative sizes of the two communities. Trinidad & Tobago remained well behind, reflecting the pattern of migration and the relative demographic positions of the Caribbean communities in Britain.[4]

In the case of Jamaica, the volume of foreign currency (including savings, investments, matured private insurance, etc.) flowing into the economy has encouraged some leaders of the returnee communities, such as John Small[5] in Kingston and Steve Batchelor[6] in Spanish Town, to argue that the returnees' contribution to the national economy has not been fully recognised. In contrast, tourism is recognised as the single largest earner of foreign currency, and appropriately a high priority is given to this sector in the country's industrial policy (Jamaica Information Service, 1996, ch. 9). It is, however, obvious that the tourist dollar does not exhibit the sterling qualities of the returnee's financial contribution: it is spent within Jamaica, it is predictable and it is reliable whereas the tourist dollar

Table 8.6 Pensions and benefits from the UK to selected Caribbean countries, 1998–99

	January–December 1998			January–December 1999		
	RP	WB	STB	RP	WB	STB
Barbados	£7,233,480.94	70,312.74	1,635.82	8,206,532.31	79,092.66	119.03
No.	3,406	41	NA	3,695	35	NA
Jamaica	£52,776,732.73	893,181.36	16,875.14	56,287,200.98	958,338.61	49,870.32
No	22,966	340	NA	23,589	341	NA
Trinidad	£1,041,284.68	12,930.41	0	1,106,644.46	14,758.99	0
No.	790	15	NA	833	16	NA

Key: RP = retirement pensions WB = widows' benefit STB = short-term benefits NA = not available

Source: International Office, Pensions and Overseas Benefits Directorate, Department of Social Security, 2001

fluctuates according to the perceptions of holiday makers and other, often external, factors. More recently, these qualities of the returnee's financial contribution to the national economy were formally recognised by the government (see Planning Institute of Jamaica, 1996, ch. 2).

Table 8.6 shows the continuing patterns of flows of returnees' pensions and benefits, particularly to Jamaica and Barbados, at the turn of the century. The importance of this contribution to the national economies is being recognised, but there is still more than a lingering unwillingness to give this the status it deserves in public policy. What is true for Jamaica is also true for some of the smaller islands, such as St Lucia and Grenada, but it is more difficult to locate specific figures for these islands, because of their relative small sizes. The figures for 2000 should indicate a continuing trend, but officials at the Department of Social Security were not able to supply figures at the time of writing.

Of course, it is a matter of speculation whether the number of pensioners will continue to increase or will decline or remain stable in the years ahead. What may be more likely is the steady decline of retired persons and perhaps increases in early retirees and those who are seeking to take advantage of employment opportunities, particularly skilled employment (cf Ministry for Foreign Affairs and Foreign Trade, 1998, appendix ii). The return of elderly people to the Caribbean is no doubt an advantage to those societies, but may be a loss to their families in the UK who continue to do without their full complement of relatives who made up the traditional extended family and household during the period of entry and settlement (see, Barrow, 1982). In other words, as Nutter suggested in his study of returnees in Kingston in the mid-1980s, some of the benefits associated with returnees are limited, despite the benefits brought to the society of resettlement (see, for example, Chevannes and Ricketts, 1997; also, Brown, 1997). This may be particularly so when we consider the vulnerability of the Caribbean communities in Britain and the possible loss of social resources through the return process.

CONCLUSION

These observations about the return phenomenon in the 1990s have implications for both policy and research in the UK and the Caribbean. These would include the relevance and impact of age and gender in the return migration process and re/settlement; reassessment of the present and potential skills and financial contribution of returnees to Caribbean economies; the impact of returnees on family members who remain in Britain, in particular the absence of grandparents in the development of the young; audit of the needs of elderly returnees and what the UK and Caribbean governments can do to help a remarkably resilient and self-reliant element of the population to help themselves and make a worthwhile contribution to civil society; the impact of returnees on housing, local communities and medical facilities. By the beginning of the new millennium the British media were covering a number of occasions when returnees to the region, particularly Jamaica, were being targeted by robbers as part of the apparent anomic violence that is becoming characteristic of the region.

These are issues for the research community to address and they provide a basis for overcoming the great divide between those scholars who see themselves being concerned with race relations matters in Britain and those who are concerned with migration and Caribbean societies. The discussion here suggests that we need to recognise more clearly the unified field in which these matters are actually enacted. After all, for the individuals and the families involved in the transatlantic world, bordered by the British Isles, North America and the Caribbean, migration is a unified experience and family networks are only temporarily fractured in the crossings of the waters.

9 Caribbeans and an Atlantic Fate

In Britain there is a widespread ignorance about the English-speaking Commonwealth Caribbean. At one level this is surprising because modern British history from the seventeenth century has been closely bound up with the Caribbean. Moreover, if only as a backdrop, the Caribbean and the experiences of Caribbeans feature prominently in much of the literature generated by cultural theorists and postmodernists. None the less, ignorance about the region is to be found at various levels in British society.

For example, the authoritative *Oxford Reference Dictionary* (1996, p. 877) claimed that the late Michael Manley of Jamaica 'became the island's first vice-president in 1955'. For Jamaicans this would have been an extraordinary situation, particularly since the dominant Jamaica Labour Party, in office from 1944 to 1955, opposed outright independence. On reading the entry I was wont to think that this is just an editorial error. However, it soon occurred to me that the compilers must have been quite unaware of the significance of the entry for a country which only in the late 1990s began seriously to debate a constitutional change in arrangements that go back to the very beginning of Britain's presence in the country from the mid-seventeenth century.

It might also sound extraordinary that a similar degree of ignorance and misunderstanding exists today about the living connections between Caribbeans in Britain and their connections with the wider world across the Atlantic. But this should not be surprising, given that there has never been a concerted effort in Britain to promote verifiable knowledge about the region. This is in sharp contrast to efforts to promote such knowledge about Africa and Asia. For example, there has not been anything comparable to the University of London's School of Oriental and African Studies in British universities. To be sure, there have been piecemeal attempts at the universities of Warwick, Goldsmiths', and North London to allow some kind of Caribbean interest. Similarly, there have long been and continue to be individual scholars scattered in several British universities (Edinburgh, Kent, Sussex, Cambridge and so on) with Commonwealth Caribbean interests. My point, however, is that none of these have amounted to a concerted effort to promote knowledge about that sub-region.

In the preceding chapters I have tried to show that the presence of Caribbeans has given new force and meaning to the African diaspora in an Atlantic order which straddles the worlds of the Caribbean, North America and parts of Western Europe, from the perspective of Britain. The discussion has focused on a number of specific aspects of what I call Caribbean transnational experiences. These included, first, the assertion that there is a common transatlantic heritage shared not only by indigenous Europeans across the Atlantic, but also by people of African and other historical backgrounds. This may be contentious or even resented by those who assume that the North Atlantic world is, exclusively, an expansion of Western Europe, and also by those who can make an unambiguous distinction between 'the West and the Rest'.

Second, this assertion led to a close look at particular aspects of Caribbean transnational experiences. These included the broadly social and political framework shared across the Atlantic; the meaning of Africa, the Caribbean and the US for Caribbean organisational, inspirational and other kinds of expressions in Britain; the nature of continuing familial or kinship relations between people in Britain and the Caribbean; and the phenomenon of 'return' from the 'Mother Country' to Caribbean points of departure.

However, these should strictly be seen only as illustrations of a living and dynamic process. By no means do they exhaust the range of experiences which demand close empirical examination. For example, the contributions of Caribbeans in Britain and other European countries to the economies of the Caribbean; the changes in the use of language; patterns of religious ties across the triangular Atlantic world, and much else cry out for such empirical research. It is the hope that as studies about representations are seen to be less than adequate in enhancing our understanding of these processes, young scholars will be drawn to reassessing the need for verifiable empirical knowledge about social action, from which useful theory can be constructed.

It was in this spirit that I suggested in Chapter 1 that these developments need to be addressed as more than mere representation, and be seen as aspects of the lived lives of real groups of people. In this concluding chapter, I want to make a few general remarks which arise from the foregoing discussion about these matters as illustrations of our common Atlantic fate.

One major assertion set out in Chapter 1 was that Caribbeans are differentially incorporated into British society. However, much of the material presented in the overall discussion suggests that Caribbeans in Britain have become significantly integrated into the mainstream of society. The question arises, therefore, of how to reconcile an apparent contradiction: the achievement of integration and at the same time differential incorporation of groups into a social order. Here we have the positive ideal of social integration and the negative social exclusion of some groups (as implied by the notion of the differential incorporation) standing side by side. The first of these is the concern of policy makers and sociologists who charted the entry and settlement of new minority ethnic communities in post-Second World War Britain from the 1950s; the second is driven by structural forces, such as institutional racism as well as other mechanisms of exclusion, such as material poverty.

What I have suggested to be a curious congruence of integration and differential incorporation has resulted in the continuation of major social patterns in the midst of change in the English-speaking Caribbean. There, the majority population are indeed integrated into the social whole; after all, they constitute the demographic majority. This majority is, however, still some distance from participating in control of the economy that would ensure full incorporation. In the Caribbean, therefore, the African or black majority remains marginal to the control of material resources. In the Atlantic world, Caribbeans constitute a relatively small population with limited access and participation in either control or ownership of resources. In the Caribbean this element of the population forms a demographic majority, but is also distanced from the 'commanding heights of the economy', particularly in terms of ownership, if not always control and decision making. In both cases, however, Caribbeans actively participate as performers in the visual and audible arts, that is, the production of material resources.

This apparent contradiction between integration and incorporation may be explained in the following manner. In the first instance, there can be little doubt that Caribbeans are indeed integrated into mainstream British society, but this integration is limited or circumscribed so that integration occurs only in some spheres of society. It is in this sense that M.G. Smith's concept of differential incorporation has to be refined if it is to be of use in explaining the paradoxical situation of Caribbeans in the Atlantic world.

In some respects, this contradiction has been recognised in Britain. For example, the point is well made by what Marian Fitzgerald's respondent told her in the late 1980s: 'I'm *very turned on* by the Asian community. *Culturally* I find Afro-Caribbeans much more difficult to get to grips with: *they're more like poor whites'* (Fitzgerald, 1988, p. 255, emphases added). Another example of this integration that emerges from time to time in the British social science community is the assertion that Caribbeans are like the Irish, whereas Asians are like the Jews – supposedly two very different forms of incorporation into British society. The model suggests that while the former are being integrated into the working classes, the latter are being integrated into the middle classes, particularly the professional, investing and ownership elements.

There is, of course, a degree of truth here. To be sure, Caribbeans are well integrated into mainstream English working-class culture and society through family membership, residence, popular culture (music, sports, outwardly expressed styles of clothing and speech, and production and consumption of entertainment forms), as well as language and religion. Some of these factors were discussed in the early chapters and need not be entered into here. Suffice it to reiterate the point that the sharing of such social factors is strong evidence of integration.

There is another sense in which integration as a sharing of value systems is becoming more common between Caribbeans and established Englishness of people and culture. In Chapter 7 it was suggested that Caribbeans have long exhibited characteristics now being described as postmodernist, particularly with regard to family and household patterns resulting from an extreme of individualisation or atomisation. These have long been characteristic of Caribbean life in the region and have taken root in Britain. It is this spirit of individualism that has dogged many decision makers or implementers of policy in the multicultural context of Britain, as expressed by Fitzgerald's respondent and any number of local government officials over the years. This is largely because many of the officials, who are sensitive and caring about the multicultural society also, unfortunately, expect members of new minorities to behave in more or less predictable and uniform ways. Caribbeans, therefore, are likely to be seen as unpredictable, and this sometimes makes it difficult for officials to know how to prepare and respond to demands from Caribbean spokespersons and communities. For example, in meeting community needs, service heads in local authorities sometimes find that the individuals they dealt with at one point in Caribbean communities are not the same ones they are likely to find a few months later. Moreover, perhaps apart from the Caribbean black-led (or, as it is being increasingly described black-majority) churches, these leaders or vocal individuals can rarely guarantee any measure of cooperation or predictable outcome to officials. Members of groups exercise their individualities. Sometimes this is done to a point that must appear anarchic to the casual external observer or to observers who expect the exhibition of traditional forms of authority based on patriarchy and other forms of pre-modern and undemocratic mechanisms of social control.

These features stand in sharp contrast with the perceived or public behaviour of other new minority ethnic communities, to which officials are more easily able to respond. It has not been my concern in this discussion to relate the transnational experiences of non-Caribbean communities in Britain, and so it would be amiss to enter into discussion here about the *leitmotifs* of other groups in these concluding remarks. It is enough to say that my point in this discussion is that, in the main, Caribbean social action in Britain is not to strike a note of difference on the basis of religion, language, values, etc., from either the indigenous ethnic majority or other new minority ethnic communities. Caribbean public voices have been heard, in the main, to join with a generalised call for broad social change under the banner of equality for all, not exclusively for themselves.

This is both a simple and a more difficult demand for officials to address, than are demands for particularistic treatment. The democratic urge which informs this kind of social perception and action comes out of the conflicting elements that moulded the dominant form of society in the Caribbean, that is, Creolism. People from the very different worlds of Africa, Asia (India, China and elsewhere), Europe, and the Middle East met in the Caribbean; some through force (slavery, indenture, asylum, refuge) and some through voluntary migration. But their meeting on common and alien ground effected a situation of what Malinowski called 'culture-contact' nearly always resulting in a transformed situation of 'culture-change'. This evolution involved the honing of mutual tolerance and (perhaps grudging) respect for each contributor to what has been called the Creole society in the region, and avoided what M.G. Smith (1965) described as the formation of socially and culturally plural social orders.

This leads back to the strength and limitation of the theory of differential incorporation as applied to Caribbeans in the Atlantic world. As noted in the preceding chapters, Caribbeans enjoy tremendous freedom of movement in Atlantic communities and their families are distributed, however thinly, throughout this vast world. While they historically differentially incorporated into the various societies of the Atlantic world after slavery, Caribbeans and others now have what Smith called uniform incorporation: equality before the law, freedom to own and live in their own property, to worship, to take up whatever occupation is considered desirable, and so on, on the same basis as any other citizen. This enjoyment is, however, limited to identifiable spheres of society with barriers placed on others.

As far as Caribbeans in the Atlantic world are concerned, therefore, the central issue in this new century of a new millennium may not be what Stuart Hall has identified as the problem of how different groups of people live with diversity. For some groups this will no doubt be the situation, but Caribbeans will be fairly well prepared for this challenge. For Caribbeans, particularly those of African backgrounds, the central problem is likely to be a continuing one: how to effect equality in access to, and participation in, the enjoyment of available material resources. This aspiration goes beyond the request for an apology for slavery and colonial exploitation. Successfully facing this problem will amount to the kind of incorporation that has so far achieved equality in integration. But this is an equality and integration into what has been limited in the main to the material poverty of the dominated.

Notes

CHAPTER 2

1. Of course, the Bahamas is larger than Jamaica, but it is made up of some 700 islands and the population is less than that of Jamaica.

2. These are changes that novelists of this great city in the ebb and flow of human society do not always see as being of historic significance (see, for example, Rutherfurd's *London: The Novel*). The city remains, however, perhaps the key measure of the development or direction of the island as a whole.

3. Much of this part of the discussion was delivered as the lecture 'From West Indian immigrants to Caribbean communities' as one of three public lectures organised by Peter Fraser at Gresham College, London entitled 'Dreams and a special destination: fifty years of Caribbean migration to Britain', Autumn 1998.

4. Of course, Lewis was never a monk. Author of *The Monk*, a contribution to the early novel, he soon became closely linked with the neo-Gothic movement in England and acquired the nickname 'Monk'. His account of his visit to his plantations in the West Indies reveals a lively and quite non-Gothic personality.

5. This section of the chapter was first given as a public lecture under the title 'The aftermath of slavery in the Commonwealth Caribbean', on 13 January 1999 to mark the commencement of the Bristol City Museum & Art Gallery exhibition on Bristol's role in the transatlantic slave trade.

6. Consider, for example, Conservative MP for Hayes and Harlington Terry Dicks' statement that West Indians are 'lazy, good-for-nothings who had come across here to sponge and to bring their way of life in the Caribbean to this country' (the *Guardian*, 2 September 1986), some two or more decades after Caribbean migration to Britain had effectively ceased.

7. In the second half of the twentieth century much the same response has been evoked by the Cuban Revolution of the late 1950s: Fidel Castro and his men from Mexico and the mountains became a fundamental aspect of the political context of the Caribbean as the region began to redefine itself after 1962. As the islands became independent states with their own flags, anthems, cabinets and so forth, the American-inspired fear of Russian-led Communism became the bogey of the region well into the 1980s. This culminated in Ronald Reagan's invasion of a Commonwealth member state, Grenada, in 1983 and provided the opportunity for visiting Secretary of State George Schultz to describe that island as a very nice piece of real estate.

8. This is a reference to the sharp and insightful riposte by the Trinidadian intellectual, J. J. Thomas in the 1890s to Froude's attack on the West Indies.

CHAPTER 3

1. This did not materialise in accordance with this timetable, but it was significant because it demonstrated a willingness on the part of small, vulnerable states to share limited resources.
2. It may be noted that Australia is also much exercised by the question of whether the British monarch should continue to be their head of state, and it was decided on 13 February 1998 at the Canberra convention by a vote of 133–17 to put this to a referendum in 1999 (see, for example, the *Independent*, 14 February, 1998, p. 11). Those in favour of the status quo have, for the moment, won the day, but there is little doubt that the question will remain on the public agenda for the foreseeable future.
3. There is provision for other Commonwealth judges to sit on this body, but this appears to be not taken up, although it was expected that Tony Blair's new judicial enquiry into the killings in Londonderry, Northern Ireland, in 1972 was expected to be headed by an English judge but with one of the other two members coming from a Commonwealth country.
4. Indeed, in the 1990s a number of these states actively took advantage of what has been called 'economic citizenship' facilities, that is, the generous endowment of citizenship to rich individuals who could insure against potential or actual insecurity in their own country in the changing circumstances of that decade. The price of such 'economic citizenship' varied, but was generally from US$50,000, as in Dominica (and I believe Canada and the UK). The popularity of St Kitts with people from Hong Kong, Taiwan and Russia has recently pushed up the price to US$120,000, and it is hoped that this will reduce demand. In the main, 'economic citizens' do not relocate, but hold their second citizenship as an insurance against future risks for themselves and their families.
5. In both Britain and Commonwealth Caribbean states such as Jamaica, residential and age qualifications by a citizen of another Commonwealth country are enough to enjoy the franchise.
6. Clare Short, at the height of the crisis and in a mood of exasperation famously declared that the people of the island would be asking for golden elephants. For several weeks the statement was used by the media to haunt her and to shroud her otherwise sympathetic approach to the plight of people in need of state assistance.
7. There were, by the end of the 1990s, apparently only 160,000 remaining persons with this form of British status, and for a variety of reasons, including security and assistance in times of natural disasters this relationship is more than likely to continue into the foreseeable future.
8. It is something of a paradox that in the post-Cold War 1990s, a number of former British semi-colonies (Cameroons, Palestine) have sought membership of the 'club', as the Commonwealth is affectionately called by members. Indeed, even former colonies which were never within the British sphere of influence let alone rule – Mozambique and Angola – have sought membership in the 1990s. Both Cameroons and Mozambique are now members.
9. Of course, traditional British economic interests in the Caribbean are promoted not only through the Foreign Office, but also through the

West India Committee and the Caribbean Council for Europe based in London. Although the functions of the Committee are now vastly diversified, the group was originally founded in the eighteenth century to defend the slave interests in the region against Parliamentary efforts to abolish, first, the slave trade and then in the following century slavery itself. Moreover, the Committee's interests today go well beyond the English-speaking Caribbean and include the region as a whole. The journal *Caribbean Insight* provides a very useful summation of news about and from the region for publics in the UK.

10. In the Caribbean region, this meant that there were discussions taking place with states such as Cuba, the Dominican Republic and Haiti about membership.

11. From this point of view it is worth noting that an important aspect of the new Labour government is indeed to reform the British constitution, including the incorporation of a written Bill of Rights, following countries such as the US and other EU members who have written constitutions.

12. For example, in the preparation of the appropriate phrasing of questions about the ethnicity of individuals in the 1991 national census the Office of Population Censuses & Surveys (now the Office of National Statistics) consulted some of these organisations.

13. The point is not, however, lost on the British black communities and press that Boateng's position as first a junior minister (in the Department of Health, then in the Home Office as minister for prisons, and after June 2001, Financial Secretary in the Treasury) was a demotion from the position he occupied in John Smith's frontbench team as spokesperson on legal affairs and earlier in Neil Kinnock's frontbench team as a treasury spokesperson. He was later joined in government by Baroness Scotland, Baroness Amos and Keith Vaz. Following a number of scandals in the last months of Blair's first government, the prime minister relieved Vaz, the only Asian politician in his administration, of ministerial responsibility after the 2001 elections. David Lammy, who had succeeded the late Bernie Grant, became a member of the Whip's office.

14. These candidates included individuals from communities other than the usual African, Caribbean and Asian groups, such as individuals form the smaller Iraqi and Chinese communities.

CHAPTER 4

1. The case of Rolan Adams is returned to later in this discussion. Aseta Simms died in Stoke Newington police station during the night of 13 May 1971. It appears that she was taken in off the street at about 11.30 p.m. and died sometime between 12.00 and 12.30 a.m. A doctor, apparently representing the police commission, who examined the body was reported to say that he could not 'say what was the cause of her death' (BUFP pamphlet, 1972, p. 3). The verdict was death by misadventure. The North London branch of the party led a campaign, involving publications, demonstrations, meetings, etc., to demand a

public enquiry into the circumstances of Mrs Simms' death (see *Black Voice*, 1972 *passim*).

2. Ron Phillips was the eldest of three well-known brothers, the others being the crime writer Mike Phillips and Trevor Phillips, chair of the London Assembly; Ron later re-migrated to the US, and died in the mid-1990s in Philadelphia.

3. The names Kwame Toure were taken from Carmichael's two heroes Kwame Nkrumah and Sekou Toure of Ghana and Guinea respectively. Kwame Toure died of cancer in the late 1990s, after living for decades in Guinea, West Africa, and gaining recognition throughout the African diaspora, including his native Trinidad.

4. The JCWI itself suffered a similar fate in the early 1990s, when its Birmingham branch separated to form an independent body from its London headquarters.

5. There were, of course, other groups, such as the Black Liberation Front headed by Tony Soares, and various collectives in different parts of London.

6. In John LaRose's view, Althea Jones (as she then was) personified black British youth protest in the 1970s. Born and brought up in a Trinidadian middle-class family, she came to England to study, and at the time of the Mangrove Nine trial Althea Jones was conducting research for a doctorate in chemistry at London University. She later became a lecturer at the University of the West Indies, where she also studied medicine, before returning to the UK, apparently as a general practitioner.

7. The term came from Harriet Beecher Stowe's novel *Uncle Tom's Cabin* published at the height of the anti-slavery movement in the Northern states of the US in the 1850s. The relevance of the epithet is discussed in the next chapter.

8. Internally, the BUFP sought to establish a women's group and a youth group. Discussions around the kinds of problems youth and women faced were promoted, but in practice the membership tended to act in unison over the general problems the organisation addressed. The group arranged discussion groups around Marxist philosophy, black history, developments in Africa, Asia, the Americas and so on. It arranged for visitors to the country to address groups in specific communities, and members met on a regular basis to monitor events in their neighbourhoods.

9. Philip Murphy, who read philosophy at the University of Southampton, went on to become a prominent Labour councillor on Birmingham City Council, and an officer at the Commission for Racial Equality in the city.

10. Roger Lofters, who had returned to Jamaica in the late 1970s and became the electrics manager at the University of the West Indies' Hospital in Kingston, came to an untimely death in an accident in the summer of 1997. A gathering in his honour was later held in Brixton, organised by young members of the then BUFP and a number of old members from different parts of the country attended.

11. Nearly all these individuals (for example, Edward Kamau Brathwaite, Orlando Patterson) were to go on to distinguished careers in the Caribbean and North America, and relatively few (such as John LaRose)

remaining in England to make a lasting mark in Caribbean communities, as is outlined in a later chapter.

12. These were George Jackson, Fleeta Drumgo and John Clutchette, whose experience in prison politicised them, and made them heroes of radical black America and Britain.

13. This date was deliberately chosen to reflect the importance of the Cuban Revolution for Caribbean people living in Britain and elsewhere.

14. This was so no doubt because the death of Mao in September 1976 and the subsequent struggle in China for control of state power revealed some of the injustices of the Cultural Revolution and subsequent abominations in the name of socialist justice in the 1980s and 1990s.

15. This concern in the black communities in Britain was to continue and was forcefully restated in the Stephen Lawrence case, as set out in the McPherson Report of February 1999.

16. Lenin argued, following Frederick Engels, that an aristocracy of labour had emerged in West Europe. This meant that with the emergence of reformist social-democratic parties and trades unions, capitalists were able to gain the support of the working classes by offering non-essential reforms of capitalism. Union leaders played a crucial part in this process, because it is through them that the 'deal', or class collaboration, has been effected.

17. Of course, the early beginnings of the black churches in the 1950s and 1960s in the rooms of devout families and individuals, involved holding Sunday schools in much the same way as these alternative classes were organised.

18. Of course, where there were cameras these were used in the belief that pictures would show the police attacking black youths. This would also have the effect of making the police think carefully before attacking these youths.

19. The *Press* reported that there were 200 people present, but this number appears to have been a way of saying that there was a large body of people, because the number turns up again and again in the major events reported during this period. In any event, there was unlikely to be an actual count, and only an estimation was possible.

20. The church – which is situated within the town's largest roundabout directly opposite Lambeth Town Hall, which together with this and the town's library forms a triangle – is now Brixton Caribbean Centre.

21. A Trinidadian young man with a young family, Edward Cole was found guilty of assaulting about forty hefty policemen single-handedly outside his home in Waterloo. Neighbours and passers-by told a different story, but the court allowed the police to have their way. This had a profoundly negative impact on family members.

CHAPTER 5

1. Baldwin's criticism of Wright's work as going 'down into the pit together' (p. 22) with Stowe, was joined by Eldridge Cleaver in the radical late 1960s. At the time Cleaver's mistaken belief that homosexuality was a white man's disease led him to develop the most devastating con-

demnation of Baldwin, particularly through his character Rufus Scott in *Another Country*: 'Rufus Scott, a pathetic wretch who indulged in the white man's pastime of committing suicide, who let a white bisexual homosexual fuck him in his ass, and who took a Southern Jezebel for his woman, the epitome of a black eunuch who has completely submitted to the white man' (Cleaver, 1968, p. 107).

2. DuBois was Harvard's first black doctoral student.

3. As expressed by the 'yes, massa' stereotypical characters portrayed in Hollywood films or the 'yes, bwana' Africans of the white hunter genre of entertainment on television in the 1950s and 1960s.

4. The majority white media often give disproportionate coverage to black and white athletes (Snyder and Spreitzer, 1983, p. 174). Mistakes by black athletes are also more likely to be exaggerated. For example, when Ben Johnson won medals he was described as Canadian, but when at the Seoul Olympics he was accused of taking steroids, the description changed to 'Ben Johnson the Jamaican-born ...'.

CHAPTER 6

1. This was later published as *A History of the Upper Guinea Coast 1545–1800* (London: The Clarendon Press, 1971).

2. Sir Philip, a white Jamaican, was himself responsible for turning the tide in the production of books for Caribbean schools, when he started in the 1930s to write for schools in the region on Caribbean experiences rather than depending on texts from England.

3. Jamaica had an elected Free Assembly until the Morant Bay Rebellion of 1865, when the plantocracy decided to hand over internal governance to the Crown out of fear that an upwardly mobile brown and black element in the population would assume control.

4. Small later returned to Jamaica and established himself as a prominent lawyer, and a major figure in the Jamaica Council for Human Rights.

5. He was later to became a prominent Stanford University academic.

6. Babu was eventually released from prison/detention in 1979, and soon migrated to the UK and the US where he took up a career as a journalist and commentator on African affairs. He returned to Tanzania in the 1990s, after the single-party regime came to an end, and competed in the presidential elections of 1995 as a vice-presidential candidate against the Cha Ma Chamapinduzi (CCM) candidate, Ben Mkapa, also an old friend of Rodney's. Bhagat returned to Tanzania in the early 1980s, turned his talents to producing schoolbooks, before migrating to India, from where his forebears had come.

7. It is worth noting that it was the year before that the Soviet writer, Anatoli Vinogradov's novel *The Black Consul* (London: Gollancz, 1935, translated by Emile Burns) about L'Ouverture's struggle against Napoleonic France and the British, became available to the English reading world.

8. Named in honour of Guyanese/Trinidadian pan-Africanist, George Padmore, who was a moving spirit at the 1945 Manchester Pan African Congress, attended by several giants of the movement, such as Kwame

Nkrumah of Ghana, Jomo Kenyatta of Kenya, and W.E.B. DuBois of the US.

CHAPTER 7

1. Subsequently a family myth developed (or was reinforced) that English training is superior to Canadian training, at least in the nursing occupation.
2. Of course, this kind of arrangement between kin members is not unusual in the Caribbean (see, for example, Gordon, 1996).

CHAPTER 8

1. In her famous poem, 'Colonization in reverse', Louise Bennett depicted Jamaican emigration to England in the 1950s as a process whereby 'Jamaica people colonizin Englan in reverse' (Bennett, 1983, p. 106).
2. These figures are likely to include spouses, dependent children and professionals, because entry into the UK was no longer open as before the 1962 Commonwealth Immigration Act.
3. There are also psychological and psychiatric conditions, which researchers at the University of the West Indies Hospital in Jamaica, and King's College Hospital in South London are collaboratively addressing.
4. Closer analysis would be required to determine whether these figures also reflect social differences between communities (that is, class differentials which would be reflected in levels of pensions).
5. John Small and his wife Jean Small are well-known figures in Britain, particularly London, for their activities as radical social workers involved with interracial adoption and legal services.
6. Steve Batchelor was a well-established figure in Birmingham Caribbean circles, having been in the forefront of campaigns about community issues for several decades before returning to Jamaica in the 1990s.

Bibliography

Abenaty, F 2000 'St Lucians and Migration: Migrant Returnees, Their Families and St Lucian Society', unpublished PhD Thesis, South Bank University, London

Abenaty, F 2001 'The Dynamics of Return Migration to St Lucia', in, H Goulbourne & M Chamberlain (eds), *Caribbean Families in Britain and the Trans-Atlantic World* (London & Oxford: Macmillan)

Abiola, Chief Moshood 1992 *Reparations: a Collection of Speeches*, compiled by Muyiwa Phillips, Lome: Linguist Service

Ahmad, W (ed) 1993 *'Race' and Health in Contemporary Britain*, Buckingham: Open University Press

Ahmad, W & Atkin, K (eds) 1996 *'Race' and Community Care*, Buckingham: Open University Press

Almond, G & Powell, G B 1966 *Comparative Politics: a Developmental Approach*, Boston & Toronto: Little Brown & Co Ltd

Almond, G & Verba, S (eds) 1963 *The Civic Culture: Political Attitudes and Democracy in Five Nations*, New Jersey: Princeton University Press

Anderson, Beatrice 1991 'Uncle Tom: a Hero at Last', *American Transcendental Quarterly*, vol 5, no 2

Anwar, M 1979 *The Myth of Return*, London: Heinemann

Anwar, M 1994 *Race and Elections: the Participation of Ethnic Minorities in Politics, Monographs in Ethnic Relations, no 9*, Coventry: ESRC Centre for Research in Ethnic Relations, University of Warwick

Appignanesi, L & Maitland, S (eds) 1989 *The Rushdie File*, London: Fourth Estate Ltd

Asante, M K 1998 *The Afrocentric Idea*, Philadelphia: Temple University Press

Baber, C & Jeffrey, H B 1986 *Guyana: Politics, Economics and Society*, London: Frances Pinter (Publishers)

Baldwin, James 1990 *Notes of a Native Son*, Boston: Beacon Press

Ballard, R 1994 'Differentiation and Disjunction Among the Sikhs', in Ballard (ed), *Desh Pardesh: The South Asian Presence in Britain*, London: Hurst & Company

Banton, M 1968 'The Use of the Useful', *SSRC Newsletter*, no 3, May

Barrow, C (ed) 1996 *Family in the Caribbean: Themes and Perspectives*, Kingston: Ian Randle Publishers

Barrow, J 1982 'West Indian Families: an Insider's Perspective', in R N Rapoport, M P Fogerty & R Rapoport (eds), *Families in Britain*, London: Routledge & Kegan Paul

Basch, L 1987 'The Vincentians and Grenadians: the Role of Voluntary Associations in Immigrant Adaptation to New York City', in N Foner (ed), *New Immigrants in New York*, London: Columbia University Press

Basch, L. et al 1994 *Nations Unbounded: Transnational Products, Post-Colonial Predicaments and Deterritorialised Nation States*, Amsterdam: Gordon & Breach

Baumann, G 1996 *Contesting Culture: Discourses of Identity in Multi-Ethnic London*, Cambridge: Cambridge University Press

Beckford, G 1972 *Persistent Poverty : Underdevelopment in Plantation Economies in the Third World*, New York: Oxford University Press

Beckford, G 1984 'The Struggle for a Relevant Economics', in H Goulbourne & L Sterling (eds), *Social Sciences and Caribbean Society*, Kingston: Institute of Social and Economic Research, University of the West Indies

Beckford, G & Witter, M 1982 *Small Garden ... Bitter Weed: The Political Economy of Struggle and Change in Jamaica*, Morant Bay & London: Maroon Publishing House/Zed Press

Bennett, L *Selected Poems*, Kingston: Sangster's Book Stores

Bernal, R. et al 1994 'Caribbean Economic Thought: the Critical Tradition', in H Goulbourne & L Sterling (eds), *Social Sciences and Caribbean Society*, Kingston: Institute of Social and Economic Research, University of the West Indies

Berrington, A 1996 'Marriage Patterns and Inter-Ethnic Unions', in D Coleman & J Salt (eds), *Ethnicity in the 1991 Census: Demographic Characteristics of the Ethnic Minority Populations*, London: OPCS, vol 1

Berry, William 1989 'Uncle Tom We Hardly Knew You', *The Swanee Review*, 97 (Fall)

Best, Lloyd 1968 'A Model of Pure Plantation Economy', *Social & Economic Studies*, vol 17, no 3

Bhachu, P 1986 *Twice Migrants*, London: Tavistock

Birch, A H 1993 *The Concepts and Theories of Modern Democracy*, London: Routledge

Blake, J 1961 *Family Structure in Jamaica: the Social Context of Reproduction*, New York: The Free Press of Glencoe

Blakemore, K & Boneham, M 1994 *Age, Race and Ethnicity: a Comparative Approach*, Buckingham: Open University Press

Boyce Davis, C 2001 'Imperialism and the Super-Exploitation of the Black Woman: Claudia Jones' Transnational Black Feminism', paper delivered at the ESRC *International Conference on the Caribbean Diaspora*, 30 August–1 September 2001, South Bank University, London

Brathwaite, E 1978 *The Development of Creole Society in Jamaica 1770–1820*, Oxford: Clarendon Press

Brathwaite, E 1997 'Pluralism, Creolisation and Culture', in F Knight (ed), *Slave Societies of the Caribbean*, UNESCO General History of the Caribbean, vol iii, London: Macmillan Caribbean

Brown, C. 1984 *Black and Brown Britain*, London: Policy Studies Institute

Brown, D 1997 'Workforce Losses and Return Migration to the Caribbean: a Case Study of Jamaican Nurses', in P R Pessar (ed), *Caribbean Circuits: New Directions in the Study of Caribbean Migration*, New York: Center for Migration Studies

Brown, J M & Foot, R (eds) 1994 *Migration: the Asian Experience*, London: St Martin's Press

Bruno F 1992 *The Eye of the Tiger: My Life*, London: Weidenfeld

Bryan, P 1990 *Philanthropy and Social Welfare in Jamaica: an Historical Survey*, Mona: Institute of Social and Economic Research, University of the West Indies

Bulmer, M 1996 'The Ethnic Group Question in the 1991 Census of Population', in D Coleman & J Salt (eds), *Ethnicity in the (1991) Census:*

Demographic Characteristics of the Ethnic Minority Populations, London: Office of Population, Censuses and Surveys (OPCS), vol 1

Byron, M & Condon, S 1996 'A Comparative Study of Caribbean Return Migration from Britain and France: Towards a Context-Dependent Explanation', *Transaction, Institute of British Geographers*, vol 21 no 1

Calley, M 1965 *God's People*, Oxford: Oxford University Press

Carnegie, J 1973 *Some Aspects of Jamaica's Politics 1918–38*, Kingston: Institute of Jamaica

Carrington, B 1986 'Social Mobility, Ethnicity and Sport', *British Journal of Sociology of Education*, vol 7, no 1

Carrington, B & Wood, E 1983 'Body Talk: Images of Sport in a Multi-Racial School', *Multi-Racial Education*, vol 11, no 2 (Spring)

Carter, T 1986 *Shattering Illusions: West Indians in British Politics*, London: Lawrence & Wishart

Cashmore, E 1982 'Black Youth, Sport and Education', *New Community*, vol x, no 2

Castells, M 1996 *The Rise of the Network Society*, vol i, Oxford: Blackwell Publishers Ltd

Chamberlain, M 1997 *Narratives of Exile and Return*, London: Macmillan

Chevannes, B & Ricketts, R 1997 'Return Migration and Small Business Development in Jamaica', in P R Pessar (ed), *Caribbean Circuits: New Directions in the Study of Caribbean Migration*, New York: Center for Migration Studies

Clarke, E 1957 *My Mother Who Fathered Me*, London: Allen & Unwin

Cleaver, Eldridge 1968 *Soul on Ice*, New York: McGraw-Hill

Coard, B 1971 *How the West Indian Child is Made Educationally Sub-Normal in the British School System*, London: New Beacon Books

Cohen, R 1994 *Frontiers of Identity: the British and Others*, London: Longman

Cohen, R 1997 *Global Diasporas: Introduction*, London: UCL Press

Cohen, R. 1998 'Cultural Diaspora: The Caribbean Case', in M Chamberlain (ed), *Caribbean Migration: Globalised Identities*, London: Routledge

Coleman, D & Salt, J (eds) 1996 *Ethnicity in the 1991 Census: Demographic Characteristics of the Ethnic Minority Populations*, vol 1, London: OPCS

Coleman, T W 1993 'Betrayed: Clarence Thomas' Former Supporters', *emerge* (sic), November

Collins, W 1965 *Jamaica Migrant*, London: Routledge & Kegan Paul

Commission for Racial Equality 1990a *Britain: a Plural Society, Report of a Seminar, Discussion Papers, no 3*, London: Commission for Racial Equality

Commission for Racial Equality 1990b *Law, Blasphemy and the Multi-Faith Society, Report of a Seminar, Discussion Papers no 1*, London: Commission for Racial Equality

Commission for Racial Equality 1992 *The Social Security Persons Abroad Regulations: an Analysis of the Conditions Governing Continued Entitlement to Disability Benefits of Persons Going Abroad and Their Implications for Ethnic Minorities*, London: Commission for Racial Equality

Crisis, November/December 1993

Cross, M & Entzinger, H (eds) 1986 *Lost Illusions: Caribbean Minorities in Britain and The Netherlands*, London: Routledge

Cumper, G E 1956 'Population Movements in Jamaica 1830–1950', *Social & Economic Studies*, vol v, no iii

Davison, R B 1962 *West Indian Migrants*, London: Oxford University Press

Deakin, N 1970 *Colour, Citizenship and British Society*, London: Panther Modern Society

Dench, G 1986 *Minorities in the Open Society: Prisoners of Ambivalence*, London: Routledge & Kegan Paul

Dench, G 1992 *From Extended Family to State Dependency*, London: Institute of Community Studies

Dench, G 1996 *The Place of Men in Changing Family Cultures*, London: Institute of Community Studies

Douglas, A 1981 'Introduction: the Art of Controversy', in Harriet Beecher Stowe, *Uncle Tom's Cabin*, New York: Penguin

Driver, G 1982 'West Indian Families – an Anthropological Perspective', in R Rapaport & M Fogarty (eds), *Families in Britain*, London: Routledge & Kegan Paul

DuBois, W E B 1965 (1903) *The Souls of Black Folks: Essays and Sketches*, London: Longmans, Green

Dummett, A & Nicol, A 1990 *Subjects, Citizens, Aliens and Others: Nationality and Immigration Law*, London: Weidenfeld and Nicolson

Durkheim, E 1933 (1893) *The Division of Labour in Society*, New York: The Free Press

Durkheim. E 1982 *The Rules of Sociological Method and Selected Texts on Sociology and its Methods*, edited with an Introduction by Steven Lukes, London: Macmillan

Eade, J 1989 *The Politics of Community: the Bangladeshi Community in East London*, Aldershot: Avebury

Edwards, A 1967 *Marcus Garvey: 1887–1940*, London: New Beacon Books

Edwards, J (ed) 1992 *Let's Praise Him Again*, London: Kingsway Publications Ltd

Egbuna, E 1971 *Destroy This Temple: the Voice of Black Power in Britain*, London: MacGibbon & Kee

Eisner, G 1961 *Jamaica 1830–1930: A Study in Economic Growth*, Manchester: Manchester University Press

Equaino, Oloudah 1969 (1789) *The Interesting Narrative of the Life of Oloudah Equaino, or Vassa Gustavus, The African*, abridged and edited by Paul Edwards, London: Dawson

ESRC (Economic and Social Research Council) 2000 *The Indian Diaspora Conference*, New Delhi, 8–10 April

Fanon, F 1968 *Black Skin, White Masks*, London: Macgibbon & Kee

Finch, J 1989 *Family Obligations and Social Change*, Cambridge: Polity Press

Fitzgerald, M 1984 *Political Parties and Black People*, London: Runnymede Trust

Fitzgerald, M 1988 'Afro-Caribbean Involvement in British Politics', in M Cross & H Entzinger (eds), *Lost Illusions: Caribbean Minorities in Britain and the Netherlands*, London: Routledge

Foner, N 1979 *Jamaica Farewell: Jamaican Migrants in London*, London: Routledge & Kegan Paul

Foner, N 1987 'The Jamaicans: Race and Ethnicity Among Migrants in New York City', in, Foner (ed), *New Immigrants in New York*, London: Columbia University Press

Foot, P 1969 *The Rise of Enoch Powell*, Harmondsworth: Penguin

Froude, J A 1888 *The English in the West Indies, or, The Bow of Ulysses*, London: Longmans, Green

Fryer, P 1984 *Staying Power: The History of Black People in Britain*, London: Pluto Press

Furnas, J C 1956 *Good-bye to Uncle Tom*, New York: William Sloane Associates

Gay, P & Young, K 1988 *Community Relations Councils: Roles and Objectives*, London: Policy Studies Institute

Geiss, I. 1974 *The Pan-African Movement*, London: Methuen & Co Ltd

Gellner, E 1983 *Nations and Nationalism*, Oxford: Basil Blackwell Publisher Limited

Gerloff, R 1992 *A Plea for British Black Theologies*, London: Verso

Gilroy, P 1993 *The Black Atlantic: Modernity and Double Consciousness*, London: Verso

Girvan, N. 1971 *Foreign Capital and Economic Underdevelopment in Jamaica*, Kingston: Institute of Social & Economic Research, University of the West Indies

Glass, R 1960 *Newcomers: the West Indians in London*, London: George Allen & Unwin Ltd

Goffman, E 1956 *The Presentation of Self in Everyday life*, New York: Anchor Books

Goldberg, S 1990 'Athletes: Why Blacks Are Better Than Whites', *International Journal of Sociology and Social Policy*, vol 10, no 8

Gordon, D 1987 *Class, Status and Social Mobility in Jamaica*, Kingston: Institute of Social & Economic Research, University of the West Indies

Gordon, S 1996 '"I go to Tanties": the Economic Significance of Child-Shifting in Antigua, West Indies', in C Barrow (ed), *The Family in the Caribbean: Themes and Perspectives*, Kingston: Ian Randle Publishers

Goulbourne, H 1980 'Oral History and Black Labour: an Overview', *Oral History Journal*, vol 8, no 1

Goulbourne, H. 1984 'Explanations of Violence and Public Order in Jamaica', *Social & Economic Studies*, vol 33, no 4

Goulbourne, H 1988a *Teachers, Education and Politics in Jamaica, 1882–1972*, London: Macmillan

Goulbourne, H 1988b *West Indian Political Leadership in Britain*, The Byfield Memorial Lecture 1987, Occasional Papers in Ethnic Relations, Coventry: University of Warwick

Goulbourne, H (ed) 1990 *Black Politics in Britain*, Aldershot: Avebury

Goulbourne, H 1991a *Ethnicity and Nationalism in Post-Imperial Britain*, Cambridge: Cambridge University Press

Goulbourne, H 1991b 'The Offence of the West Indian: Political Leadership and the Communal Option', in M Anwar & P Werbner (eds), *Black and Ethnic Leaderships: the Cultural Dimensions of Political Action*, London: Routledge

Goulbourne, H 1998 *Race Relations in Britain Since 1945*, London: Macmillan

Goulbourne, H (ed) 2001 'General Introduction', *Race and Ethnicity: Critical Concepts in Sociology*, 4 vols, London: Routledge

Goulbourne, H & Lewis-Meeks, P (eds) 1993 *Access of Ethnic Minorities to Higher Education in Britain: Report of a Seminar at King's College Cambridge*, *Occasional Paper in Ethnic Relations No 10*, Coventry: Centre for Research in Ethnic Relations, University of Warwick

Goulbourne, H et al 1995 *The Needs of the African Caribbean Community in Coventry: a Report*, Cheltenham: Centre for Policy & Health Research, Cheltenham & Gloucester College

Goulbourne, S 2001 'The Caribbean Court of Appeal: Intimations of Change?', paper delivered at the ESRC *International Conference on the Caribbean Diaspora*, 30 August–1 September 2001, South Bank University, London

Greene, J E 1974 *Race vs Politics in Guyana: Political Cleavages and Political Mobilization in the 1968 General Election*, Kingston: Institute of Social & Economic Research, University of the West Indies

Hall, S 1990 'Cultural Identity and Diaspora', in J Rutherford (ed), *Identity: Community, Culture and Difference*, London: Lawrence & Wishart

Hall, S 1993 'The West and the Rest: Discourse and Power', in, S Hall & B Gieben (eds) *Formations of Modernity*, London: Polity Press

Hall, S 1995 'Negotiating Caribbean Identities', *New Left Review*, 209, January–February

Hall, S et al 1978 *Policing the Crisis: Mugging, the State and Law and Order*, London: Macmillan Press

Hamilton, C V and Carmichael, S 1967 *Black Power: The Politics of Black Liberation in America*, New York: Random House

Harris, W 1967 *Tradition, the Writer and Society*, London: New Beacon Books

Haskins, E 1988 *The Crisis in Afro-American Leadership*, Buffalo: Prometheus Books

Hebdige, D 1998 'Reggae, Rastas & Rudies', in S Hall & T Jefferson (eds), *Resistance Through Rituals: Youth Subcultures in Post-War Britain*, London: Routledge

Heineman, B 1972 *The Politics of the Powerless*, Oxford: Oxford University Press

Henriques, F 1953 *Family and Colour in Jamaica*, London: Eyre & Spottiswoode

Hesse, B (ed) 2000 *Un/settling Multiculturalisms: Diasporas, Entanglements, Transruptions*, London: Zed Press

Higman, B W (ed) 1999 *UNESCO General History of the Caribbean: Methodology and Historiography of the Caribbean*, vol vi, London & Oxford: UNESCO Publishing/Macmillan Education Ltd

Hill, C S 1963 *West Indian Migrants and the London Churches*, London: Oxford University Press

Hinds, A 1992 *Report on Organisations Serving the Afro Caribbean Community*, London: West Indian Standing Conference

Hintjen, P 1985 'Ethnicity, Class and Internal Capitalist Penetration in Guyana and Trinidad', *Social and Economic Studies*, vol 34, no 3

Hintjens, H 1995 *Alternatives to Independence: Explorations in Post-Colonial Relations*, Aldershot: Dartmouth Publishing Company

Hintjens, H 1997 'Governance Options in Europe's Caribbean Dependencies: the End of Independence', *The Round Table*, 344

Hiro, D 1971 *Black British White British*, London: Eyre & Spottiswoode

Hooker, J R 1967 *Black Revolutionary: George Padmore's Path From Communism to Pan-Africanism*, London: Pall Mall Press

Humphry, D & John, G 1971 *Because They're Black*, Harmondsworth: Penguin

Hylton, C 1997a 'Caribbean Community Organisations in Leeds', unpublished PhD thesis, Department of Sociology, University of Leeds

Hylton, C (ed) 1997b *Black Men in Britain: Marching into the Millennium*, Leeds: Bogle-L'Ouverture & Black Men's Forum

Ingman, T 1996 *The English Legal Process*, London: Blackstone Press Limited

Jackson-Leslie, L 1991 'Tom, Buck and Sambo or How Clarence Thomas Got to the Supreme Court', *The Black Scholar*, vol 22, nos 1 & 2

James, C L R 1982 'Walter Rodney and the Question of Power', in E Alpers & P-M Fontaine (eds), *Walter Rodney – Revolutionary and Scholar: a Tribute*, Los Angeles: Centre for Afro-American Studies & African Studies Center, University of California

James, W & Harris, C (eds) 1993 *Inside Babylon: The Caribbean Diaspora in Britain*, London: Verso

Jenkins, Roy 1967 'Racial Equality in Britain', in A Lester (ed), *Essays and Speeches by Roy Jenkins*, London: Collins

John LaRose Tribute Committee, 1991 *Foundations of a Movement: a Tribute to John LaRose*, London: John LaRose Tribute Committee

Johnson, H & Watson, K (eds) 1998 *The White Minority in the Caribbean*, Kingston: Ian Randle Publishers

Johnson, James Weldon 1990 *The Autobiography of an Ex-Coloured Man*, New York: Penguin

Johnson-Jackson, J 1991 ' "Them Against Us": Anita Hill v Clarence Thomas', *The Black Scholar*, vol 22, nos 1 & 2

Jones, E 1965 *Othello's Countrymen: the African in English Renaissance Drama*, Oxford: Oxford University Press

Jones, E 1971 *The Elizabethan Image of Africa*, Charlottesville: University of Virginia

Keith, M 1990 'Misunderstandings?: Policing, Reform and Control, Co-Option and Consultation', in H Goulbourne (ed), *Black Politics in Britain*, Aldershot: Avebury

Keith, M 1993 *Race, Riots and Policing: Lore and Disorder in a Multi-Racist Society*, London: UCL Press

King, R 1986 'Return Migration and Regional Economic Development: an Overview', in King (ed), *Return Migration and Regional Economic Problems*, London: Croom Helm

Lacey, R 1977 *Violence and Politics in Jamaica 1960–70*, Manchester: Manchester University Press

Lasswell, H 1958 (1936) *Politics: Who Gets What, When, How*, Cleveland/New York: Meridian Books

Lasswell, H & Kaplan, A 1950 *Power and Society*, New Haven/London: Yale University Press

Latin American Bureau, 1984a *Guyana: Fraudulent Revolution*, London: Latin American Bureau (Research and Action) Ltd

Latin American Bureau, 1984b *Grenada: Whose Freedom*, London: Latin American Bureau (Research and Action) Ltd

Layton-Henry, Z 1992 *The Politics of Immigration*, Oxford: Blackwell

Lewis, D L 1993 *W.E.B. Dubois: Biography of a Race 1868–1919*, New York: Henry Holt

Lewis, R 1987 *Marcus Garvey Anti-Colonial Champion*, London: Karia Press

Lewis, R 1998 *Walter Rodney's Intellectual and Political Thought*, Mona & Detroit: University of the West Indies Press & Wayne State University Press

Lewis, R and Bryan, P (eds) 1986 *Garvey: His Work and Impact*, Mona: Institute of Social & Economic Research, Univerity of the West Indies

Lewis, R and Warner, M (eds) 1988 *Garvey: Africa, Europe, The Americas*, Mona: Institute of Social & Economic Research, Univerity of the West Indies

Lewis, W Arthur 1939 *Labour in the West Indies*, London: Fabian Society

Lewis, W Arthur 1958 'Economic Development with Unlimited Supplies of Labour', in A N Agarwala & S P Singh (eds), *The Economics of Underdevelopment*, London: Oxford University Press

Little, K 1947 *Negroes in Britain*, London: Kegan Paul

Lord Chancellor's Advisory Committee on Legal Education and Conduct 1997 *Report of the Consultative Seminar on Standards and Regulation of Immigrant advice*, London: Millbank Tower

Lyons, A 1991 'Towards an Understanding of Black Ethnic Minorities' Involvement in Sport', unpublished MA dissertation, University of Warwick

Madison, Donna & Landers, D 1976 'Racial Discrimination in Football: a Test of the "Stacking" of Playing Positions Hypothesis', in D M Landers (ed), *Social Problems in Athletics*, Urbana: University of Illinois Press

Malinowski, B 1961 *The Dynamics of Culture Change*, Westport: Greenwood Press

Malinowski, B 1963 (1913) *The Family Among the Australian Aborigines: a Sociological Study*, New York: Schocken

Manley, M 1974 *The Politics of Change: A Jamaican Testament*, London: Andre Deutsch

Mao Tse-Tung 1967 'On Contradictions', in *Selected Works of Mao Tse-Tung*, Peking: Foreign Languages Press, vol i

Marienstras, R 1989 'On the Notion of Diaspora', in G Chaliand (ed), *Minority Peoples in the Age of Nation-States*, London: Pluto Press

Marx, K 1974 (1867) *Capital: a Critique of Capitalist Production*, vol 1, Moscow: Progress Publishers

McPherson, Sir William 1999 *The Stephen Lawrence Inquiry*, CM 4262–1, London: The Stationery Office

Mendes, A H 1934 *Pitch Lake*, London: New Beacon Books

Messina, A M 1989 *Race and Party Competition in Britain*, Oxford: The Clarendon Press

Milbrath, L 1965 *Political Participation*, Chicago: Rand McNally

Miles, R 1993 *Racism after 'Race Relations'*, London: Routledge

Mills, C Wright (1959) *The Sociological Imagination*, Oxford: Oxford University Press

Mintz, S 1993 'Goodbye, Columbus: Second Thoughts on the Caribbean Region at Mid-Millenium', *Walter Rodney Memorial Lecture*, Coventry: University of Warwick

Mintz, S & Price, R 1992 *The Birth of African-American Culture: an Anthropological Perspective*, Boston: Beacon Press

Mirzoeff, N (ed) 2000 *Diaspora and Visual Culture: Representing Africans and Jews*, London: Routledge

Mishan, E J 1988 'What Future for a Multi-Cultural Britain?', *The Salisbury Review*, June, pp 18 ff and September, pp 4 ff

Modood, T & Berthoud, R et al 1997 *Ethnic Minorities in Britain: Diversity and Disadvantage*, London: Policy Studies Institute

Modood, T 1988 '"Black", Racial Equality and Asian Identity', *New Community*, vol xiv, no 3

Mohammed, P 1988 'The Caribbean Family Revisited', in Mohammed & C Shepherd (eds), *Gender in Caribbean Development*, Cave Hill: The University of the West Indies

Morrison, Toni 1978 *Song of Solomon*, London: Picador

Munroe, T 1972 *The Politics of Constitutional Decolonization: Jamaica 1944–62*, Kingston: Institute of Social & Economic Research, University of the West Indies

Myrdal, G 1944 *An American Dilemma: The Negro Problem and Modern Democracy*, London & New York: Harper & Brothers

Myrdal, G 1969 *Objectivity in Social Research*, London: Gerald Duckworth & Co Ltd

Nettleford, Rex 1972 *Identity, Race and Protest in Jamaica*, New York: William Morrow & Company, Inc

Nettleford, Rex 1978 *Caribbean Cultural Identity: The Case of Jamaica – An Essay in Cultural Dynamics*, Kingston: Institute of Jamaica

Newman, P & Smith, A 1997 *Social Focus on Families*, London: The Stationery Office

Nutter, R 1986 'Implications of Return Migration from the United Kingdom for Urban Employment in Kingston, Jamaica', in R King (ed), *Return Migration and Regional Economic Problems*, London: Croom Helm

Olwig, K 1996 'The Migration Experience: Nevisian Women at Home and Abroad', in C Barrow (ed), *Family in the Caribbean: Themes and Perspectives*, Kingston: Ian Randle Publishers

Owen, D 1996 'Size, Structure and Growth of the Ethnic Minority Populations', in, D Coleman & J Salt (eds), *Ethnicity in the 1991 Census: Demographic Characteristics of the Ethnic Minority Populations*, London: HMSO

Owen, D 1994 *Black People in Great Britain: Social and Economic Circumstances*, 1991 Census Statistical Paper No 6, National Ethnic Minority Data Archive, University of Warwick

Patterson, O 1967a *An Absence of Ruins*, London: Hutchinson

Patterson, O 1967b *The Sociology of Slavery*, London: Macgibbon & Kee

Patterson, O 1968 'West Indian Migrants Returning Home: Some Early Observations', *Race*, 10

Patterson, O 1982 *Slavery and Social Death: a Comparative Study*, London: Harvard University Press

Patterson, O 1999 'The Afro-Atlantic Diaspora: A Sociohistorical Overview of "Race" and Ethnicity in the UK and Americas', paper presented at *Race, Ethnicity and Mobility Conference*, Bath, 24–27 June

Patterson, S 1965 (1963) *Dark Strangers: a Study of West Indians in London*, Harmondsworth: Penguin

Payne, A. 1991 'Britain and the Caribbean', in P Sutton (ed), *Europe and the Caribbean*, London: Macmillan

Payne, A. 1994 *Politics in Jamaica*, Kingston: Ian Randle Publications

Peach, C 1968 *West Indian Migration to Britain: a Social Geography*, London: Oxford University Press

Peach, C 1991 *The Caribbean in Europe: Contrasting Patterns of Migration and Settlement in Britain, France and The Netherlands*, Research Papers in Ethnic Relations no 15, Coventry: Centre for Research in Race Relations, University of Warwick

Phillips, M & Phillips, T 1998 *Windrush: The Irresistible Rise of Multi-Racial Britain*, London: HarperCollins Publishers

Philpott, S B 1973 *West Indian Migration: The Montserrat Case*, London: Althone

Pilkington, E 1988 *Beyond the Mother Country: West Indians and the Notting Hill White Riots*, London: I B Tauris

Post, K 1978 *Arise Ye Starvellings: The Jamaican Labour Rebellion of 1938 and its Aftermaths*, The Hague: Martinus Nijhoff

Premdas, R 1995 *Ethnic Conflict and Development: the Case of Guyana*, Aldershot: Avebury

Pryce, K 1979 *Endless Pressure: a Study of West Indian Life-Style in Bristol*, Harmondsworth: Penguin Books

Rampton, A 1981 *West Indian Children in our Schools: Interim Report of the Committee of Inquiry into the Education of Children from (sic) Ethnic Groups*, Cmnd 8273, London: HMSO

Rex, J 1983 *Race Relations in Sociological Theory*, London: Routledge & Kegan Paul

Rex, J & Moore, R 1967 *Race, Community and Conflict*, London: Oxford University Press

Rex, J & Tomlinson, S 1979 *Colonial Immigrants in a British City: a Class Analysis*, London: Routledge & Kegan Paul

Richardson, B 1985 *Panama Money in Barbados 1900–1920*, Knoxville: University of Tennessee Press

Richmond, A H 1955 *The Colour Problem: a Study of Racial Relations*, Harmondsworth: Penguin Books

Ringer, B 1983 *'We the People' and Others: Duality and America's Treatment of its Racial Minorities*, London: Tavistock

Roberts, G & Mills, D 1958 *Study of External Migration Affecting Jamaica 1953–55*, Mona: Institute of Social & Economic Research, University of the West Indies

Robinson, Randall 2000 *The Debt: What America Owes to Blacks*, New York: Putnam/Penguin

Robotham, D. 1984 'The Emergence of Sociology in Jamaica', in H Goulbourne & L Sterling (eds), *Social Sciences and Caribbean Society*,

Kingston: Institute of Social and Economic Research, University of the West Indies

Rodney, Walter 1981 *A History of the Guyanese Working People, 1881–1905*, London: Heinemann Educational Books

Rodney, W 1969 *The Groundings with My Brothers*, London: Bogle L'Ouverture Publications

Rodney, W 1972 *How Europe Underdeveloped Africa*, London: Bogle L'Ouverture Publications

Rose, E J B et al 1969 *Colour and Citizenship: a Report on British Race Relations*, London: Oxford University Press

Rubin, V (ed) 1960 *Social and Cultural Pluralism in the Caribbean*, New York Academy of Sciences

Runnymede Trust 2000 *Report of the Commission on the Future of Multi-Ethnic Britain*, London: Profile Books

Ryan, S D 1972 *Race and Nationalism in Trinidad and Tobago: a Study of Decolonization in a Multi-Racial Society*, Toronto: University of Toronto Press

Saggar, S 1992 *Race and Politics in Britain*, London: Harvester Wheatsheaf

Scarman, Rt Hon Lord Leslie 1982 *The Brixton Disorders 10–12 April 1981*, Cmnd 8427, London: HMSO

Seabury, P & McDougall, W A (eds) 1984 *The Grenada Papers*, San Francisco: Institute for Contemporary Studies Press

Segal, R 1967 *The Race War: the World-Wide Conflict of Races*, London: Penguin Books

Sewell, G W 1862 *The Ordeal of Free Labour in the West Indies*, New York: Harper Bros.

Sewell, T 1993 *Black Tribunes: Black Political Participation in Britain*, London: Lawrence & Wishart

Sheffer, G. (ed) 1986 *Modern Diasporas in International Politics*, London: Croom Helm

Sherwood, M (ed) 1999 *Claudia Jones: A Life in Exile*, London: Lawrence and Wishart

Shukra, K 1990 'Black Sections in the Labour Party', in H Goulbourne (ed), *Black Politics in Britain*, Aldershot: Avebury

Shyllon, F O 1974 *Black Slaves in Britain*, London: Oxford University Press

Sivanandan, A 1986 *From Resistance to Rebellion: Asian and Afro-Caribbean Struggles in Britain*, London: Institute of Race Relations

Smith, D 1977 *Racial Disadvantage in Britain*, Harmondsworth: Penguin

Smith, M G 1962 *Kinship and Community in Carriacou*, New Haven: Yale University Press

Smith, M G 1965 *The Plural Society in the British West Indies*, Berkeley & Los Angeles: University of California Press

Smith, M G 1974 *Corporations and Society*, London: Duckworth

Smith, M G 1984 *Culture, Race and Class in the Commonwealth Caribbean*, Mona: Department of Extra-Mural Studies, University of the West Indies

Smith, M G 1988 'Pluralism, Race and Ethnicity in Selected African Countries', in J Rex & D Mason (eds), *Theories of Race and Ethnic Relations*, Cambridge: Cambridge University Press

Smith, R T 1963 'Culture and Social Structure in the Caribbean: Some Recent Work on Family and Kinship Studies' *Comparative Studies in Society and History*, vol 6, no 1

Smith, R T 1988 *Kinship and Class in the West Indies: a Genealogical Study of Jamaica and Guyana*, Cambridge: Cambridge University Press

Smith, R T 2001 'Caribbean Families: Questions for Research and Implications for Policy', in H Goulbourne & M Chamberlain (eds), *Caribbean Families in Britain and the Trans-Atlantic World*, London & Oxford: Macmillan

Snyder, E E & Spreitzer, E A 1983 'The Black Athlete', in *Social Aspects of Sport*, London: Prentice Hall

Solomos, J 1988 *Black Youth, Racism and the State: the Politics of Ideology and Policy*, Cambridge: Cambridge University Press

Stephens, E H & Stephens, J D 1986 *Democratic Socialism in Jamaica: the Political Movement and Social Transformation in Dependent Capitalism*, London: Macmillan

Stone, C 1983 *Democracy and Clientism in Jamaica*, New Jersey: Transaction Books

Stone, C & Brown, A (eds) 1977 *Essays on Power and Change in Jamaica*, Kingston: Jamaica Publishing House

Supperstone, M & O'Dempsey, D 1996 *Supperstone and O'Dempsey on Immigration and Asylum*, London: FT Law & Tax

Sutton, C & Chaney, E 1987 *Caribbean Life in New York: Socio-Cultural Dimensions*, New York: Centre for Migration Studies

Swann, Lord Michael 1985 *Education for All: Report of the Committee of Inquiry into the Education of Children from Ethnic Minority Groups*, Cmnd 9453, London: HMSO

Talburt, T (2001) *The Lome Conventions' rum protocol and Development Policies in the Commonwealth Caribbean*, PhD thesis, South Bank University, London

Tebbitt, N 1990 'Fanfare of Being British', *The Field*, May

Thatcher, M 1988 *Britain and Europe: Text of a Speech Delivered in Bruges by the Prime Minister on 20 September 1988*, Conservative Political Centre

Thomas, J J 1969 (1869) *The Theory and Practice of Creole Grammar*, London: New Beacon Books

Thomas-Hope, E 1980 'Hopes and Reality in West Indian Migration to Britain', *Oral History Journal*, vol 8, no 1

Thomas-Hope, E 1992 *Explanation in Caribbean Migration*, London: Macmillan

Thomas-Hope, E. 1998 'Globalisation and the Development of a Caribbean Migration Culture', in M Chamberlain (ed), *Caribbean Migration: Globalised Identities*, London: Macmillan

Thompson, P 1978 *The Voice of the Past: Oral History*, Oxford: Oxford University Press

Tinker, H 1974 *A New System of Slavery: the Export of Indian Labour Overseas, 1830–1920*, Oxford: Oxford University Press

Tomlinson, S 1983 *Ethnic Minorities in British Schools*, London: Heinemann Educational Books

Van Sertima, I 1968 *Caribbean Writers*, London: New Beacon Books

Vansina, J 1965 *Oral Tradition: a Study in Historical Methodology*, Harmondsworth: Penguin

Walker, R 2000 *The Classical Roots of Black Culture*, London: Bogle L'Ouverture

Walmsley, A. 1992 *The Caribbean Artist Movement 1966–1972: a Literary & Cultural History*, London: New Beacon Books

Walvin, J 1973 *Black and White: the Negro in British Society*, London: Allen and Unwin

Walvin, J 1982 *Slavery and British Society, 1776–1846*, London: Macmillan

Warnes, T 1996 'The Age Structure and Ageing of the Ethnic (*sic*) groups', in D Coleman & J Salt (eds), *Ethnicity in the 1991 Census: Demographic Characteristics of the Ethnic Minority Populations*, vol 1, London: OPCS

Weber, M 1930 *The Protestant Ethic and the Spirit of Capitalism*, London: Allen & Unwin

Weber, M 1995 *Max Weber: Selections in Translation*, R W Runciman (ed), trans E Matthews, Cambridge: Cambridge University Press

Weeks, J et al 2001 *Same Sex Intimacies: Families of Choice and Other Life Experiences*, London: Routledge

Western, J 1992 *A Passage to England: Barbadian Londoners Speak of Home*, London: UCL Press

Williams, E 1963 *British Historians and the West Indies*, London: Andre Deutsch

Williams, E 1964 (1944) *Capitalism and Slavery*, London: Andre Deutsch

Williams, E 1962 (1964) *History of the People of Trinidad and Tobago*, London: Andre Deutsch

Williams, M W (ed) 1993 *The African American Encyclopaedia*, New York: Cavendish

Wood, D 1968 *Trinidad in Transition: the Years After Slavery*, London & New York: Oxford University Press

Wright, Richard 1964 *Native Son*, New York: Signet Classics

INTERVIEWS

Steve Batchelor, returning residents' leader, Spanish Town, Jamaica, 5 August 1996

Lloyd Bradshaw, Head, National Insurance Board, Bridgetown, Barbados, 1 August 1996

Don Brice, Director, RFFU, Ministry of Foreign Affairs, Kingston, Jamaica, 7 August 1996

Charles Corbin, Chief Welfare Officer, Bridgetown, Barbados, 1 August 1996

Melvin Drayton, returning resident assocations leader, Bridgetown, Barbados, 2 August 1996

Arthur Harper, Chief Immigration Officer, Trinidad, Port of Spain, 29 July 1996

Eric and Jessica Huntley, London, 1992

John LaRose, London, 1991

Dr Beverley Miller, Chief Medical Officer, Ministry of Health, Bridgetown, Barbados, 1 August 1996

Dr Peter Phillips, Minister of Health, Kingston, Jamaica, 25 July 1996

Jennifer Sampson, Permanent Secretary, Ministry of Health, Port of Spain, Trinidad, 29 July 1996.

John Small, Department of Sociology, University of the West Indies and
returning residents' leader, researcher and Lecturer in Sociology, 7 August
1996

From the ESRC project, *Living Arrangements, Family Structure and Social Change
of Caribbeans in Britain*, ESRC Grant No L31523009:

BG 070/2 Tape 3, Side A/p. 4
BG 120/1, Tape 2 Side A/pp. 8–9
BG 091/3 Tape 1, Side A/pp. 4–5, 7–8
BG 091/3, Tape 2, Side A/pp. 4–5

JF 002 Tape 1, Side B/p. 1
JF 020 Tape 1, Side A/p. 12
JF 021 Tape 1, Side A/p. 2
JF 022 Tape 1, Side A/pp. 3, 9
JF 022 Tape 2, Side B/pp. 5, 7, 13

TO 01 Tape 1, Side A/p. 1
TA 015 Tape 1, Side A/p. 14
TA 015 Tape 1, Side B/p. 8

NEWSPAPERS, COMMUNITY AND MISCELLANEOUS PUBLICATIONS AND SOURCES

Black Liberator, passim
Black Unity and Freedom Party (BUFP) pamphlets and files, 1970–91
Caribbean Insight, passim
Black Voice, 1971–91, passim
Caribbean Times, 1992–4, passim
Crisis, November/December, 1993
New York Times, 1992, passim
Guardian, passim
Independent, passim
The Lawyer 1998–2001 passim
New Nation, passim
South London Press, passim
Sunday Times, 2001, passim
The Times, 16 August, 1985
The Voice, 1992–94, passim
Weekly Gleaner, passim
Weekly Journal, 1992–94, passim
Time, 8 August, 1994

GOVERNMENT/OFFICIAL SOURCES

Facilitation Unit for Returning Nationals/Ministry of Foreign Affairs, 1996
Returning Nationals Booklet, Barbados: Facilitation Unit for Returning
Nationals/Ministry of Foreign Affairs

Home Office, 1998 *Fairer, Faster and Firmer – a Modern Approach to Immigration and Asylum*, London: The Stationery Office Limited

Jamaica Information Service, 1996 *National Industrial Policy: a Strategic Plan for Growth and Development*, presumably Kingston: Jamaica Information Service

Ministry of Foreign Affairs and Foreign Trade, 1998 *The Returning Residents Programme: Mandate, Operation, Direction*, Kingston: Returning Residents Facilitation Unit/Ministry of Foreign Affairs and Foreign Trade

Pensions & Overseas Benefits Directorate, 1997 *Overseas Pensions and Benefits*, Newcastle: Pensions & Overseas Benefits Directorate

Pensions & Overseas Benefits Directorate, 1998 *Overseas Pensions and Benefits*, Newcastle: Pensions & Overseas Benefits Directorate

Pensions & Overseas Benefits Directorate, 2001 *Overseas Pensions and Benefits*, Newcastle: Pensions & Overseas Benefits Directorate

Planning Institute of Jamaica, 1996 *Economic and Social Survey Jamaica 1995*, Kingston: Planning Institute of Jamaica

RRFU (Returning Residents Facilitation Unit/Ministry of Foreign Affairs and Foreign Trade), 1995 *Numbers of Returning Residents*, Kingston: Returning Residents Facilitation Unit/Ministry of Foreign Affairs and Foreign Trade

RRFU (Returning Residents Facilitation Unit/Ministry of Foreign Affairs and Foreign Trade), 1997 *Numbers of Returning Residents*, Kingston: Returning Residents Facilitation Unit/Ministry of Foreign Affairs and Foreign Trade

RRFU (Returning Residents Facilitation Unit/Ministry of Foreign Affairs and Foreign Trade), 1998 *Numbers of Returning Residents*, Kingston: Returning Residents Facilitation Unit / Ministry of Foreign Affairs and Foreign Trade

Index

Compiled by Sue Carlton

238   Caribbean Transnational Experience